acting foolish

acting foolish

lewis j. stadlen

BearManor Media
2009

Acting Foolish

© 2009 Lewis J. Stadlen

All rights reserved.

For information, address:

BearManor Media
P. O. Box 71426
Albany, GA 31708

bearmanormedia.com

Cover design by

Typesetting and layout by John Teehan

Published in the USA by BearManor Media

ISBN—1-59393-329-0

Table of Contents

acknowledgements i

preface 1

PART ONE
    tics and foibles 9

    Photo Section A 105

PART TWO
    the opposite of brilliance 191

    Photo Section B 205

PART THREE
    what the hell happened to you? 297

    afterword 325

*To Zero Mostel, Sam Levene, David Burns
and Stella Adler—
all of whom acted with size.*

Acknowledgements

My thanks to Daniel Okrent, my initial reader, who made several valuable literary suggestions as well as passing the manuscript on to Chris Jerome who did more than edit, she untangled passages of jumbled syntax that I would never have accomplished on my own. To Dennis Brown, the most insightful drama critic in the country, whose kind words gave me the confidence to presevere. Edward Hibbard who worked to get it published. Nick Santa Maria whose recommendation did get it published.

Preface

I'm sitting in the bowels of the Bob Carr Auditorium, in Orlando, Florida, awaiting the start of the first performance of a hastily thrown-together touring company of *The Sunshine Boys*. It stars Mickey Rooney and Donald O'Connor as the fictional vaudeville team of Willie Clark and Al Lewis. I am playing Ben Clark, Willie Clark's nephew, the role I had introduced in the show's original Broadway run, eighteen years earlier.

The room is large, empty, and beneath the glare of the overhead fluorescent lights, nondescript, a way station that separates my civilian life from the world of the professional theater. I've been rehearsing with Rooney for three weeks, so I flatter myself into thinking I understand what he's about.

At the end of our first day of rehearsal in our sun-drenched studio in Burbank, I mentioned that I might be coming down with something; did he know of a good doctor?

"Why don't you let me take a look at you?" offered the rotund sixty-eight-year-old legend.

"*You*?" I asked, nonplussed. "I need to see a doctor—someone who can prescribe some antibiotics."

"That's why I'd like to take a look at you," said Mickey. "You know I was very nearly a doctor?"

"You were *very nearly* a doctor? Where? In a *Doctor Kildare* movie? Were you assisting Lew Ayres?"

"What are you talking about?" said Mickey, clearly distressed. "I was very nearly a great doctor!"

"I have to tell you something, Mick," I said, certain he was pulling my leg. "If I was being wheeled into the operating room and just before they put me out, I looked up to see that Mickey Rooney was about to operate—I'm not sure I'd be too thrilled about that."

"What are you talking about?" he said, his great pink jowls vibrating. *"I was very nearly a great surgeon!"*

In the three weeks since then, I'd come to love and hate the man who at sixteen had become the biggest movie star in the world. I'd watched with fascination as he'd progressively forgotten the twenty or so lines he had managed to memorize. In exactly five minutes the two of us would be stepping onto the stage to begin the play. I could hardly imagine what was going through Mickey's head, knowing he was about to perform in a play he was now barely acquainted with. What I had begun to fathom about Mickey Rooney was that he was so consistently wrong about everything, he was almost right.

Suddenly the icon gestured for me to take a seat beside him. "I want to tell you something," he said, shaking his head like a sweet-tempered professor who was completely off his rocker. "This play is never going to be *Sweet Bird of Youth!*"

"No, it's not, Mickey," I said. "But it is *The Sunshine Boys.*"

"Do you have cancer?" he asked me.

"Do I *what?*"

"Do you have cancer?" he repeated through his trademark buck teeth.

"No, I don't have cancer," I said, uncomfortable even repeating the word.

"Well," he said, before ascending the stairs that led to the stage, "what the fuck are you worried about?"

No one threw me onto the stage at three years of age the way they had Mickey Rooney; nor was I born into a family of acrobats touring the vaudeville circuit like Donald O'Connor. Neither boy had much of a choice when it came to choosing his destiny. I did.

My story is several degrees removed from anything close to motion picture fame, but as a forty-year survivor of the American theater, my attempts to fight my way out of that insular world have met with little success. Even my worst battle scars involve a narcotic self-love that usually ends in a good belly laugh.

To quote my wonderful acting teacher, Stella Adler: "If you don't keep working on what your soul needs, you are going to be wiped out."

In 1981, at age thirty-four, experiencing a certain erosion of the soul, I decided I was tired of reinventing myself. Why reinvent myself when I didn't know who the hell I was in the first place? Who said acting was the only thing I could do? I had been traveling for several months in minor league baseball circles. My friend Jim Paul, who owned the El Paso Diablos of the Texas League, had introduced me to his world while making it clear that he believed everyone's grass looked greener from the outside. He loved show business and I loved baseball. His appreciation for showmanship had helped him usher in a renaissance in his field. He had bought the team for a fifty-thousand-dollar debt in the early seventies, and when he eventually sold it in the mid-nineties the price was in the millions. His formula was baseball as family entertainment. Every game featured exotic giveaways, homespun cheerleaders, a public address announcer who was more like a stand-up comedian. Ah, the incorruptibility of America's national pastime. Who needed show business?

By the time I returned from El Paso to New York in the early autumn, I had tracked down a ramshackle baseball franchise in the Single A Carolina League whose asking price was $125,000. The owner of the Winston-Salem Spirits was even willing to throw in the team bus. This is not a memoir of how a Jewish boy from the city bought a minor league baseball team. It's about a lifelong fascination with a subject I actually know something about: the implausibility of sustaining a major league acting career.

I was deep into my fantasy of entrepreneurship when I got a phone call from my young female agent, who had recently graduated from some fancy women's college. Having listened long enough to an endless list of complaints, she asked innocently enough, "So, Lewis? If things are actually as bad as you say they are, have you ever considered giving up the business?" Life is tough enough without your personal representative egging you on to an early retirement.

"I have an audition for you down at the Public Theater," she said. "Three one-act plays by a Czechoslovakian playwright whose name I can't pronounce." (It turned out to be Vaclav Havel.) The director is Lee Grant." Lee Grant was an actress I had always admired. She had reputedly hunkered down before the House Committee on Un-American Activities, and those who had refused to name names during the blacklist had been exalted as heroes in my youth.

The play, *A Separate Peace*, concerned a married couple living under a totalitarian regime who were seduced by material possessions. The regime survives as the couple chooses comfort over dissent. Their tranquil life is interrupted by the arrival of an old friend who's just been let out of prison, where he'd been incarcerated for protesting the state's violation of human rights. The play is about Czech Communism, but the message extends to anyone willing to ignore their conscience in order to add another wing to their house. The twenty-four-page play was witty and disturbing, opening with the couple showing off their bounty and acting as generous hosts until they recognize they've unwittingly collaborated with their friend's jailers.

Preparing to audition for a play is similar to the way a professional chef plans a meal. It's about making decisions that best showcase your conceptual talents. A chef may choose a tomato-and-onion salad to go along with a rib-eye steak. An actor decides that this character has deluded himself by wearing rose colored glasses. This coffee table he has just purchased in West Germany has made him ecstatic. He can't wait for his friend to arrive, to prove to him that life after prison can be wonderful.

Acting is an interpretive art, and the interpretation usually begins at the audition. At this one, however, I was distracted because I was waiting for a phone call from the guy who owned the North Carolina baseball team. I sat in a hallway beside an actor I'd recently done a movie with. Regarded as a handsome leading man because he had a strong jaw and a headful of tight curls, his major talent lay in making you believe he found you fascinating. I thought he was one of the worst actors I had ever worked with, and I resented his ability to convince people otherwise. I mention this because besides deciding who your character will be, you must supply the intellectual side with energy and temperament. Anger is an easy emotion to dredge up. A few minutes later I auditioned for Lee Grant, smiling affably through my resentment. "I'll show you who the better actor is" was the gas that fed my engine. The moment my audition ended, I forgot all about it.

Two weeks went by before I learned that the Winston-Salem Spirits were about to be sold to a professional baseball man whose father had spent fifty years working for the Boston Red Sox. As I watched my fantasy recede into the weeds, a late-afternoon phone call came from the agent who'd suggested I leave the acting profession.

"I have an audition for you tomorrow morning," she said.

"Damn it! How many times have I told you I need time to prepare for an audition? It's already six o'clock. I haven't even read the play."

"It's the same play that's being directed by Lee Grant," she told me. "I'll leave the script with my secretary, and you can pick it up on the way."

I have always been a reluctant auditioner, but never more so than at that moment. I wanted to own a baseball team in North Carolina; I didn't want to act in an Off Broadway play at the Public Theater. So I decided to do what I had done several times before: audition just well enough not to embarrass myself but not well enough to get the job.

The next morning I arrived at my agent's office to find that she had forgotten to leave the script with her secretary. As I cursed her I also felt a measure of gratitude. This would add legitimacy to my not auditioning well. At the Public, I stepped off the elevator to find only a large, effeminate receptionist and a row of empty chairs. Here was more good news. My nitwit agent had not only forgotten to leave the script, she had also gotten the time of the audition wrong. I would stay for ten minutes beyond my appointed time and then leave, pretending I had some pressing engagement.

A few minutes after eleven I made my way up the hall and was about to step onto the elevator when a phone was answered by the large fey man at the desk.

"Is there a Lewis J. Smoller here?" he asked in that brain-dead voice certain low-level employees use when addressing actors.

"You mean Lewis J. Stadlen?" I answered unwisely.

"Yeah, Lewis J. Strabler."

"Stadlen!" I said. "It's like Stadler Shoes with an *n* instead of an *r*."

"Well, whatever your name is, Rosemary Tischler wants to speak with you." Rosemary Tischler was the casting director for the Public Theater.

"Lewis," she said, "didn't your agent tell you that your audition has been changed to twelve o'clock?" This was just the news I was hoping for.

"No, she didn't," I said, adding a harried tone to my voice. "I'm sorry, Rosemary, I was told eleven and I'm already late for another appointment."

"What appointment is that?" she asked. "When I spoke to your agent last night she wasn't aware that you had another appointment."

"I suppose she didn't know about it. I have an audition for a whole flock of voice-over commercials on the other side of town."

"Auditions?" she said quizzically. "Couldn't you ask her to move them to another time?"

"Did I say auditions? I meant bookings. I have five voice-over bookings."

"Well, that beats all," Rosemary said with a sigh. "I'm so damned angry with your agents. They must have known about these commercials. I'm going to get on the phone and give them a piece of my mind."

"*No!*" I yelled back at her. "You see, they don't know anything about them. I'm doing this for a friend. He owns a baseball team in El Paso. We're doing the session nonunion." I'd just lied myself into being a scab.

"I see." Rosemary seemed somewhat confused. "What time is it now? Lee really wants to see you. I mean, it's already close to eleven thirty. Can't you ask your friend to put off the session for another half hour?"

"Well, I'll try," I said stupidly. "You know these studios cost a lot of money. That's why we're doing it nonunion."

"Please try," she said. "Lee's really interested in you for the part."

"I'll call him up right now," I told her. "I hope I brought his number with me."

"Please try," she reiterated, and hung up.

Having totally confused myself, I stepped onto the elevator and took it down to the street, where I walked briskly around the block remembering how tantalizingly close I had come to escaping. Five minutes later I returned to the receptionist's desk and had him buzz Tischler.

"They're being incredibly generous," I blathered. "They've put the session off till twelve forty-five."

"Thank you," said Rosemary, evidently relieved. "I'm certain this is all going to work out for everyone. Lee just loved your first audition. I'll be right up."

"Well, I don't know," I said, not wanting to raise her hopes. "I have a number of important things going on in my life right now."

Twelve o'clock rolled around and no Lee Grant. By twelve fifteen Rosemary was frantic as I kept pointing to my watch and rolling my eyes. At twelve twenty-five Grant sauntered into the room, accompanied by her young male assistant and an actress who looked extremely familiar.

"Lee!" said Rosemary, enormously agitated. "Lewis has been kind enough to put off a pressing engagement. He should have been out of here five minutes ago."

Suddenly I recognized the actress as Concetta Tomei. I'd seen her the week before in the play *Cloud Nine*, in which she had been brilliant. So this was the actress they'd cast to play the wife.

"Can we please get started?" pleaded Rosemary, as Grant's assistant languidly removed several containers of coffee from a large paper bag. Lee just stared out at everyone, unconcerned.

By the time I began to read with Concetta, who was as glorious as I remembered her, my objective was to make a speedy exit. This caused an explosive churning beneath Vaclav Havel's words. The two of us performed an inspired scene, until I gazed down at my watch and in a dramatic flourish allowed my script to fall from my fingertips to the floor. "I'm very sorry," I announced, "but that's all they wrote." A second later I was out the door with Lee Grant in hot pursuit.

"I want you to play this part!" she called out before I could step onto the elevator.

"No!" I replied.

"What do you mean, no?"

"When do you go into rehearsal?" I asked her.

"Next Monday."

"Well, there you go, I can't do it. Many pressing matters."

"What pressing matters?"

"Private stuff," I said, clearly exhausted. "Listen, you know what? I'll think about it."

Lee Grant, Academy Award-winning actress that she was, looked penetratingly into my eyes. "Don't think," she said. "*Do!*"

"I am so fucking late," I said, stepping onto the elevator. Moments later I found myself racing along Lafayette, desperately trying to wave down a cab. "Wait a minute," I told myself. "What just happened here? You don't need a taxi. There's no place you have to go! You just did everything in your power not to get a job, and the damned fools gave it to you anyway."

Welcome to the world of the American theater!

PART ONE

tics and foibles

Chapter 1

I got into it because of the women I saw on the stage. They had painted faces and beautiful bodies and long silky legs. It got more complicated as I went along, but as a child sitting in a Broadway theater, it was the smell of female perspiration, pancake makeup, and the look of mesh stockings caressing a woman's legs that ignited my desire to enter the privileged world of The Theater.

I wish my motives had been more complicated. In his definitive theatrical memoir, *Act One*, Moss Hart theorizes that "the theater is an inevitable refuge of the unhappy child." I don't believe I was any unhappier than most, but I do remember from an early age lying beneath my sheets at night thinking that my life would certainly be better if I could share it with someone who wanted to love me and kiss me all over.

My day-to-day existence attending public schools and competing in athletic events above the blacktopped garage that was the center of my Forest Hills apartment complex afforded little of the world of fantasy and panache that I yearned for. From the sound of the alarm clock that woke me at seven each morning, nothing seemed to make much sense. My dear mother, wishing only to do her best, would secretly break a raw egg into my chocolate milk so I would go to school replenished and energetic. (Why did the chocolate milk served at my friends' houses always taste so much more like chocolate milk?)

I'd head off to school wearing my Davy Crockett coonskin cap, the cheap model with fur on the sides and brown vinyl on the top (my mother had picked it up at Alexander's department store on Queens Boulevard) and dash into classrooms presided over by Mrs. Soskis, Mrs. Baum, Mrs. Bison, or, every fifth grader's most horrific nightmare, Miss Eleanor Biddlecomb. To quote Woody Allen, I attended a school for emotionally disturbed teachers. Only my sixth-grade teacher, Mrs. Bobko, took a liking to me. During a spelling bee she threw me a softball, asking me to spell the word *marriage*. I returned the favor by spelling it m-a-r-r-a-g-e. That word—and that state—was never to be my specialty.

My parents divorced when I was ten, and although I was soon to learn that in the outside world divorce was not an aberration, in the neighborhood that I grew up in, it was. All my friends' parents stayed together no matter how miserable they were. My favorite family belonged to my friend Robert Goldhammer, whose mother was always so hammered when I went over there that she'd answer the door in a slip and a pair of translucent plastic wedgies that revealed the separation between her long painted toes. I was never aware that she was snockered, just that she was always half naked. I longed to have Mrs. Goldhammer as my mother so I could be a member of a normal family.

For the first thirteen years of my life nothing seemed to be working out. Three times a week I would be called from my classroom so a speech therapist could help me differentiate *r* sounds from *w*s. I can assure you that this minor speech impediment was treated with the greatest sensitivity by my fellow grade-schoolers, many of whom were otherwise busy stealing automobile ornaments off the hoods of Mercedes-Benzes.

The predominantly Jewish middle-class Queens neighborhood where I was raised wasn't far from the Big Apple. By the time my parents moved there in 1953, the neighborhood was going through a boom, housing the families of returning GIs. Six- and ten-story redbrick housing developments were going up on every vacant lot. A mile to the east stood the symbol of establishment Queens, Forest Hills Gardens, home to the U.S. Open tennis tournament, a serene, ivy-covered Tudor landscape that stood in direct contrast to the déclassé neighborhood in which I resided. There seemed to be no delicatessens or Chinese restaurants in Forest Hills Gardens. We children were advised that we were no more welcome there than the black tennis star Althea Gibson, who generated much controversy by having the temerity to compete and triumph at the Open.

There was a prickly sensitivity about growing up Jewish in the years after World War Two. My family passed judgment on every individual according to their religious or political affiliation. My grandmother's brother, Zack Becker, was the family's lone Republican, and only his kind heart and the prestige that went with his job as a treasurer at the CBS television network saved him from excommunication. Not that I can recall ever being in Zack's presence without a screaming political argument erupting. Toward the conclusion of every dispute, Zack would turn his chair around so whoever he was fighting with would have to argue to his back. It would only be a matter of time before someone made a door-slamming exit from our apartment. The names Joseph McCarthy, Richard Nixon, and Thomas E. Dewey were invoked at our dinner table with such regularity that a place should have been set for all three of them. That reactionary rag, the *Daily News* was allowed in our home only once when McCarthy died of liver cancer, so the family could rejoice at the block letter headline SENATOR JOE, DEAD AT 57!

As a substitute for talking about how we felt about each other, there were endless discussions about Nazis hiding in South America, who had the atomic bomb, how many times Israel could outsmart its hostile Arab neighbors, and, the most frightening possibility of all, President Dwight D. Eisenhower succumbing to a heart attack and being replaced by the avid red-baiter Richard M. Nixon. That possibility had the power to reduce family conversations to silence.

My family suffered from a scarcity of forgiveness. Little slack was afforded those who towered above us, and even less those who sat around our kitchen table. The adults were smart and for the most part well-informed, but it was our ability to dissect the faults of others that met with the greatest affirmation. We performed for each other, competing for the most valuable insights. There was much laughter beneath my roof, but someone always paid the price at the punch line.

The chief architect of my worldview was the family patriarch, my maternal grandfather, David Chassler, who was known to the end of his long life as Poppa. He sat me down on his paternalistic knee when I was six and informed me that the worst Democrat was better than the best Republican. His opinions carried enormous weight because he was handsome, very smart, hilariously funny, and wealthy. He dressed like a dandy and entertained himself in the summer heat by sitting shirtless on a lawn chair, a handsome straw boater on his well-groomed head, sending horseflies to their final reward with a green plastic swatter. One of his major themes was that it was incumbent upon Jewish Americans to remain oblique in the face of superior numbers, although he rarely took his own advice. I remember a June evening on the beach at Coney Island when he wrapped his arms around me during a fireworks display, convincing me that without my Poppa's protection I would be snatched from the earth by the exploding tentacles of light. I never doubted him for a second.

My grandfather's influence dominated the family dynamic, especially in the case of my mother, who simultaneously adored and loathed him. She strove for his unconditional love while searching for some knight errant who could run him through. Eventually she found my father, who took a shot at it, but my mother's conflict would prove too heady for any man. By the time I was ten my father had packed his bags and finalized a divorce in Mexico. That left me to take on the aging colossus, which I had no intention of doing because I was crazy about him.

From the time I first knew my grandfather he was wealthy, although it was considered the worst possible form to admit it. To acknowledge his wealth was to accept the existence of far wealthier men, mostly Republicans, who had dedicated their lives to the sole pursuit of gain. My grandfather had simply outsmarted the schnooks who thought they were so bright just because they had a high school education. In a world filled with utopian political theories, Poppa was a passionate New Dealer, an idolizer of Franklin Delano Roosevelt and a generous employer—as long as everyone acceded to living under his thumb. I remember a night in his modest home in Flatbush, watching the Friday night fights on his black-and-white Philco. In an unusually spirited and bloody affair, Archie Moore was fighting a Canadian boxer. Taking a puff on his cigar, Poppa turned to me and said, "Root for the colored guy. They've got enough problems without getting knocked on their ass."

He drove a Cadillac but nobody else in the family was allowed to buy one; that would be flaunting their wealth. He traveled the world with my grandmother and their platinum blond friend, Shirley Horowitz, who doubled as Poppa's secretary and whom my mother, for reasons unknown, seemed to loathe. She was fond of telling the story of the day Shirley, then in her mid-sixties and wearing a bathing suit that revealed her ample cleavage, came upon an elderly man with a long beard sunning himself on a Miami beach. "Are you a rabbi?" she asked him. "No," he replied. "Are you a whore?"

I was deeply fond of Shirley, who had a low whiskey voice, a kind smile, and a far more relaxed manner than any of the other women in the family. Whenever we were together she would press her hand on mine, ask me about myself, and regale me with stories of what a caring and wonderful man my grandfather was. Our conversations never lasted more than a few minutes before my mother intervened and yanked me to the far side of the room. Years later I was told by a favorite uncle that besides being my grandmother's best friend, Shirley was Poppa's lover, and that my grandmother found the arrangement preferable to having to guess where her husband might be. How they worked out their living arrangements while on vacation can only be imagined. Shortly before Poppa died, he digressed from a political discussion we were having about Ronald Reagan's almost certain prospects for a second term. Pouring us both a shot of Jack Daniel's, he confided, "Your grandmother is a wonderful woman, but after she gave birth to the twins, she was never the same again."

My grandfather always spoke his mind. It was one of his more admirable traits, something he did with the confidence of knowing he was the family pooh-bah. From the start I revered his candor and intelligence, and embraced his worldview. I knew that to win his favor, I would have to express myself candidly, to distinguish myself from the bullshit artists he constantly railed against. The true currency in my Poppa's eyes was authenticity. Before taking you seriously, he insisted that you accomplish something.

My mother, Vivienne Chassler, was a twin, born two minutes ahead of my uncle Seymour, who went on to father two sons and a daughter. I grew up an only child. Seymour's son Joseph, two years older than me, was said to possess a genius IQ. His mental capacities had a significant effect on my family's sense of its intellectual heft. So precocious was my first cousin that my father, struggling to be an actor and writer, wrote a television play entitled *The Devil Wears Short Pants*. The plot centered on a six-year-old genius with an antisocial personality who figures out how to build an atomic bomb in his room. While unsure I'd ever be able to identify the words in my first grade reader; my eight-year-old cousin, meanwhile, would sit in the living room of my grandparents' summer cottage in Mahopac, New York, speed-reading *The Sound and the Fury*.

Although my family disagreed about nearly everything, the one thing everyone believed was that Joseph was destined to be the next Albert Einstein. This left me in the uncomfortable position of scrounging for an alternative identity. The one I invented for myself was that I was basically a good-natured, accessible little fellow, when in truth I was neither. What I found most confusing was that despite Joseph's exalted status, nobody much liked him. The poor boy was a freak who seemed to know too much about the human condition without much experience to back it up. From the beginning he was a nihilist. God knows the pressures he must have endured, being the family trophy. Besides his ability to digest a full page of Faulkner within ten seconds, it was anybody's guess how much of *The Sound and the Fury* he actually assimilated. He was a genius at shutting people out. From day one he was my archrival for the family's affection, and although it was inconceivable to me at the time, I was most certainly his.

Everything seemed to come easy to Joseph, excluding the small pleasures associated with childhood. He disdained athletics and had few friends because there was no one bright or unhappy enough to share his emotional frequency. One day while we swam together in Lake Mahopac, he must have decided to rid himself of me forever. While my father sunned himself on a raft near shore, Joseph grabbed my head and forced me underwater while my ten-year-old lungs strained for air. I was seconds from drowning when he must have thought better of murdering me and at the last possible moment loosened his grip so that the episode could be explained as a childish prank. No amount of sputtering outrage on my part could convince my father that I wasn't behaving like a baby. Later in the day, after we changed out of our wet swimsuits, Joseph returned to a comfortable chair in the living room and with ferocious intensity polished off the last few pages of *Crime and Punishment.*

There is no doubt that my childhood competition with Joseph influenced the road I would travel. If being a genius meant living Joseph's unhappy existence, I would find a different way of getting attention. Who needed to share a ten-year-old's conviction that we were all human garbage? My priorities were simpler. I wanted to avoid being the last one picked in a touch football game, and I wanted to plant a kiss on my freckle-faced third-grade classmate Emily Fisher, whose dainty little face peered out beneath a row of neatly trimmed bangs. She wore white starched blouses, pleated plaid skirts, and adorable crimson penny loafers. As detestable as I found the daily grind of school, I entertained myself staring across the invisible divide that separated me from my first love. (My grandfather referred to her as Emily Pisher.) Emily's inevitable response to my overtures was an upturned lip that suggested weary contempt.

The earliest recollection I have of a creative leaning that differentiated me from my peers had to do with the endless games of World War Two we played with fiendish gusto on the vacant lots that were rapidly disappearing from the neighborhood. Most of us had toy guns, and those who didn't would substitute a long stick for a rifle, a large stone for a hand grenade. We would choose up sides for different armies and disperse to the far corners of the lot. After each of us found a hiding place, our mission was to seek out the enemy and shoot them dead.

I was the only one who insisted on assuming a fictitious name—always Charley, because my father had a handsome friend of this name who had coarse, straight black hair that reminded me of the man who ran the Chinese laundry. I hated my own hair, which was curly. My choice of name seemed to annoy my friends, who wanted to get on with the action. My favorite part of the game was when I was alone, making my way through the brush in search of my quarry. I would carry on an animated conversation with myself, imagining that the girl waiting for me back home was Emily Fisher, who spent her every waking moment praying I would not be killed. It was my first attempt at dramatic monologue. I imagined myself a soldier in a war movie—not a hero or a leader of men, but an infantryman tenuously surviving.

When the moment of confrontation came I would point my stick at the enemy and shoot him right through the heart. Invariably my victim would scream, "You missed me!" or "I was wearing a bulletproof vest!," but when it came my time to die, I would embrace the moment with a flourish. Reacting to the spray of machine-gun fire, I would clutch my mortal wound, fling my weapon to the ground, and tumble down the steepest incline I could find. As I was about to expire I would imagine the grief visited on my inconsolable Emily Fisher. She would be hard-pressed to find another man like her Chinese laundry, straight-haired Charley. Good men like Charley were always the first ones to die.

My friends were perplexed by my enthusiasm for dying and taking myself out of the game. Wasn't the purpose of any game to survive to the last? "Stadlen always dies," I would hear them mutter under their breath. But it wasn't Stadlen who always died, it was Charley, a man who was deeply loved and would be sorely missed—the man I might have been if I hadn't been stupid, vainglorious me, reveling in my own defeat, the only boy in the neighborhood who, when shot through the heart, allowed himself to die.

Chapter 2

The Broadway theater scene that existed from the 1950s through the mid-1960s was ablaze with energy, rhythm, and talent. Perhaps it was the introspection in the aftermath of a terrible war that incited writers to write, composers to compose, and commercial producers to take a gamble on what they hoped might turn a profit. Whatever was in the drinking water at the time seemed to motivate the most talented people in the country to continue evolving a medium that had been experiencing a renaissance since the 1920s.

Alan Jay Lerner and Frederick Loewe, Frank Loesser, Leonard Bernstein, Betty Comden and Adolph Green, Richard Adler and Jerry Ross, Jule Stein, Stephen Sondheim, Jerry Bock and Sheldon Harnick, Arthur Miller, Tennessee Williams, William Inge, just to mention a few, had been influenced by their brilliant predecessors—George and Ira Gershwin, Larry Hart, Jerome Kern, Kurt Weill, Bertolt Brecht, Eugene O'Neill, George S. Kaufmann, Thornton Wilder—while the likes of Richard Rodgers and Oscar Hammerstein, Cole Porter, Irving Berlin, Howard Dietz and Arthur Schwartz, Harold Arlen, Yip Harburg, Johnny Mercer, and Burton Lane were still contributing dazzlingly in the present.

What gave this decade and a half its distinction was the contribution of a handful of directors and choreographers, some of whom had begun their careers in the 1920s, '30s, and '40s but were now at the peak of their creative powers: Elia Kazan, George Abbott, Harold Clurman, Moss Hart, Jerome Robbins, Agnes de Mille, Michael Kidd, Jack Cole, Bob Fosse, Herbert Ross, and a host of others who, if not particularly innovative, had absorbed the craft of moving the play's story forward, regardless of how the New York theater critics might react. As for the performers, an unintended benefit of the period was the Hollywood blacklist, which had left many of America's finest actors with no option than to leave California and scamper back to the commercial theater from which they had come. There was no blacklist in the theater.

This was the environment I was exposed to by my culture-addicted parents, who had filled four drawers of our coffee table with playbills from their nights together at the theater.

It was my recently divorced mother who decided that I had the talent to stand before a group of strangers and emote. She and I hadn't been on the best of terms since my father had moved to glamorous surroundings across the East River, a duplex apartment on West Fifty-seventh Street. Heartbroken, she was left to badger me nightly about doing my homework and achieving passing grades, a task I studiously avoided from the seventh grade on.

I lived for the alternate weekends I spent with my father, who would ply me with toys from F.A.O. Schwarz. We passed endless hours bowling. (A few establishments still employed gnarled, middle-aged pinsetters, whom my father would dutifully tip after every game.) We ate most of our meals at restaurants, with an occasional take-out order of Chinese food, fried chicken, or pizza. We would scour the city in search of the ultimate hamburger, hot dog, and egg cream. No weekend was complete without our taking in a double feature in Yorkville or a trip to Forty-second Street, where I was introduced to the intoxicating grubbiness of ten-cent French fries and fifteen-cent hamburgers at Grant's.

It was a thirteen-year-old's idea of paradise, but it ended like clockwork at six- thirty every other Sunday when my father, with false cheeriness, would ask me to pack my bag. We'd drive across the Queensborough Bridge and be greeted by my mother, who would offer civil but icy pleasantries, accept my father's alimony check as if it was infected with cholera, and walk miserably around the kitchen table looking like she had a lot more to say but it would be hopeless to say it. My father would kiss me good-bye and say, "I'll see you in two weeks, monkey." Without exchanging more than a few words with my mother (whom I blamed for everything), I'd head straight for my room, where I would shuffle papers and push pencils around my desk as if I were doing my homework.

There's nothing quite like the mindset of a thirteen-year-old only child. Believing only in a furious disregard for authority, I would pass the hours dreaming of the day I could pack my bags and disappear. Very little interested me beyond having my mother replace the swinging door that connected my bedroom to the kitchen. I wanted a door I could close and lock. At any moment my mother or even the local handyman could come bursting through that three-inch no man's land that separated the world from my dirtiest thoughts. Lying in bed at night, obsessing over the possibility of an early death, I would stare toward that hated slab of wood I shared with the rattling kitchen utensils and await the *whoosh* that accompanied an unannounced presence. If much of my personality can be attributed to being born feet-first with my umbilical cord wrapped around my neck, a second factor in my romance with escape has everything to do with that blasted swinging door.

Chapter 3

On a late summer evening in my thirteenth year, my father and I took a leisurely walk down Broadway, heading toward the Lunt-Fontanne Theater, where Mary Martin was performing in Rodgers and Hammerstein's final collaboration, *The Sound of Music*. The street was alive with scurrying patrons mingling with faces I vaguely recognized but could not name. "There's Cyril Richard," my father whispered as a tall, exquisitely tanned gentleman in a tweed jacket and green alpine hat picked his way through the evening crowd, making certain he would be recognized. Tipping his hat as he brushed the elbow of a well-dressed matron, he headed toward the stage door of the Music Box Theater, where he was costarring with Cornelia Otis Skinner in *The Pleasure of His Company*. All around me a swarm of well-dressed men and attractive women were heading toward some brightly lit marquee.

Seated inside the Lunt-Fontanne, I experienced the radiating warmth of Mary Martin, who cavorted through the Austrian Alps teaching a flock of tow-headed Aryan children the choral harmony that would eventually save them from the Nazis. I had seen better musicals than this one—*My Fair Lady* and *West Side Story*, to name two—but never with the original casts or from the exclusive seats arranged by my father's friend John Randolph, who was appearing in the play as the butler Franz. (John had been a victim of the Hollywood blacklist.)

It was after the curtain came down that the evening turned electric. My father took me through the stage door, where John had left our names with the doorman, and up several flights of stairs to John's dressing room, where I watched enraptured as he removed his makeup with gobs of cold cream. We were then escorted onto a bare stage illuminated by a single lightbulb, where I was introduced to Mary Martin.

She greeted my father and me with the graciousness one might expect from an old friend.

"She stays for hours after every performance," John told us as we exited the stage door onto Forty-sixth Street. "She autographs playbills and takes down addresses so the next time she appears anywhere, she'll send out postcards asking people to come and visit their old friend Mary Martin. Quite the cagey gal. I've made a reservation at Downey's. It's hot, and Sardi's is too stuffy."

In 1960 there were two prestigious after-theater watering holes: Jim Downey's, on Eighth Avenue and Forty-fourth Street, attracted a casual bicoastal clientele. As I made my way to the men's room that evening I passed John Wayne sitting in a leather booth knocking down a few with several oversized buddies. On the way back I caught a glimpse of Shirley Shrift, aka Shelley Winters, who in a few years would play a significant role in indoctrinating me into the realities of big-time show business.

The other theater restaurant, Sardi's, catered to actors who considered themselves more elegant. Even the drunks at the bar dressed in jackets and ties. A joint with pretensions to theater history, Sardi's was frequented by managers and investors and actors who worshipped the likes of the Barrymores and the Algonquin Round Table and considered the Hollywood movie scene ridiculous. Actors with egalitarian impulses, people who had endured the indignities of McCarthyism, preferred winding down at Jim Downey's. The Sardi's experience was still a few years away.

What I remember about that transforming evening was that I was seated next to a black actor named Osborne Smith, who took a kindly (and probably sexual) interest in me. A member of the ensemble of the hit musical *Irma La Douce*, he probably realized that every word he uttered sounded magical to my virgin ears as he plied me with stories of his struggles as a black actor driving a taxicab in Chicago. I wished I could visit Jim Downey's nightly, my sole responsibility in life to step onto the stage of the Plymouth Theater six days a week and twice on Wednesdays and Saturdays. By the end of the evening I longed to be black and driving a taxi in Chicago.

My second transformative experience happened a few months later, when my mother, much to my indignation, decided we would take a five-day excursion to the revolutionary war colony in Williamsburg, Virginia. My Christmas break was only ten days long, and I was convinced that since my father and I saw each other for a mere four days a month, it was only fair that I would spend my entire vacation with him. The divorce agreement read otherwise, however, and for weeks I was left to conjure the numbing prospect of sitting beside my mother as she drove six hundred miles over slippery terrain in her Nash Rambler.

Adolescent sullenness aside, I had good reason to fear such a trip. My mother was a dangerous driver. Martyred, by her reckoning, because she had been born a twin—a twin whose other half was masculine—she drove an automobile with an indifference bordering on belligerence. She believed the highway, like most other things, was out to get her. Simple rules of the road, such as knowing who has the right of way when turning left into oncoming traffic, eluded her. Looking for automobiles over her right shoulder when changing lanes, or even checking the direction of the arrow when turning onto a one-way street, was not her responsibility.

For a full week before we departed for Virginia, I prayed to God that we would avoid a major accident—and I was not in the habit of praying to a God my father insisted did not exist. (I continued my supplications throughout the trip, until we were two days from home. Sure that I was simply being paranoid, I stopped praying, and the next day my mother nearly drove us off a bridge in Northern Virginia.)

We left New York on a Sunday and headed toward the exotic environs of Baltimore, where we would spend our first night in a hotel before continuing south. I entertained myself on the ride down listening to the National Football League championship game being played between the Philadelphia Eagles, with whom I had fallen in love a few years before because they were the worst team in the league and because I was partial to their Kelly-green-and-white colors, and the Green Bay Packers, who had also been the worst team in their division until they came under the aegis of coach Vince Lombardi. Never before had two such hopeless underdogs made it to the championship game.

If ever I need a reminder of the joys of listening to a sporting event rather than watching one, I think back to that broadcast. The specificity of television has made the world a more linear place. I'd rather imagine my own camera angles, fantasizing my way through a turnstile on the way to my seat than be seduced by the horizontal imagery of the television screen.

The game that day was one of high drama. It ended on the final play, with Green Bay needing a touchdown to win the game. With no time left on the clock, the Packers fullback Jim Taylor took the ball on the Eagle five-yard line and burst through the entire defense, except for

Philadelphia's heroic middle linebacker, Chuck Bednarik, who was playing the final game of his career. The son of a Pennsylvania coal miner, Bednarik was the last professional football player to play a full sixty-minute game, center on the offense and linebacker on the defense. In arguably the greatest moment of his career, Bednarik wrapped his arms around the hard-driving fullback and wrestled him to the ground as time expired. The Philadelphia Eagles were the champions of the world, while the Packers would have to wait another year before beginning their football dynasty. The Eagles were never to be champions again.

This drama happened in my mother's car, as we turned off the exit ramp and spent what seemed an eternity navigating the one-way streets of Baltimore.

Baltimore was the first small city I had ever visited, and by 1960 it was in decline. Raised in New York, I had no idea what other cities looked like. After checking into our hotel, my mother arranged for us to see a play at the city's last remaining legitimate theater, the Ford. For someone who'd experienced the bustle of Broadway, the deserted streets of Baltimore on a Sunday evening mystified me. I imagined live theater was the sole province of New York. Who would buy tickets, and what actors would perform, in a landscape so deserted?

To my surprise, the play we were attending was *The Pleasure of His Company.* But instead of Cornelia Otis Skinner and Cyril Richard (he of the green Alpine hat), this production featured Donald Cook and onetime movie star Joan Bennett. I remember little of the play, other than that it was a comedy concerning high-born sophisticates who bantered in a way I could barely comprehend. What I do recall is that when the curtain came down with a thud to conclude the first act, an enormous cloud of brown dust descended on the orchestra, providing the audience with the biggest laugh of the evening. We were told at intermission that the theater was soon to be demolished, and cleaning the curtain wasn't worth the expense.

What was far more interesting to me than the play was how its cast had gotten to Baltimore in the first place. On the walk back to our hotel, my mother attempted to clarify matters.

"This is the road company of the same play that's appearing on Broadway," she explained, "but with different actors playing the same parts."

"Do the actors live here?"

"No. They're probably staying at a local hotel."

"Does the play run as long here as it does on Broadway?"

"I can't imagine they stay anyplace longer than a few weeks. Then they pack up and move to another city."

"Together?"

"I would imagine so. It's called a touring company. They all travel together by bus or train or automobile or airplane."

"Like a family."

"I suppose. Like a family, yes."

This was an idea so tantalizing that my preoccupations—spending vacations with my father, fiery car crashes in Virginia, championship football games—receded into inconsequence. It occurred to me that being in a touring company might just be my ticket out of the doldrums of childhood. I could spend every night in a hotel and eat every meal in a restaurant. The only problem was that I was still thirteen, and we had more than four hundred miles to drive.

Chapter 4

The irony of my mother's life was that she adored the theater, but because my father and his friends were part of it she felt deeply estranged from the individuals onstage who brought her such pleasure. When they were still married, my father would wait until my mother and I had traveled upstate to Mahopac and then sneak his actor friends out to our apartment in Queens. In fact, it was not until they separated that I learned that my father had any actor friends.

My mother found the actors she knew to be insincere and emotionally overbearing. They would prattle on about their hits and misses, their sexual peccadilloes, without expressing the slightest interest in what was happening to her. Within this small circle of theater people, she believed she would be forever out of the loop. The duality of her feelings confused me and made me think that what my father did for a living was infantile. She would be rapturous describing Rex Harrison's performance in *My Fair Lady,* and in the next breath would refer to him as "a disgusting person" because he had jilted Lili Palmer in order to marry Kay Kendall (even though Kay Kendall was one of her favorite actresses). She believed all actors were adulterers, loudmouths, wannabe gangsters and whores—and that included Sir Laurence Olivier and everyone else who spoke the Queen's English. Dean Martin she gave a pass to because he openly admitted to being a bum. In spite of all this, she was generous enough to explore the possibility that she may have given birth to an actor.

From the time I was a toddler my mother suspected that I was a performer. My father, however, was dubious. Pretending to be playing the piano by banging on the keys was an act my father believed needed polish; there was a difference between uninhibited behavior and talent. But my mother persisted, to the point where competition between my father and me began to cloud the debate. Even though my father was the professional actor and family breadwinner, she seemed more embarrassed than supportive of his gifts. About me, she seemed to harbor no doubts.

After I had spent several summers at sleepaway camps that ranged from the conventional coed athletic program to a ranch where each child was assigned his or her own horse, my mother decided she would enlist her brother's expertise (he was editor of *Redbook*) to find a summer program that catered exclusively to the arts. A camp called Gray Gables Theatrical Workshop, about thirty miles north of Manhattan, was recommended by one of the magazine's staff, and whoever that person was, I will be eternally grateful to him or her.

Of course I took to the idea of attending a theater camp with my customary grace: "I'm not going!"

"Why not?" asked my father.

"Because I want to go back to the ranch camp."

"Your mother and I won't let you. The last time we visited you there it was so filthy we were afraid there'd be an outbreak of bubonic plague."

"I love it there. All my friends are there."

"You'll make new friends."

"I don't want to make any new friends."

"I'm sorry, but you're going."

"I'm not going!"

On a clear summer day in late June, my father drove his Chrysler Imperial past two stone pillars that separated the Gray Gables Theatrical Workshop from the rest of the world. By the time we arrived at the hilltop estate in Kitchawan, New York, the sun was nearly down. Although this camp had been my mother's brainchild, she thought it best to stay behind and let my father do the dropping-off, since we were on far better terms. I was so angry and frightened I could barely breathe. It had come down to a matter of principle, and here was more proof that when it came to my welfare, I had no power other than to throw a fit.

There's no more hopeless feeling than watching your father remove a metal foot locker from the trunk of his car, kiss you good-bye, and drive away in a cloud of dust. Somewhere up a gravel road I could hear a camper singing "In the jungle / the mighty jungle / A lion sleeps tonight." The trees were festooned with strings of colored lights.

A short woman with a pretty face but whose jaw was cast iron greeted me with a smile that exposed a pronounced overbite. This was Carol

Renner Melnick, who had dreamed up the place. I wasn't sure whether she intended to embrace me or wrestle me to the ground. Her belligerence seemed a match for my own.

"You're Stadlen, aren't you? We met a few months ago when I showed you around. You were pretty unhappy then. Are you still unhappy?"

"I'm fine," I said. Better to sulk than appear frightened.

"I think you've come to the right place. Then again, maybe you haven't." She reached down into a bag and pinned a plastic name tag on my chest. "You can call me Aunt Carol—or anything else you want to call me." She laughed at her own joke. "You'll be all right, Stadlen. Let's get you situated with the others."

She led me up a narrow path to a freshly painted wooden stage that faced an open field, where the inhabitants of my new world were either chatting, singing, or playing musical instruments. Everyone around me was my age or slightly older, and all of them seemed more talented, better looking, and more at ease in their own bodies. I decided I would cry.

There is a theatrical muse who watches over young people who find themselves in the right place at the right time, even though they haven't yet figured out a thing about themselves. As I stared past the modest white buildings that comprised the camp, I was handed a plastic glass filled with fruit punch.

"Drink it, Lew," said a strange, manicured boy dressed in a seersucker suit, madras shirt, and white patent leather shoes worn with no socks. Rings adorned three of his fingers, and a gold bracelet hung from one wrist. When he spoke his lips produced a hissing sound like the vibration of a bee's wings. "I see you've already met Aunt Carol, Lew. Watch out for her. I wouldn't trust her as far as I could throw her."

The boy was handsome, except for his insinuating mouth, which was frozen in a perpetual leer. He engaged me as if we had been friends forever.

"Go easy on the Hawaiian punch, Lew. I can't believe she's budgeted for seconds." He clinked his plastic glass against my own.

"I came up here with my mother in February. A fifty-mile shlep from Belle Harbor, where I live. What does she offer in the way of refreshments?" He took a long, dramatic pause. "A cool, refreshing glass of spring water. Her words, Lew, not mine! I'm sorry! You don't woo potential customers by offering refreshments that run under your property."

He sat me down on a wooden chair, then took the seat beside me. "Let's figure out what we're paying. Are you on scholarship?"

"I don't know what that is," I told him.

"It's a fancy word for discount. She'll knock a few bucks off her asking price if you get up at five o'clock in the morning and slave in the kitchen."

In my fourteen years, I had never been asked to make my own bed or wash a dirty dish.

"I don't think I'm on scholarship," I responded, staring at the name tag that identified him as Michael Aptner.

"You're better off. For the few extra dollars you'd be saving, she'd have you living in a hole."

Who was this strange boy, and why was he wearing clothes that made him look like a middle-aged Miami businessman? When he stood, his double-jointed knees hyperextended, a teenage boy who had never picked up a baseball bat or taken a gym class in his life. This fellow was a revelation to me. It no longer mattered how I stacked up in the pecking order of the Gray Gables Theatrical Workshop. Sitting beside me was a kindred spirit far stranger than me. He structured every sentence like our neighbor, Bea Schultz. His eyelids drooped like the gangster Meyer Lansky's. He comported himself fearlessly. He was my first friend in the theater.

Gray Gables was a twenty-acre estate reachable via the Hudson Valley line out of Grand Central to Ossining, or you could drive up the Taconic and get off at Pinesbridge Road. If you stared up at the blue sky before lowering your gaze to the trees that ringed the property, you could convince yourself you were sitting beneath an enormous transparent dome. How the Melnick family had come by the place was anyone's guess. They were hardly wealthy people, and although the property was oversized for their needs, a threadbare aura could be detected. The property resembled the setting of a Chekhov play in which a family of limited means struggles to maintain a country estate.

Everything about Carol Melnick, a pretty, round-faced, middle-aged woman of ample bosom and short legs, reeked of unrequited love. She identified herself in the camp's brochure as a child counselor, although she really made her living dispensing tickets behind the bars of a box office at the Broadway Theater. Her husband, Dan, from whom she appeared to be estranged, had once been the general manager for the flamboyant Broadway producer Billy Rose. In recent years he had been relegated to working as box office treasurer at the theater where Carol worked. He seemed merely an observer, dropping by unexpectedly a few hours a week, his demeanor suggesting that he'd learned detachment in order to safeguard his health.

Camp headquarters was a large Victorian house where we all ate our meals. On the second and third floors, thirty-five teenage girls were shoehorned into rooms of varying size. A gravel pathway led to a two-story barn the Melnicks had converted into a small theater. The lower floor was separated into two sections, one a dressing area, the other a dormitory that slept the eight older boys who doubled as kitchen help.

To the left of the barn a white clapboard bungalow housed me and seven other boys. Up an incline stood a modest two-story dwelling for the staff. Behind the bungalow was an outdoor stage used as a dance space, and beyond the staff house a gravel path passed through a stand of pines to a neglected swimming pool that nobody ever used. Two former chicken coops served as costume and scenery shops, and past the outdoor stage there was a field where a dilapidated baseball dugout hung on against the elements, the preposterous suggestion being that if anyone was interested in athletics, a ballfield was at their disposal.

The Melnicks had three daughters, two in their early twenties and the youngest in her late teens. All were beautiful. Helena, the oldest and loveliest, was a recent graduate of Briarcliff Junior College. A dead ringer for Susan Hayward, she was scheduled to direct our first play. Judith, the youngest, was a sexy, laconic redhead who spent all her time flirting with the older boys and wishing she were someplace else. Ellen, the middle daughter, was pretty and blond, although her appearance was compromised by a slight Tolstoyan mustache. All the boys who doubled as waiters were madly in love with her, for she inspired obsessive loyalty in the kitchen, which she controlled with the singlemindedness of Annie Oakley. The rest of the working family included a very sexy teenage niece, two nephews, and an aunt who spoke with a thick European accent and spent most of her time locked in an attic, working on the books. Everyone had been enlisted to serve in an enterprise that could not have netted the family much of a profit.

That summer day, Gray Gables awaited the arrival of sixty teenagers, some of whose parents had been divorced two, three, even four times.

It was if the lot of us were being led through two stone pillars in manacles and striped pajamas to discover the impracticality of a creative existence.

On our first morning we assembled on the outdoor stage to learn a dance combination taught by the resident choreographer, Joe Vilane. Joe was a prematurely balding, no-nonsense fellow in his early thirties, kind and unpretentious, ferociously honest and intelligent. Within an hour he had taught a dozen of us a rudimentary vocabulary of dance: how our bodies performed when our shoulders rotated backward and forward, how our arms extended through our fingertips to complete a fluid movement that had begun at the center of our torsos. Like all good teachers he made an adventure of the unknown. And then there was the sweat. The occasional breeze that wafted far above us mixed with our perspiration and gave our beating hearts a sense of purpose. He started us off to the beat of African drums—shoulders back, back straight, bend at the knees. He taught us how to do a ballet barre, and when he was done he let us lope across the stage, each of us doing what little we knew as best we could. I had never participated in a group physical activity in which I wasn't terrified of screwing up. For the first time in my life I granted myself permission to succeed.

An hour later I was passing through the white picket fence that surrounded my bungalow when I encountered, walking in the opposite direction and carrying a Samuel French edition of *Look Homeward, Angel,* a tall blond girl wearing a white blouse unbuttoned down to her cleavage and a pair of cut-off jeans that revealed the longest, shapeliest legs I had come across in my brief tenure on the planet. When she addressed me, her voice was cool and pitched like a flute. Our conversation, mostly one-sided, concerned the hardships she had endured at the hands of her parents. She lived in New Haven, where her father was a professor of South American antiquities at Yale. So misunderstood by her family was she that she had been sent away to St. Margaret's Episcopal boarding school in Waterbury, where the nuns had dedicated themselves to ridding her of her free-spirited ways. Though she took pains to forgive her oppressors, she knew that she was destined to experience the innumerable pleasures missing from her parents' loveless marriage. I immediately fell in love with her.

Laney Kubler was the first of many young women who emitted a cold heat I could not resist. From an early age I chased after women I believed to be the opposite of my mother, not realizing that what they all had in common was an ambivalence about who I was and a conviction about who they did not want me to be—specifically, myself. Since I hadn't the faintest notion who I was, I was open to any suggestion, as long as they would passionately desire me one moment and insist I get lost the next. Laney Kubler was the embodiment of the female temptress who passionately wanted me to leave her alone. The lousier she made me feel, the more I desired her.

But I'm getting ahead of myself. At fourteen I stood a full foot shorter than her, and when she sat in the grass in her cut-offs, the crease in her thigh seductive above her bent knee, she was intoxicating. Never before had I conversed with a contemporary who quoted from James Joyce: "And then I asked him with my eyes to ask again. Would I yes to say yes, my mountain flower, and then I drew him down to me so he could feel my breasts yes. All perfume yes, and yes I said yes, I will yes."

Oh, baby. This was truly the beginning of the end, yes.

I don't remember having much to say, other than confiding that I had a pretty terrible life of my own that wasn't half as sexy as hers. I sensed that I was having the first adult conversation of my life and that the bondage my childhood represented had more past than future. This was the girl I would con into relieving me of my virginity. If misery loved company, who better to spend it with than Laney Kubler? I don't believe I would have dared to entertain the notion of pursuing such a girl if not for the heady possibility of my new surroundings, for she appeared to me that day as an aberration, much the way Omar Sharif and his black stallion first appeared in the film *Lawrence of Arabia*, as a cloud of desert vapor before metamorphosing into a man and horse.

The mission of Gray Gables was to create what every actor and actress would like to experience in a professional environment. On the fourth day of camp we were asked to audition for the first of two plays the camp would present over an eight-week session. We were to rehearse each play for three weeks, then perform it for five performances before audiences of parents and guests.

I was never very good when it came to tests: my mental processes would shut down and I would rage at the indignity of being judged. Mathematics was a special bugaboo. I reasoned that there was no point in being an acceptable student when I stood in the shadow of my genius first cousin. I seemed to earn affection when I presented myself as someone who swam against the tide. I excelled at imitating my English teacher, who crossed and uncrossed her legs so that those of us in the front rows would be unable to peek up her skirt. That was my single academic achievement. I refused to believe that acceptance at a good college was my ticket to a life of emotional security. Who needed security, when all I wanted was to bathe in the warmth of a good laugh? Not that I was lighthearted: I sat next to the kid who was lighthearted. In short, my most fervent desire was to get out without formulating a way of getting in—until I auditioned for the camp's first play, *Anastasia*, a melodrama about a group of crooks attempting to cash in on the possibility that the czar's daughter, Anastasia Romanov, had survived the mass murder of her family by the Bolsheviks. Here at last was a vehicle that might allow me to shine.

I auditioned that day in the carefree mental state of believing I would never get the part. It was assumed that only kids returning from previous summers would be cast in the good roles; at least this was the information gleaned by Michael Aptner, who seemed forever ahead of the curve.

"It's a racket, Lew," he confided. "First-year kids get the crumbs. Next summer they soak you for another two grand."

The beautiful Helena Melnick was the auditioner. Also in attendance was Joe Vilane, who would direct Rodgers and Hammerstein's *Oklahoma!* later that summer. All of us were abuzz, because Joe had danced in the original production on Broadway. I entered through the barn door with the smell of cedar in my nostrils and was asked to stand on my very first stage and audition for the role of the artist Petrovin, one of two sidekicks of the play's male lead, Prince André Bounine. My first lines were "He's not at home? This house is cold. You need a stove. Maybe I'd better draw one on the wall, one of our big Russian *pechas*."

My line readings elicited a delightful nasal giggle from the unbearably beautiful Helena. As I continued her laughter increased, which surprised me, because the last thing I wanted to be was funny.

"He's used to living with beautiful things. His villa in the Crimea was a delight." More roars of laughter, this time from Joe Vilane. Why were they laughing, when I was never more serious? When I finished I felt a warm pounding in my chest. When they asked me what plays I had performed in, I told them I had never actually performed in a play, but I had sung along with a lot of my parents' cast albums. This elicited more laughter. They thanked me for stopping by and said I would be hearing from them one way or another in the next twenty-four hours. As I left, the distance between the stage and the barn doors seemed much farther apart than when I'd walked in. My lungs seemed to lack the oxygen needed to complete the journey. Still, it had been a relatively painless first attempt. There were worse experiences then having beautiful people laugh in my face.

The next morning the entire camp was summoned to the barn, where the cast list was posted on the door. To my surprise, not only was I cast as Petrovin, but the role of the second sidekick, the accountant Chernov, had been awarded to my skeptical friend Michael Aptner. At last I had wandered into a place where fairness and justice ruled supreme.

We apprentices at the Gray Gables Theater Workshop were a diverse group. Parents like my own must have concluded that here was a place where an overweight, ungainly daughter might learn poise, or a stutterer could be cured of his impediment. Here a boy with no interest in playing sports but who enjoyed shopping for dresses with his mother could prosper in a sympathetic environment. Most of the girls and a few of the boys were attracted to the dance; others enjoyed working on sets and costumes, and sprinkled among the sixty of us was a smaller core who imagined themselves the next generation's gift to the commercial theater. There weren't any of the ultra-ambitious, monomaniacal types I would encounter a few years later when I turned professional. We were a good-natured group of hormonal teenagers who sensed that whatever adulthood had in store for us, to this point in our young lives something had definitely been missing.

To succeed at anything, one has to be good, but equally, lucky. I didn't know it at the time, but Gray Gables was in its heyday. What had started as a creative workshop for a number of Carol's relatives and local children had reached its apogee at the exact moment I arrived. The camp was to last only three more summers, as the connective tissue that united the staff soon disintegrated over creative differences.

What distinguished that summer from any other were the talents of the two directors, Helena Melnick and Joe Vilane. They were as talented as any director or choreographer I would find in the professional theater. (I'll make an exception for Agnes de Mille.) Helena was very young and extremely marriageable, and one of the more insidious aspects of her mother's influence was that Carol, for all her romantic notions, believed that none of her daughters could marry too much money. She saw her loveliest daughter as the most likely to attract wealth, and Helena was doing everything possible to comply with her mother's wishes.

Only fourteen at the time, I perceived Helena to be an adult, but she couldn't have been more than twenty-two, and how seriously she took her gifts as an artist was eclipsed by her search for a wealthy spouse. This was a pity, because she possessed exceptional communication skills and was devoid of the slightest pretension—pretension being something I would soon learn is the hallmark of the stage director who doesn't know what the hell he's doing. Helena communicated what she knew, and if she didn't know something, she didn't pretend she did. Her modesty about her talents helped set our artistic guidelines. She had no interest in being perceived as a guru who had all the answers. Her job was to direct *Anastasia*, with a cast of teenagers of varying talent and devoid of craft, in less than three weeks.

Working under the tutelage of Joe Vilane was incredible good fortune. Joe offered the best vision for creating theater: he just wanted it to be good. Not different, good! His great ambition was to teach. He lacked the stomach to compete against those who excel at talking the talk. I've met many people over the years who have held themselves back with a crippling form of self-criticism. Perhaps I'm one of them. All true artists have it, but those who make a name for themselves in the popular culture know that whatever personal dissatisfaction they may feel about themselves, their lives would be unbearable if they gave in to this negativity. What complicates the picture are those whose sole talent lies in perpetuating an unquenchable ambition. They have a more pedestrian definition of achievement, and there are far too many of them. Joe Vilane's purpose was to teach young people craft, structure, and art. To us kids, all sexed up and armed with nothing more than enthusiasm, he was a gift from above.

In the days that followed, Aunt Carol became the personification of the meddling theatrical producer. After all, had it not been for Carol there would be no Gray Gables, no production of *Anastasia*, no money to pay the staff. Like all producers, powerful or marginal, after conceptualizing the enterprise she felt locked out of the creative process, which had passed to her daughter. In the days and weeks ahead, therefore, she attempted to exercise leverage by insinuating herself into our personal lives. This was pretty exciting stuff. Never before had anyone cared enough to interject themselves into my emotional life, except for my parents, and they didn't count because they were my parents. Aunt Carol was greatly troubled that I seemed to be carrying a torch for Laney Kubler.

What if my fascination with the girl distracted me from committing fully to the play? At the time I thought that all actors did was memorize their lines and emote on the stage. I never realized that my own personality would be interesting enough to inspire an offstage drama. I was so stimulated by all this attention I wanted to pinch myself.

Working on the play was a labor of love. I didn't have the faintest idea what I was doing, but every morning I would brush my teeth, wet down my hair, and go out and do it. A few of my colleagues were extremely gifted, yet I never felt overwhelmed or in over my head. It was quite different from the anxiety I always felt participating in other team events. Here there were no losers. We were like living building blocks that accumulated over rehearsal time to form something infinitely larger than victory or defeat. There was no defeat. If you weren't holding up your end of the bargain, you could go back and try it again. There was an element of patience that translated into good feeling. No one could be heard snickering in the bleachers, and of course our leader was the beautiful Helena, who laughed and exhorted us to be better, always reminding us that we had a story to tell.

We must have been at it a week when I was given a break while the other actors rehearsed a scene I wasn't in. I walked out onto a wooden balcony that faced the scenery shop and experienced a feeling of peace I had never felt before. I was an actor in a play called *Anastasia*. We would open out of town in Philadelphia before moving to New York. I would stay in a very nice hotel, and after the performance we would go to a restaurant that was the equivalent of Jim Downey's and talk about the show. This was all a person like me could ever ask for, and now it would come to pass. People were paying attention to me and worrying that my emotional life might interfere with some of their own plans. I was a bit of a big deal. I knew from that moment on that this was what I was meant to be.

Be careful what you wish for.

The moment I remember most during our rehearsal process for *Anastasia* was a scene in which Michael Aptner, I, and the leading man (an enormously gifted fellow named Eric Berne, who was a few years our senior) were sitting around a table plotting some mischief, when a book that was one of the props was inadvertently pushed off the table and fell to the floor. Since the fallen book was nothing we had planned, the three of us stared down at it dumbly and continued on with the scene. After we had finished, Helena told us that if such a thing had happened in real life, one of us would certainly have retrieved the book and put it back on the table. I quickly assimilated this observation, and although it might seem pedestrian, I can assure you that I have seen any number of professional actors who, finding themselves in similar circumstances, will stare down blankly at a fallen book and wait for the scene to end, even though they're being paid handsomely for their time. A mere tadpole, I never imagined that an observation this simple could contain more content than a year and a half of study at a prestigious New York acting school.

When the moment came for the cast of *Anastasia* to perform before a paying public (so to speak; I'm certain they came for free), we acted with great elan, and the response was that we were a smash hit. All of the parents seemed mesmerized with our depiction of adults, and although Michael and I were starving at intermission and decided to scrape some smelly fish eggs off some perfectly tasty Ritz crackers and into the garbage, our opening night was an unqualified success.

Laney Kubler, who was not in the cast, was so impressed that she followed me home as I walked beneath the towering pines and asked me to sit on a large boulder near the tennis court. Helping me unhook her brassiere (left to my own devices this would have taken me the better part of the summer), she whispered to me, "You are a very nice boy." And I kissed her breasts and yes I said yes, I will yes.

My self-image that summer stood in direct contrast to the person I perceived myself to be the other nine months of the year at Highland Prep. I had been a student there for a year, after my parents, fearing I would be swallowed up in overcrowded classrooms where no one would pay much attention to me (and where I would pay even less attention to them), had wisely moved me out of the public school system. After the eighth grade I had completely given up on myself as a student; it was only the public school bureaucracy, not my own efforts, that pushed me forward from grade to grade. By the time I entered private high school I was so far behind that each morning I had to overcome severe anxiety about surviving a five-hour day by completely faking it. With the exception of social studies and certain aspects of tenth-grade English, I was hopelessly lost, to the point where anything learned in eighth-grade math had long been forgotten. Now they expected me to pass a more advanced form of math called geometry.

At the beginning of the school year, before I knew anything about Gray Gables, my class was informed by our geometry teacher, Mr. Hyman (you can imagine the hours of entertainment that name provided) that since geometry was based on logic, he expected all of us to get straight A's. It didn't take me long to conclude that what seemed logical to Mr. Hyman was completely illogical to me. I was clueless as to why I should take this leap of faith concerning the square of the hypotenuse when I was having a difficult enough time in English class figuring out what the subjunctive was. For a month or two I struggled, failing every pop quiz, until God intervened. Mr. Hyman's son was seriously injured in a trampoline accident, and he stopped teaching. One substitute teacher followed another, and by the end of term I knew no more about geometry than I had on my first day of class. By the time we were about to take our final exam, I was already stressing about the summer, although by then anything seemed preferable to the battery of tests I would be forced to take to receive even minimum passing grades.

The last of our geometry teachers, a Mr. Gross (we had gone from a Hyman to a Gross), informed us that for our final he would be using an old New York State Regents' exam, a test required by all public schools in the state but not private ones. This information was a great gift to us, because past Regents' exams were published in a small book that could be purchased as a study aid. Hoping to help us prepare for our finals—or perhaps daring us to expose ourselves as the cheating dogs we were—Mr. Gross daily revealed to us the very geometry problems we would be tested on in our final exam.

None of this information was of any use to me because I was so far behind. I could never figure out what old exam he was planning to use, but several of my classmates, also on the cusp of failing, could. After weeks of sleuthing, my good friend Barry Sternlieb announced to the rest of us that he had broken the code. All we had to do was purchase the old Regents' booklet, hide it under our desks on the day of the exam, and copy the answers down. Ignorant as I was about things academic, I was much less the fool when it came to persuading our teacher that four of his worst students had crammed just hard enough to manage a better-than-anyone-could-possibly-have-expected passing grade. Alas, my idiot friends saw it differently.

"I'm going to give myself 100," said Arnold Chusid. Arnold was destined for a career in medicine.

"No, no, we can't do that," I told him.

"The way I figure it, I need about 120 to finish up with a 65."

"Nobody gets a perfect grade. If the four of us do too well, they'll know we all cheated."

"I figure I need at least 90 to pass," said Barry. Barry would later become a gifted poet.

"Let's give ourselves an 80," I suggested. "Anything more than that and they'll figure it out."

"An 80 won't do it for me. I haven't passed a test all year," said Barry.

"It's creating the illusion that we *tried*," I posited. (By this time I had actually convinced myself that I had.) But I couldn't convince my pals. Even though I gave myself a modest 78, Mr. Gross linked me to the others, and I was told a week before the school year ended that I would have to get up at six every morning, whether I attended Gray Gables or not, and go to summer school, because Mr. Gross had failed me in geometry. Was there so little gratitude in the world, after I had worked my tail off to get a respectable 78?

The threat of summer school had hung over my head from the time I entered junior high. Only the prospect of being left back a grade was more hideous than going to summer school. Basically I regarded grade school as a twelve-year sentence in the big house. I would keep my nose clean and do my time, but learning something—anything—was just not part of the deal. You can thus imagine my feelings when Aunt Carol dropped me off at six-thirty in the morning on the steps of Ossining High, where I was surrounded by more Irish and Italian teenagers than I had ever seen in my life, to be introduced to my latest geometry teacher. A barrel-chested gentleman in his mid-thirties with a prematurely balding pate, Mr. Eli's first words to us were that passing his course was not going to be any snap. The midterm exam would take place in three short weeks, and we all had a lot of studying to do. I had always imagined summer school as a punishment designed to destroy my summer vacation, but never in my wildest dreams did I imagine I would have to accomplish in eight weeks what I had been incapable of accomplishing in eight months.

Every morning at dawn I would throw my clothes on and walk over to the main house, where I would tiptoe up the stairs to the room Laney Kubler shared with five other girls and sneak beneath her covers, nudging myself closer to the accumulated heat beneath her cotton nightgown, the smell of her day-old Canoe cologne tantalizing me. Feigning indifference, she would stretch her long body like a cat, cast a sleepy glance to see if it was indeed me, whereupon she would make the sweetest female whimper before turning on her side, allowing me to spoon. Fifteen minutes later I would sneak downstairs to await my chauffeur, who would drop me a few feet from my geometry classroom, where I whiled away the next three hours playing dice baseball under my desk.

I scored 38 on my geometry midterm. Apparently the prospect of being thrown out of Highland Prep wasn't having much effect on me. What did I care if my twelve-year sentence at school was reduced to ten? Now that I was going to be an actor, who cared if I had a high school diploma? Somewhere in the back of my mind was the knowledge that state law mandated that I finish high school, but there was time to jump off that bridge when I came to it. Let my parents experience the sting of my misfortune; I had just been cast as Will Parker in *Oklahoma!* Every morning I was cuddling with my blond, six-foot cutie, and my voice hadn't even changed yet. Was I an actor or a mathematician? I was fully committed to taking advantage of my good fortune, and the summer still had four weeks to go.

Sensing imminent danger, Aunt Carol concocted a strategy intended to save my ass. "I'm going to invite your geometry teacher to a performance of *Oklahoma!*" she told me the morning she got my test marks.

"That's crazy!" I told her. "There's a hundred kids in the room. I sit in the back of the class. He doesn't know I exist."

"That's exactly why I'm going to invite him. Find out if he's married; I'll send them both an invitation." Then she gripped my nose between her second and third fingers and gave it a squeeze. "And stay out of Laney Kubler's bed in the morning! What kind of camp do you think I'm running here? If that girl's mother starts yelling bloody murder I'll be out of business."

The rehearsals for *Oklahoma!* were what every rehearsal process should be (and often isn't). We were to perform the play as written by Rodgers and Hammerstein, exploring the social conditions that existed when it was first presented while integrating our directors' vision so that the final product would be amusing, sexy, well paced, and full of heart. It was not Joe Vilane's intention to reinvent the play's original meaning. *Oklahoma!* had been written in the midst of an international conflagration to honor the guileless optimism of the American pioneering spirit. We were fighting the fascists, and Oscar Hammerstein chose the very center of the country as a metaphor for what was right, wrong, and silly about the people who called themselves Americans. It wasn't written to explore the dark underbelly of the republic. It wasn't about the genocide the settlers perpetrated on the American Indian nations. It was about a very good girl who could hardly keep her hands off the most charming cowboy in the territory, while all around her the secondary characters "just couldn't say no." An underlying theme concerned farmers' and cowboys' differing ideas about what livestock—cattle or sheep—should rule the range. Thrown into the mix was an extremely dim field hand named Jud Fry, who caused a lot of trouble by obsessing over the very good girl (Laurie) because he couldn't get it through his thick skull that she found him repulsive and kind of scary.

When the show was first presented it was hailed as revolutionary because of Agnes de Mille's act-ending Dream Ballet, which was motivated by the good girl taking a sniff of a cocaine-laced elixir given her by a randy, comic Jewish peddler, aka Ali Hakim (he gives himself a Persian name so he won't be unmasked as a peddler from Delancey Street).

That's all there is to it. The characters are robust and slightly immature, not unlike the territory known as Oklahoma that had yet to gain enough confidence to become a state. The music is fabulous and, as in all musical comedies, the love story is interrupted by scenes of comic relief that point up the foolishness of the human animal. It isn't brain surgery, but to do it right, it helps if the director and choreographer maintain a respect for the intentions of the original collaborators.

For the only time in my acting career, I was cast as a character who was really dumb. Will Parker is a guileless, dancing cowboy who is madly in love with Ado Annie. Their subplot involves Will's unending romantic frustration, because Annie is a hopeless, kind-hearted flirt who is pretty dumb herself, except when it comes to roping her man. Rodgers and Hammerstein wrote the Will Parker character two great comic numbers. Will is introduced to the audience with "Everything's Up to Date in Kansas City," a song that limns the pleasures and temptations of urban life. In the second act he and Ado Annie sing a comic love duet, "All or Nothing."

Joe Vilane cast Rita Schwalb, a diminutive fifteen-year-old strawberry blonde with a faceful of freckles, to play Annie. The best dancer at Gray Gables, Rita performed with an elegant economy that set her apart from the rest of the girls. Whatever she was asked to do she did with warm-hearted precision. She was a thoroughly delightful girl whom I decided I loved like a sister.

Throughout the summer Joe had been teaching us a vocabulary of dance, which he now used to make the story of *Oklahoma!* come alive.

He had a straightforward, authoritative style, and he was always prepared. (It was inconceivable to me that he wouldn't be; after all, he was the director.) Good-natured, always encouraging and accepting of other people's ideas, Joe Vilane was a true mensch. He had cast the best people in camp in the major roles.

One advantage our youthful company possessed was that as teenagers we were not only acting out our roles in the play, we were acting out our roles in life. The rehearsal process was a huge social event in which, instead of searching for our inner child, we were searching for our inner adult. How did older people react to real-life situations? The challenge to appear older than we were unleashed our imaginations and gave many of our performances a sense of irony and a heft that only the better professional actors can summon.

To save money, Carol hired a college professor named Clarence "Beeb" Salzer to design a simple set, brightly painted cloth panels mounted on ropes ranged around the stage like clotheslines. The costumes were either made or rented from the Eaves Costume Shop in New York. (Carol called in all the favors she could from the Broadway theater community.) The musical accompaniment consisted only of a piano and a drummer, but what was lacking in talent was made up for in enthusiasm.

Joe directed all the scenes with faithfulness to the original. Because his sole object was to enhance the play's entertainment value rather than bring glory on himself, our production of *Oklahoma!* was an unqualified success. I dwell on this experience because I remember my father taking me aside after a performance and offering a prescient assessment. "Lewis," he said, clearly moved by what he'd just seen, "hopefully you will have a fine career in the theater that will span a lifetime. What I am about to say may sound absurd. You have wandered into this place during its renaissance. It may be years before you are treated to such a pure and creative experience again. Theater does not get much better than this."

I was thrilled that he'd enjoyed the performance, but I thought he was completely daft.

On the last day of summer school I was to take my final Regents' exam. Either I'd pass or in the fall I'd be expelled from my private school (a school that gave its students every benefit of the doubt because it was in its financial interest to do so). On that last Friday of summer term I sat at my desk with a sharpened pencil in my hand, conscious that I knew considerably less about geometry than I ever had. With a certain self-pity, I realized that among the hundred or so morons now putting pencil to paper, I was perhaps the most ignorant and uncaring of the lot. The questions before me could as well have been written in the original Greek. It would have been folly to attempt to answer any of them, so I took my sweet time darkening the small windows that made up the multiple choice section. Knowing that it would be unseemly to stand up after thirty minutes and walk out of a test scheduled to last three hours, I decided as my final act of rebellion to compose a letter to the authorities:

Dear Mr. Eli and the New York Board of Education:

> If I asked you what the potential weekly gross of the Winter Garden Theater was for its current production of *The Unsinkable Molly Brown*, you wouldn't be able to answer it. If you asked me what the square of the hypotenuse is to the right triangle, I wouldn't be able to answer that either. Why must my life depend on answering questions I know will have nothing to do with my life in the future? I am not interested in geometry and you are not interested in the theater. Etc., etc.
>
> Sincerely,
Lewis Stadlen

No sooner had I finished my declaration of independence and started to stand than a forceful if not unfriendly hand pushed me back into my seat. Looming above me was the composed presence of Mr. Eli, who reached for the letter with one hand while his other remained clamped to my shoulder. During the minute it took for him to read the letter, it occurred to me that the system of oppression I was attempting to ignore was about to descend on me like the hammer of Thor. What was I but a cog in a mighty machine, my escape a mere delusion?

Mr. Eli gently put the letter down on my desk and sat down in the seat beside me.

"My wife and I saw you in that play the other night. It was wonderful. You were wonderful. Is that what you want to be, an actor, Lew?"

"Yes," I said, barely able to credit the civility of his tone.

"Then that is what you *should* be." He took his hand off my shoulder and shook mine. "Lew, it has been a great pleasure to meet you, and I hope someday you become a very successful actor." Before walking away he gave me the most sympathetic of looks. With nothing left to do but be embarrassed, I stumbled out of his classroom.

The following Monday I received word I had scored an 18 on the exam, but Mr. Eli gave me a passing grade for effort. That fall I was readmitted to Highland Prep to finish my senior year. Thank you, Mr. Eli, wherever you are!

Chapter 5

On my father's fortieth birthday I accompanied him to a performance of *A Funny Thing Happened on the Way to the Forum*, starring the comic genius Zero Mostel. In the middle of the second act my father laughed so hard he vomited a small part of his seafood dinner onto the carpeted floor of the Alvin Theater. He spent the rest of the evening surreptitiously attempting to blend it with his shoe into the fabric, where I'm certain it still remains. After the performance we went backstage to congratulate David Burns, who played (magnificently) the delusional Senex. For the first time I realized how tiny a Broadway dressing room could be. David Burns sat staring into his mirror, a forlorn figure pouring sweat.

"I can't take it anymore!" he said in his gravelly, dirty-old-man voice. Everything about him bespoke comedy. "Zero is driving me crazy. Jack [Gilford] can take it. For him it's water off a duck's back. After tonight I'll never perform on the stage again."

Mostel was famous for his ability to shanghai a production with his subversive comic brilliance. This made things difficult for the cast but well worth it for the audience.

"Davy, I want you to meet my son, Lewis," my father said. "He's going to be an actor."

"Don't be an actor. If I had it to do all over again I would have completed my studies and become an amateur gynecologist. Did you enjoy the show?"

"We loved it!" I said.

"That's good, because Zero is driving me crazy. Listen, Al," he intoned, leaning toward us. "Next year I'm gonna work with that cunt you had in your show. What's her name?"

My-sixteen-year-old head snapped back. Was I actually dreaming? I'd never heard such language coming from an adult. Davy Burns had made the word *cunt* sound like poetry.

"I don't know who you mean," said my father.

"You know, that cunt you had in your show. God, I'd love to fuck her!"

"You mean Eileen Brennan?"

"Yeah, yeah, that's her. God, I'd love to fuck her."

That such an accomplished artist was allowing a sixteen-year-old into his privileged kingdom was a gift beyond reckoning. My father looked over at my startled face. He had always loved David Burns, and this was a historic moment.

"Really? 'Cause I find Eileen Brennan very cold."

"Yeah, yeah, she *is* very cold."

"And very asexual."

"Yeah, yeah, she's cold and asexual." He raised an eyebrow and looked straight at me. "But I'd still love to fuck her."

Chapter 6

I had accomplished the impossible and managed to earn a high school diploma. And I hadn't just gone along with the company line and committed myself to some third-rate college that would have had me. Chico State and Marlborough Junior College would have to find themselves another boy. There was, however, another institution that was dying to have me as a member, and that was the United States Army, which was busily defoliating Vietnam. Today the Vietnam war is analyzed in terms of the crisis of confidence our armed forces suffered because they couldn't get the job done. It has become about the politicians who made the army fight with one arm tied behind its back, or about the tragedy of our troops not being honored for their service to our country. It's not about it being one murderous botch that killed millions of people.

In 1964 a young man of draft age had several options. He could accept the argument that Vietnam was not so much a real country populated with human beings as it was the first in a line of dominos: If Vietnam were to fall to a Communist insurgency, so would Cambodia, Laos, and every other country in Southeast Asia. Forget the fact that the two Communist behemoths of the world, the Soviet Union and China, were using these countries as proxy states to advance their own foreign policy goals and that historically everybody who shares a common border tends to hate its neighbor. Listen, everybody has the right to earn a decent living, and that includes McGeorge Bundy, Walt Rostow, and especially Henry Kissinger. If you weren't buying that argument, you could do what everybody else I knew did. One, you could go to college and get a student deferment. Two, you could tell the army you were a homosexual. Three, you could get a psychiatrist to write a letter to your draft board saying you were nuts.

Not for one instant did my conscience suffer over the fact that I was destined to become a draft dodger; it was just a matter of what route I was prepared to take to get out. Since I intended to be an actor, and since I was residing in Manhattan, where there were hundreds of thousands of poor kids with no one to advise them against being turned into cannon fodder, I enrolled in a two-year acting program at the Neighborhood Playhouse School of the Theater and for the time being avoided the draft.

Five distinguished acting teachers dominated the New York landscape in the 1960s, all of them veterans of the Group Theater, an acting troupe that in the 1930s had dedicated itself to social themes. All were disciples of Stanislavsky and his Moscow Art Theater; each had his or her interpretation of Stanislavsky's theories. Lee Strasberg was the resident guru of The Actors' Studio. Stella Adler had her own conservatory, above a French bistro opposite Lincoln Center. Harold Clurman and Bobby Lewis taught in rented studios around the city, and Sanford Meisner was head of the acting department at the Neighborhood Playhouse School of the Theater.

I knew nothing much about acting other than that it made me feel good. This was lucky, because Meisner told me that anything I had experienced before meeting him was useless.

"If you want to learn to play the piano," he told us that first day, walking over to a piano in the corner of our classroom, "you don't start playing a sonata. You start with the scales."

He was a slight, nearsighted, natty little man who began every class by having his male assistant place one of his cigarettes in a tortoiseshell holder and light it for him. This same gentleman would then be responsible for teaching us the Sandy Meisner acting method three times a week, knowing that the day before we had watched him lighting Sandy Meisner's cigarettes.

The Meisner method was predicated on the theory that all of acting was reacting, as if a ball were being passed back and forth between two combatants. If the ball was headed for your feet, you would react by bending over to catch it before it hit the ground. If it was thrown at you with maximum force, you'd catch it or it might wind up hitting you in the face. This exercise would be played out verbally. Called the Repeating Exercise, it consisted of your partner saying something rather innocuous, such as "You're looking at me." Then it would be your turn to repeat the phrase, picking up on the attitude with which it was delivered. Was the person implying that he was displeased that you were looking at him? In that case you had options, either throwing the phrase back with even greater displeasure, or perhaps with greater patience than your partner's displeasure deserved.

For close to a year, eighty of us, paying thousands of dollars apiece, would while away the hours in front of Mr. Meisner doing that blasted Repeating Exercise.

"You look unhappy."

(Exasperated) "I look unhappy?"

(Impatient with the exasperation) "That's right. You look unhappy!"

(Insulted by the impatience with the exasperation) "I am not unhappy."

"Then why are you angry?"

"I am *not* angry."

"*You're not angry?* Then why are you raising your voice?"

"No. *You're* the one who's raising his voice."

"I am not."

"You are."

"Now *you're* the one who's angry."

This was pretty boring stuff, but what made it unbearable was that no matter how many times we did the Repeating Exercise, to Sanford Meisner's trained eye none of us ever got it right. Occasionally he would bestow on one of us his only compliment: "Not bad. Who's next?"

There was one other exercise, in which one of us had an Independent Activity, meaning we were doing something when the exercise began, and the other person had an Objective with which he'd enter the room. He could never divulge his Objective, though, because if he did, the exercise would be over. I never figured that one out. When these two exercises grew tedious, we were treated to Mr. Meisner telling some student, usually a not very talented, absurdly trusting twenty-year-old girl from Kansas, that she was wasting his time if she believed she had what it took to be an actress, let alone master the intricacies of the Repeating Exercise.

I had been studying at the Playhouse for close to a year when I encountered a second-year student on the street. (It was Meisner's decision whether you would be invited back for the second year.) The girl asked me what I thought of Sandy Meisner and I told her that I was tired of doing the Repeating Exercise and I thought he was a cruel bastard and an egomaniac. The girl smiled at me the way one might smile at a three-legged dog. "Well, I think that all great men are egomaniacs. I think that Winston Churchill [who had died the day before] was probably an egomaniac."

"Winston Churchill and Sandy Meisner?" I asked incredulously. "I always knew that Churchill, Roosevelt, and Stalin were at Yalta. Was Sandy Meisner there too?"

I wasn't invited back for the second year.

I don't mean to leave the impression that I accepted my first major show business rejection cavalierly; I was deeply distressed and at a loss as to why this injustice had befallen me. I saved my amour-propre by focusing on several students I felt were totally undeserving of promotion but had been handed a kinder fate. It was the first time I compensated for personal rejection with narcissistic rage.

Actually, the atmosphere at the Neighborhood Playhouse School of the Theater was decidedly anti-theater. The school's message was mostly about imperfection, as interpreted by the one man in the world with the ability to recognize it. There was no discussion of the theater's grand and amusing history, and only rarely was a kind word uttered about a respected actor's work. Christopher Plummer was a ham! Sir Laurence Olivier was a technician! Marlon Brando (Meisner always called him Marlon, as if that actor never made a move without him) was a great talent who had squandered his potential. Only Eleonora Duse passed the Sanford Meisner truthfulness test. If you weren't dead, forget it!

I remember as a Playhouse student attending a performance of *Tartuffe*, at the Lincoln Center Repertory. William Ball had restaged a production he had originally directed for his own company, A.C.T. The role of Tartuffe was played by Michael O'Sullivan, who performed with a comic bravura that left me and most of the audience breathless. At the intermission I ran into a number of second-year students and began gushing about one of the great performances I had seen on the stage.

"His acting is awful!" said the most outspoken student in the group. "Why, the poor man is indicating all over the place" (*indicating* being Meisner code for untruthful acting). At the Neighborhood Playhouse it was more useful to focus on the truthfulness of the woman selling orange juice in the lobby than to appreciate the imagination of a fearless farceur.

Rejection hurts, but sometimes it's the best thing that can happen to you.

I was walking down the street, my new draft card heating up my wallet, when I ran into my old Neighborhood Playhouse classmate Andrew Precopio. Andrew had also not been asked back.

"Hey, I'm studying with someone I think you'd really like. She's a little crazy, but she's a real gas. Stella Adler."

"Yeah, Stella Adler." Her name had the familiar ring of some obscure baseball player. I had heard of her, but I didn't know where.

"She has a reputation for being tough on women," Andy said, "but I think the two of you would get along. I mean, she's very theatrical. She's kind of the opposite of Sandy Meisner." The opposite of Sanford Meisner! That was good enough for me.

The next day I was ushered into Stella's office for an interview. Sitting in a high-backed chair that resembled a papier-mache throne was a woman in her early sixties who looked like the queen mother of a country whose major export was sex. She was beautiful in the same way a showgirl is beautiful, but this woman emanated intellectual authority. She spoke with a midatlantic accent tempered by a touch of New York. She had a regal Roman nose and a voluptuous painted mouth that looked like it had seen a lot of action. Everything about her, including the scent of her perfume, radiated size. She looked me over with the expression of someone who was prepared to have a major influence on my life, if I was man enough to accept it.

"Where have you studied?"

"The Neighborhood Playhouse."

"Sandy."

"Yeah."

"You mean, Yes, darling. People who say *yeah* drive buses for a living. What do you want from me?"

I wanted to say Keep me out of the draft, but I didn't.

"My friend Andy Precopio said you're a wonderful teacher. I've been doing this Repeating Exercise for a year, and I want the chance to do some real acting."

"You'll have to start at the beginning, my Principles 1 and Principles 2 courses. My scene study class might be too advanced."

"Miss Adler..."

"Stella, darling. Call me Stella."

"Stella," I repeated awkwardly, "I've got to do something besides these acting exercises."

"My exercises are very different from Sandy's." She said *Sandy* as if she were speaking of some child who had lost his way in a Grimm's fairy tale. "Did you get along with Sandy? Obviously not. I've known him for many years, darling. We're all very worried about Sandy. Go see my secretary, Mary, and have her sign you up for my two Principles courses. I shall allow you to audition for the scene study class. I won't promise you anything." She concluded our interview by indicating with her long eyelashes that I should leave the room. "Now say 'Good-bye, Stella.'"

"Good-bye, Stella."

"Not like a mouse. Like you want to command the stage. *Good-bye, Stella!*"

"*Good-bye, Stella!*"

"Better, darling." Then she rose to her full height, which was six feet in heels. "Go talk to Mary! You'll find me quite different from Sandy."

"Yes," I said.

"Sign up with Mary."

I did.

What is the mindset of a young man who knows nothing except his desires? I wanted to be a professional actor, successful enough to wreak revenge on Sanford Meisner. I wanted a woman to love me. I wanted a life lived publicly and rewardingly enough that everyone I had previously known would notice me for at least two seconds and recognize that I was not the hapless idiot I sometimes believed myself to be. I wanted plenty, but I knew nothing.

On the day I was to audition for Stella Adler's scene study class I was called at the last moment and informed that I would be auditioning not at the studio but at Ms. Adler's apartment, opposite the Metropolitan Museum of Art off Fifth Avenue. I arrived with a friend, Matthew Chait, who had graduated from Cornell and had casually dated my great obsession, Laney Kubler, in college. Apparently he didn't think that much of her ("She's all right"). Most important, Matthew had been invited back to the second year of the Neighborhood Playhouse. He was five years my senior, and although I was not impressed by his acting ability, I regarded him as my superior in every other way. We had worked up a scene from *The Ballad of the Sad Cafe*, a Carson McCullers novella that Edward Albee had adapted for the Broadway stage the year before.

Stella Adler's apartment building was as grand as the lady herself. We were ushered upstairs by a uniformed elevator operator who left us in a tiny vestibule. I had never been in a building with such an arrangement. It felt as if I were paying respects to royalty. Having rung the bell, the two of us stood dumbly outside for a good two minutes before the door was opened by an attractive East Indian woman dressed in a black maid's outfit that appeared to have been borrowed from a summer stock production of *Private Lives*. The girl looked mischievous and seedy. We were led to a living room chockablock with Louis XIV furniture, some of it tipped over in the aftermath of what had obviously been a wild party the night before. Coffee and end tables were littered with half-full brandy glasses and ashtrays overflowing with cigarette butts. Like the French maid, the furniture looked borrowed from the backlot of some 1940s MGM costume drama. Even the blasé Matthew appeared dumbfounded.

A good fifteen minutes went by before the maid returned to the living room and informed us we would be auditioning for Ms. Adler in her bedroom. Leading us down a long hallway, she ushered us into a luxuriously appointed boudoir where the great lady, in a silk dressing gown beneath satin bedcovers, reading glasses propped on her prominent nose, was reading a book.

"What have you prepared for me, darling?" she said, barely taking notice of my friend but exuding warmth and grace nonetheless.

This, I thought, is already a hundred times more interesting than a year's worth of the Repeating Exercise at the Neighborhood Playhouse.

I don't remember much about my audition, other than that I felt a kind of encouragement coming from her perfumed bed. Stella told me I had performed well enough to be part of her scene study class, which meant another $250 in her pocket. After we had concluded that negotiation she held out her hand and asked me to kiss her on the cheek. At the last moment she turned her head and I inadvertently planted a wet one on her lips.

Everything about Stella Adler exuded theatricality. After a year of studying in a place with gray institutional walls, I had just gained entry to Stella Adler's bedroom. A woman who dared to appear ridiculous to a world she herself found absurd. Had it been only a week since I'd bumped into Andrew Precopio?

It took exactly ten seconds in Stella's presence for me to learn a craft element I would apply to my work for the rest of my life. That first day of Stella's Principles 1 class she asked for two volunteers to address the question whether it was possible to live an actor's life while being married and raising a family. An effeminate young man argued that such a thing would be *impossible,* to Andy's and my snickers, while the East Indian woman I'd last seen in a maid's uniform, now in civilian attire, passionately argued the opposite. When they had finished, Stella rose from her throne and announced that we had just witnessed a political argument, that all of life could be summarized as a series of arguments, and that a play was nothing more than life reduced to a three-hour sliver of time.

"What side of the political argument is your character on, darlings? What is the play about? Why did the author write it? How does the character you're playing fit into the puzzle of the play? When does the play take place? Because, darlings," and here she pointed to a girl slouching in her chair in the first row, "if it were to take place in any time other than the informal present, you would notice that the bustle you're wearing would be cutting into your bosom and making it all but impossible to breath, let alone to disrespect that chair. Sit up straight, darling! Your posture is giving me a headache!"

The best was to come on the Friday afternoon of my first scene study class. I had prepared the final monologue of Tennessee Williams's *Glass Menagerie.* I was as preposterously wrong for the character of Tom then as I would be now, but the speech was beautiful, and I was anxious to make a rousing impression on my new teacher.

"Blow out your candles, Laura," I intoned in my New York accent. "Time is the greatest distance between two places. Today the world is lit by lightning.... And so goodnight!"

I looked over at Ms. Adler, who took a moment to compose herself on her throne. She was taking on a new generation of young people who watched a good deal of television but had probably never heard of Anton Chekhov or Leo Tolstoy. For the next six months she would dedicate her talent and intellect to those seated before her, knowing that if she could help even two of us become the kind of actors she could tolerate, let alone admire, her burden would be eased and she would not have to go screaming into the night.

After a moment she inquired with an eerie calm, "Are you Jewish?"

"Yes."

"You are from Brooklyn?"

"Queens."

"You're nice," she told me. "You are a nice Jewish boy from Brooklyn." Then she shifted her gaze so that she was no longer talking only to me but to the entire class. With a towering passion that originated in her diaphragm and exploded upward, she continued, *"But that is not good enough!* You are playing Tennessee Williams himself. You are no longer representing a nice Jewish boy from Brooklyn. You are representing everyone on earth who possesses a poetic sensibility. This is war, darling! The play concerns a world where most people can see only the meaning of what things cost! I recognize this glass because I remember the day I paid five bucks for it." She thrust her arm above her head and uttered a command. "This glass is mine, damn it! It's mine because I paid for it and nobody is going to drink from it without asking my permission!"

I had spent a year listening to Sanford Meisner eviscerate his students in cadences calculated to make the rest of us feel we were accomplices to his cruelty. You were either with him or the object of his scorn. Now I found myself alone on a tiny canvas stage while this formidable woman was screaming that I was wasting her and the playwright's time.

"Then there are those on the other side of the human equation who cannot conceive of how an object so delicate and beautiful as a drinking glass could have found its way into this world. Only God could have conceived this miracle from which I drink!" She settled back on her throne. "This is the personality that sees the world in the abstract. The poet. The creative soul. That is who you must understand in order to play the role of Tennessee, darling. Do you understand?"

"I think so, yes."

"Then if you understand, say '*Yes, Stella!*'"

"*Yes, Stella!*"

"Good, darling. When you answer me, answer me with *size!* There is no size on the stage anymore. It's all *pitse-cocka!* The man who sells me coffee in the morning does not have to perform with size. The actor does."

With supreme gratitude, "*Yes, Stella!*"

I studied with Ms. Adler at her studio above the French Fondu restaurant for a year and a half. She drove home the idea that the responsibility of every good actor is to exercise his brain. Instead of aspiring to achieve the isolated real moment, we were advised to be *interesting*. If we approached the text with knowledge and craft, presuming we were talented enough, we could create the illusion of truth. Acting was an interpretive art, a shared responsibility for honoring the playwright and respecting our fellow cast members.

During one scene study class a freakishly handsome boy who looked as if he had just rolled out of bed without showering, who was obviously in the thrall of Steve McQueen and Marlon Brando, began the class by performing the "To be or not to be" speech from *Hamlet*. His interpretation was marred by contemporary tics and mannerisms. When he had finished, Ms. Adler asked him what type of fellow he believed Hamlet to be.

"Well," he answered in the sloppiest, pseudo-naturalistic diction possible, "I think this Hamlet is a guy who's a lot like me."

Ms. Adler rested her large head on the back of her chair and then, with a deliberation we had all come to recognize as the calm before an explosion of temperament, asked the boy, "Are you Danish?"

"No."

"Are you a prince?"

"No."

"Do you have extended conversations with your dead father?"

"No."

"Then perhaps," said Ms. Adler, "you are not as much like this guy Hamlet as you think you are."

On another occasion she directly addressed an issue that had been torturing me since childhood. Were all actors and actresses what my mother perceived them to be, egocentric fools of the lowest moral common denominator?

"To be an actor in the theater is a noble calling," she declared after one student had made substantial progress in her class. "For two generations every member of the Adler family has become an actor, except one. He became a brain surgeon, and the rest of us refuse to talk to him!"

During my second year, a Christmas party was held at the studio before we broke for the holidays. Everyone had been celebrating for at least three hours before Stella made her entrance. The studio space was so unprepossessing that when Stella entered, in a provocatively low-cut evening gown, her face painted like a Greek fury's, her hair teased high above her regal head, her appearance had the effect of high comedy. For what seemed like forever she made her way silently and dramatically around the room, greeting us all individually. Sometimes she would kiss a female student on the forehead or hold out her hand, popelike, waiting for a male student to take it and bring it to his lips. Throughout the royal progress the room remained silent, every one of us waiting our turn to kiss the ring of this preposterously theatrical woman. When she had finally made physical contact with each of us, she took my hand so I could help her up the small step that separated the rest of us from the elevated platform.

Standing on the shabby stage that represented her life's work, she intoned, "Let that be a lesson to you! You can be a phony in life, but you can't be a phony on the stage!"

It had been two and a half years since I had graduated from high school, and although I considered my year with Meisner a waste, I had survived an early test of rejection and somehow discovered the perfect mentor. Interestingly, the kind of people who were students at the Neighborhood Playhouse and at the Stella Adler Studios were much the same. Few were destined to go beyond the conservatory process and make their way into the real world of show business. (An exception was Rita Schwalb, the young woman who had played Ado Annie at Gray Gables and had later begun studying with Stella on my recommendation. Rita had become disenchanted with the drama department at Boston University and had promptly become one of Stella's star pupils. She possessed an indefinable inner light that presaged great things.)

One of the failings of the Meisner method was the contempt in which it held the professional theater. It would come as a great surprise to those graduating from the Playhouse that the professional theater did not care with whom you had studied. How effortlessly you could reduce yourself to tears or how truthful you were being while you engaged in your Independent Activity were irrelevant. Nobody gave a damn about your Independent Activity. The only thing the professional theater cared about was your ability to blow the audience away.

The day after you conclude your studies it dawns on you that your time is now totally your own. Everything you need to accomplish is entirely up to you. There are no schedules except the ones you make for yourself. Most daunting of all, you're competing against every young person in the country who wants to occupy the space you've reserved for yourself. This is a brutal realization, and sadly enough, many young people with more than enough talent to succeed become discouraged by the enormity of the task and give up.

Shortly before I was to embark on a professional career, Stella Adler asked the class: "What do you want to be, darlings? Do you want to be an actor, or do you want to be a star?"

I remember sitting with Rita in the back of the room that day, thinking Stella's question was ridiculous. Of course I wanted to be a star! If I were a star I'd have a shot at all the good parts. I dismissed the question as the ravings of an eccentric old woman. Several years would pass before I could understand the distinction.

Chapter 7

Early in his acting career my father changed his name to Allen Swift because when his real name was spoken carelessly, Ira Stadlen occasionally tripped off the tongue sounding like Iris Adlen. Show business is a difficult enough racket without uncertainty about your gender.

It was my father's nature to weigh the nuances separating failure from success. He was a child of the Great Depression whose family sometimes changed its residence several times a year. His father, Max, had emigrated from Romania as a young man and then earned a law degree from the University of Pennsylvania. Shortly thereafter he made a fateful decision by marrying my grandmother Sally in order to get closer to her married sister Esperanza, with whom he had fallen madly in love. Their mutual attraction significantly shaped my father's childhood.

Max Stadlen was known to all (except his wife) as the kindest of men. His life's ambition—to build affordable housing in a kind of prewar Levittown—was washed away when the stock market crashed. He spent the rest of his life writing plays that were never produced, collecting stamps, and doting on children. What money he provided his family was minimal, which meant that my father's older brother, Cal, left home as a teenager to labor at a series of unfulfilling jobs. Similar sacrifices were made by my father's sister, Esther, as well as the assortment of relatives who shared whatever abode the Stadlens were occupying.

My grandmother Sally, embittered by her husband's emotional betrayal, cooked the family meals and although she was a skilled seamstress never took an outside job. To do so would let her chronically unemployed husband off the hook. From an early age my father was influenced by an aunt's comment that he was destined to be the family's financial savior. He took this responsibility seriously enough to become a conjurer. My father has always viewed the world through the eyes of an illusionist.

He began his career as stand-up comedian, eventually working his way to the zenith of show business bookings, a week at the Palace theater in New York. Spending the majority of his time on the road, he began to notice that as more people, especially on the East Coast, began buying television sets, nightclubs began shortening their work week. The phenomenal success of Milton Berle's *Texaco Star Theater* was essentially turning nightclubs into weekend businesses. Within a year he had directed his attention to live television, appearing on several Bob Hope specials and doing numerous guest spots with Uncle Milty. A few years later he was able to enlist his brilliant talent for mimicry by becoming a regular cast member on *The Howdy Doody Show*.

The Howdy Doody Show has become an icon in television culture, but people forget that it was conceived as a long-running soap opera for children. Doodyville was just another scandal-ridden community, like the ones portrayed on *The Edge of Night* or *One Life to Live*. Howdy Doody was the good guy attempting to maintain a moral universe while fighting the likes of the town's selfish bigwig, Mr. Phineas T. Bluster. Live characters like Clarabell the clown and the show's somewhat cynical host, Buffalo Bob Smith, interacted with Doodyville's inhabitants, most of whom were marionettes. My father not only reinvented himself as a puppeteer, but he supplied the voices for Mr. Bluster and a puppet of indistinguishable origin named Flubberdubb. Several seasons later, after Bob Smith suffered a heart attack on a Friday afternoon, my father on the following Monday became the voice of Howdy Doody himself.

Eventually he had his own children's television show on WPIX, portraying a grizzled old seaman, Captain Allen Swift, who introduced a new generation of children to Max Fleisher's *Popeye the Sailor* cartoons. My father was a major celebrity to the children I grew up with—after all, he had the power to announce my friends' birthdays at the conclusion of every show.

When it came time for me to embark on my professional acting career, he devised a scheme so original that it has remained a family secret until now. By the time I was a teenager my father had become enormously successful as a voice-over actor on radio and television commercials, promoting himself as "the Man of a Thousand Voices." To trumpet his achievements he threw a gala for himself, claiming he had just completed his ten thousandth commercial. This was preposterous. Anyone who did the math would have realized that he'd have to have averaged nine and a half commercials per business day for eleven years—perhaps within the realm of possibility, but highly unlikely.

My father believed that 8x10 glossies and resumes were merely used to shield those who cast plays, movies, and television shows from the multitude of aspirants knocking on their doors. What use was the resume of a nineteen-year-old whose total experience amounted to a summer and a half as an apprentice in a nonunion stock company, a season at a teenage theater camp, and a year and a half at an acting school? What the gatekeepers of the industry really wanted to see on a resume was a record of success in a field where so many others had failed.

My father advised me to research twelve years of Broadway history to see what plays I *might* have been in had I begun my career as a child actor. This task I performed cheerfully, since I enjoyed nothing more than thumbing through old *Theater World* books, *Theater Arts* magazines, and my mother's extensive collection of playbills. Eventually I had a list of a half dozen Broadway shows I might have appeared in, along with several national tours and two ignominious flops that had closed out of town.

The problem was that I was a poor liar. The prospect of being cornered like a rat by someone in the know filled me with such fear that I insisted there be a second, honest resume to mitigate the one that made me seem a close second to Sir Herbert Beerbohm Tree. To this my father acceded, but with the provision that my fake resume must proclaim, under the Television heading, "Over one hundred appearances on live TV!" I reluctantly agreed. Anything to gain entry into the world of David Burns.

My fraudulent resume was merely the anchor in a far more creative scam. A renaissance man who delighted in sleight of hand, my father had been nursing an idea he believed would, in his words, "show the proper amount of disrespect for the people in the industry." Once again I was given a homework assignment, this time to compile a list of prominent theatrical producers. These luminaries were going to be sent a letter alerting them to the existence of an actor none of them had ever heard of, a callow fellow by the name of Lewis J. Stadlen.

This brainstorm had occurred to my father when he learned that his brother Cal was planning to take an Adriatic cruise from Venice to Dubrovnik. He would compose a longhand letter generic enough in content that it could be written to any of the theatrical producers and signed by a guy named Dave. No last name. He got a printing shop in New Jersey to mass-produce the letter and its envelope. When the letters had been addressed to the producers on my list, they were taken to Europe by my uncle, who dutifully mailed them from a post office in Yugoslavia. The most artful aspect of the fraud was the water-stained return address in the top lefthand corner of the envelope. Only the name Dave survived the cross-Atlantic mailing: Dave's last name and his return address had been smudged beyond recognition.

The letter went something like this:

January 16, 1967

Dear [first name of producer],

What a time we've been having in Europe. The crazy blonde and I have been revisiting the site of our greatest crimes. At the moment I'm sitting in a waiting room at the Dubrovnik hospital after the crazy one tripped as we descended the gangplank. Could it have been too much Bosnian wine?

We're here for three days before ending our trip in London. Good theater and awful food awaits us. (In the food department the Brits make the Yugoslavs seem like the French.) Anyway. A crazy thing happened while we were sitting in the dining room of this adorable little ship, the *Labornia*. (First-class accommodations with five meals for less than two hundred dollars in nonrefundable Communist currency. That means we could capitalize a musical here for well under fifteen hundred dollars.)

So the two of us are digging into yet another variation of East European goat when we strike up a conversation with this couple from New York. He produces TV commercials, she's a social worker. The man introduces himself and his wife as Cal and Florence Stadlen and I'm telling you for the life of me I am trying to figure out how I know that name. Three hours go by. The crazy blond and I are wrapped in each other's arms. I'm not certain if we were in the throes of passion or whether the Adriatic was doing a number on our stomachs. I'll cut to the chase. He turns out to be the uncle of that kid Lewis Stadlen we were talking about. What were the chances of that? So here's his phone number. (212) CI6-5573. Do with it what you wish or I'll call him when we return Stateside.

There she is. She has just emerged from the operating room looking more ravishing than ever. What does it say about me that I still I go nuts whenever she limps into a room?

See you in ten days.

Love you guys,
Dave

This letter was mailed from Dubrovnik to twenty-five Broadway producers. Three responded.

First to bite was Mike Ellis, who produced summer theater at the Bucks County Playhouse in New Hope, Pennsylvania. In the early 1960s he had taken a chance on a young writer from the *Sid Caesar Show* named Neil Simon and produced his first play, *Come Blow Your Horn*. Using Bucks County as an inexpensive out-of-town tryout, Ellis produced it on Broadway the following season, where it opened to mostly positive notices and ran for two years, never grossing much above its weekly budget but rarely losing money either. It put Neil Simon on the map as a promising playwright and established Mike Ellis as something other than a producer of summer theater.

The following season Ellis produced another Broadway show, *The Beauty Part,* written by notable Bucks County resident S. J. Perelman and starring, in a multitude of different roles, the magnificent Bert Lahr. The play received raves from the critics but had the misfortune of opening during a newspaper strike, so the public never got the chance to read the reviews, nor could the play be properly advertised. It limped along for several months and closed a victim of circumstance.

By the time I was invited to Ellis's midtown office, he was searching for an inexpensive play to produce and was hardly a major player. I'd never been inside a producer's office. The walls were lined with framed posters of shows he had produced, mostly at Bucks County. A tall gentleman with a prominent nose who wore a bright madras sports jacket, he seemed more like a fellow hugging the rail at a racetrack than a producer of plays.

"Do you know this fellow named Dave?" he asked me.

"Dave?" I said. "Dave who?"

"I don't know Dave who. That's my problem. Do you know a guy named Cal Stadlen?"

"Yes, he's my uncle."

"So he must know this guy Dave." I stared back at him blankly. "Dave met your uncle on a boat, and he wrote to me about you."

"My uncle?"

"No. This guy Dave."

"I don't understand."

"Neither do I."

He looked around the room and then straight at me. He seemed to want to tell me how badly the world had been treating him lately. Who the hell had ever heard of Neil Simon until he, Mike Ellis, had given him his big break? And then what does Simon do? He ditches him and takes his next play, *Barefoot in the Park,* to a fancy-schmancy producer, Saint Subber, and the play becomes a megasmash. Two road companies crisscrossing the country with one fucking set, and to make matters worse now he's sitting across the desk from some kid he's never heard of, asking him about some guy the kid has never heard of, and all he wants to do is scream out the window at a totally uninterested Broadway!

"So, you're an actor?"

"Yes. Just starting," I said unwisely.

"Everybody wants to be an actor. Listen, I asked you here because whoever the hell this Dave is, he thinks you're worth meeting. He'll be home in a few days so I guess I'll find out then. What would Dave have seen you perform in?"

"I was in the *Spoon River Anthology* at the Gene Frankel Workshop."

"Well, that's just great. Listen, I don't mean to be discouraging, but if you don't get rid of that New York accent you'll never work in this business. You talk like I do, for Chrissakes! You got to get up in front of people and show them you're a big deal! I'm sorry. That's all the advice I can give you." And with that I was shown the door.

The next producer to take the bait wasn't a producer at all but a Broadway composer. Albert Hague had written a charming musical about the Pennsylvania Dutch, *Plain and Fancy,* as well as *Redhead,* a vehicle for Gwen

Verdon. He was on my list because he was attempting to raise money for a project of his own. He invited me to his sprawling apartment on Central Park West, where I was supposed to perform a song I'd prepared. Hague was an optimistic, erudite, middle-aged gentleman who spoke with a European accent. He introduced me to his wife, the actress Renee Orin, about whom he waxed rhapsodic as soon as she disappeared into the kitchen after leaving a plate of cookies.

"I received this letter from Yugoslavia," he said. "You wouldn't by any chance know anything about it?"

"A letter?"

"It doesn't matter. It may be a hoax of some kind. Whatever it is, it's very clever, and here we both are. Have you brought me a song?"

"Yes," I said handing him the sheet music to *Who Can I Turn To?*, a ballad co-written by my current idol, Anthony Newley.

Hague placed it on his grand piano and began playing as I launched into the song. A sequel to Newley's more eloquent mea culpa *What Kind of Fool Am I?*, *Who Can I Turn To?* deals with a man feeling very sorry for himself, which was what Anthony Newley did best.

> *With no one to guide me,*
> *And no one beside me,*
> *I'll go on my way,*
> *And after the day,*
> *The darkness will find me.*
> *And maybe tomorrow,*
> *I'll find what I'm after,*
> *I'll throw off my sorrow,*
> *Beg, steal or borrow,*
> *My share of laughter.*
>
> *With you I can learn to,*
> *With you on a new day,*
> *But who can I turn to*
> *When you turn away?*

A real epic. I performed it with my jacket slung over my shoulder like Frank Sinatra. When I finished, Hague handed me back the sheet music and invited me to take a seat on the couch.

"It's an interesting question, isn't it?" he asked from his piano bench.

"What is?" I felt I had performed the song with eloquent self-pity.

"Who can you turn to?" said Hague. "So let's get right down to it. How old are you, Mister Stadlen?"

"I'm nineteen."

"So basically, you could turn to just about anyone." He began quietly playing the song to underscore our conversation. "You could turn to your parents. You could turn to the milkman. You could even turn to the taxi driver who brought you to my apartment. Do you mind if I call you Lewis?"

"Of course not."

"You are too young to sing that song. Only a man who has lived long enough to have tasted defeat can sing that song, and unless my eyes deceive me, you are at the very beginning of what we both hope will be a promising career."

Albert Hague was a very nice man. In the next half hour he gave me two more pieces of wisdom I still use.

"Never sing an audition song associated with a famous performer. Let Judy Garland sing *Somewhere over the Rainbow*. Leave that one to Judy. And don't audition with a song that's currently popular, because when they hear you sing it with a piano they'll long for full orchestration. People don't have that much imagination. They'll be looking around for Nelson Riddle."

My Dear Dave letter had exposed me to two very different Broadway types. One told me that if I didn't improve myself, I'd end up staring out the window at someone else's name on a sign; the other was kind enough to provide an hour's worth of generous and constructive criticism. Only those with more knowledge than you can unclutter the confusion of an eager mind.

Then came the third bite.

In the fall of 1964 my mother and I attended a matinee performance of *Fiddler on the Roof* at the Imperial Theater. A few weeks earlier, at a dinner party given by my father, I listened to his friends Jack and Vivian Farren (Jack was a Broadway producer) describing *Fiddler*'s opening night.

"It made us both so proud to be Jewish," Jack said. "Zero Mostel's performance is transcendent, one of those rare experiences when your entire life is validated by an evening of theater. At the curtain call Vivian and I were too moved to speak."

Being seventeen and ambivalent about my Jewish roots, I rolled my eyes. I was in no mood to join any club that would have me as a member.

Fiddler on the Roof turned out to be everything the Farrens had claimed. Zero Mostel was the genius actor of my dreams, a creature so homely he redefined beauty, his Tevye the milkman a masterpiece of interpretive artistry. Everything about *Fiddler* was near perfection. The director-choreographer Jerome Robbins had micromanaged the production, sometimes pitting cast member against cast member. His re-creation of shtetl life was a seamless circle of color and movement. Boris Aronson's sets recalled Chagall's impressionistic paintings. Jerry Bock's score merged klezmer music with the Broadway idiom, while the libretto by Joseph Stein and Sheldon Harnick's lyrics artfully evoked the Shalom Aleichem folk tales on which the musical was based.

But carrying everything was Zero Mostel, with his fat-man balletic grace and his oversized temperament. In the years to come it would become fashionable to say that those who succeeded him in the role of Tevye were his equal or, more shamelessly still, his superior. Then again, there are those who believe Picasso is overrated. Mostel was a genius and so was Jerome Robbins, and after seeing that show I would never be the same again.

There was another man who had given life to *Fiddler*, a man who had decided to risk producing it after many others had pronounced the idea commercial suicide. His name was Harold Prince. The final response to my Dear Dave letter came from Prince's in-house casting director, Shirley Rich. Ms. Rich called me to set up an interview to verify a suggestion made by one of Prince's friends. She asked that I send her a picture and a resume so that when we met she'd be acquainted with my professional background. I at once reached into a stack of newly printed resumes and sent her the truthful one listing my meager credits.

Prince's spacious but modestly furnished suite lay in the heart of Rockefeller Center. It reminded me of my grandfather's house in Flatbush, or perhaps the compound of a fabulously wealthy Mafia don, the sanctum of a high achiever without a hint of ostentation. Shirley Rich began the interview by asking me what year I had performed the role of Angie in the musical *Gypsy*.

"I believe that was nineteen sixty-two, at the New London Barn Playhouse," I dutifully responded.

"No, no," she said. "What year did you do *Gypsy* on Broadway with Ethel Merman?"

I snatched the page from her and immediately saw that I'd sent her the wrong resume, the one my father so charmingly described as The Big Lie, fifteen years of fraudulent accomplishments including, at the top of the page, a play Harold Prince himself had produced. I became my worst fear, a frantic laboratory rat running a maze.

"Ah, the Broadway *Gypsy*, yes. That was during the second year of the run," I told her. "Actually, I joined the company during the week Jane Romano performed for Ms. Merman when she took her summer vacation." (Thank goodness for *Theater World*.) "I did perform with Ms. Merman for another nine months before leaving to do the ill-fated *Isle of Children*. That was a big mistake. We closed out of town in Boston."

Shirley shot me the knowing smile of one who had been associated with a few clunkers herself.

"We have to recast the part of Mendel the rabbi's son in the national company of *Fiddler*," she said. "It's currently sitting down in Chicago. Would you have any objections to going on the road?"

"No, no," I assured her. By this time there was so much adrenaline coursing through my veins I could have convinced myself I'd once played Tevye.

"I'm going to recommend to Hal that you be seen for the part," she said. "Tell me, what was it like to work with Ethel Merman?"

"Ohhh, very nice. She was always very nice to me. Bruce Yarnell actually named his daughter Ethel. That was after they worked together in the revival of *Annie Get Your Gun*, at Lincoln Center."

"I never knew that," she said.

"Oh, yes. We never talked much, but she was always very nice to me." With that I stood up and beat a purposeful retreat past the great director George Abbott, whose office was across the hall from Shirley's.

What a liar I was! I could barely live with myself.

"The reason we're doing this," my father had explained patiently, "is to give you the opportunity to be *seen* for the job. Once you get that opportunity, the rest is up to you."

Within days I was walking through the alley that led to the stage door of the Majestic Theater, home of *Fiddler on the Roof*. It was the first time I had entered a stage door as an actor. A youth not much older than myself, sporting a dark mustache and an air of melancholy, led me onto the stage, past a piece of scenery I recognized as Tevye's house. The house appeared to be sleeping in a fetal position. I could barely resist the urge to walk over and touch it.

"This is Lewis Stadlen," announced the young man, whereupon my attention shifted to the great shell of upholstered seats, lighting fixtures, and cornices that forever altered my perspective of what a theater looks like. Never again would I see myself as an audience member staring up at a proscenium arch. From then on my perspective shifted to that of the player staring down at the void that separated himself from the audience.

Harold Prince walked down the aisle from the back of the orchestra. Tanned and cheerful, with a smile that suggested he had found the perfect life for himself, the glasses propped on his balding pate made him look as if he were mulling a multitude of creative ideas.

I had been asked to prepare the song "Miracle of Miracles," which I had listened to on my mother's record player at least a hundred and fifty times. Auditioning for the role of a nebbishy Jewish tailor was not an enormous stretch. I may have been ambivalent about my Jewish heritage, but my Jewish heritage wasn't ambivalent about me. I sang the song effortlessly, considering that my left leg was vibrating like a tuning fork. Asked to read Motel's two scenes, I performed them well enough to suggest that I could mimic the rhythms of Austin Pendleton, who had originated the role. Make no mistake about it: at nineteen I was a mere impostor. My sole talent lay in my ability to lift the essence of another performer's work. (When I played the role of Will Parker in *Oklahoma!*, my inspiration came from Gene Nelson's movie performance.) Forty years have passed since that audition for Harold Prince, and I still consider my major strength to be my ability to lift the comic and creative essences of actors I admire. Only a man with an oversized ego will refuse to steal from his betters.

When I'd finished, Prince looked me straight in the eye and said, "I see you've worked for me before." This was the very issue I dreaded. In discussing the possibility of being tripped up in a lie, my father had assured me that a man of Harold Prince's stature would never remember all the people he'd employed over his long and illustrious career, especially some child actor who had appeared in one of his least successful ventures, *Poor Bitos*, half a dozen years before. I was now facing the moment of truth. Would I admit that I was a sham, or would I take a deep breath, collect myself, and gut it out?

"Yes, I have," I answered with as much simplicity as I could muster. "I was the understudy to the third kid on the left."

"And I see you performed in *Inherit the Wind* as well?"

"Yes, sir. The national company, with Melvyn Douglas."

Prince gave me his full Cheshire grin. He probably didn't believe a word I was saying, but perhaps he remembered the time when he had needed a pretext to introduce himself to *his* mentor, George Abbott. He gracefully allowed the matter to pass, thanking me cordially for taking the time to audition.

Later that afternoon Shirley Rich sent word that I had gotten the part.

As excited as I was, a matter of grave importance remained: a conversation with my beloved teacher, Stella. Late one afternoon I listened as she addressed us with her usual blend of passion and intellect.

"We are living in a disposable world," she bellowed. "There was a time when the rules of society were handed down by the aristocracy. Today the family heirloom has been replaced by the cardboard cup. A marvelous invention, but meant to be lightly regarded, to be discarded in the ashcan along with the baseball cap. When aristocrats controlled society, people wore crowns. Crowns were not thrown in the ashcan. Crowns were assumed to have value."

She paused to pour herself some coffee from a large metal thermos. "The end of the aristocracy was a good thing for the common man but a terrible thing for the *theater*! All of you speak in a way that can hardly be understood. You slouch in life instead of standing erect. You lessen the meaning of life instead of elevating it. It is an actor's responsibility to elevate life, and until you do so, every one of you will be unfit to walk on the stage."

When the class was over I followed her into her office to tell her my good news.

"I'm afraid I'm going to have to leave the class," I said.

"Then you are making an enormous mistake. You have only just begun to learn your craft."

"I have gotten a job as an actor."

"That is impossible!" she said imperiously. "No true actor would allow you on the stage."

"Well, I hope they will. I've been cast in the touring company of *Fiddler on the Roof* starring your brother, Luther."

She visibly softened. No woman I have ever known could affect a look of such imposing gravity, her chin raised in contemplation, her eyes misty with memory. Never to be pleased, thankful to be undone. How fortunate I was to have encountered her majestic presence.

"Luther." She shook her head with pride and pity. "You are going to work with Luther. I shall write him a letter, tell him you are coming."

She looked over at me. "You remind me of the Englishman, Sellers. Peter Sellers."

"I'm not as good as Peter Sellers."

"Of course you're not, darling. You're a baby! What I'm saying is you have the gift for comedy, and comedy is something that cannot be taught."

I remember kissing her good-bye on the lips and walking down the narrow hallway toward the stairs that led to the street. I was about to descend when she shouted at me from the doorway of her office.

"I've helped you, haven't I! You came from Sandy and you were a vegetable. He destroyed your confidence and now you are about to work with Luther."

"Yes, Stella. You helped me!" I yelled back at her.

"Yes, I helped you," she said softly, and with that she turned away. Seconds later I walked out into the real world.

Chapter 8

I packed my two suitcases and flew to Chicago the following Monday. With the exception of summer camp, I had never lived away from home before. From the moment I stepped off the green airport bus onto Michigan Avenue and dragged my luggage two blocks to the Croyden Hotel, every sight and sound reverberated for me. I was like a newborn.

At my Uncle Cal's house in Far Rockaway the day before, I had asked him to describe Chicago, a city I associated only with its baseball teams and my memory of Osborne Smith, the black actor who had once driven a cab there.

"It's like a very large Brooklyn," said my father.

"No, it's more like two Newarks," said Uncle Cal, and everyone around the table broke up. That was the last time the nuanced opinions of my immediate family were taken as gospel. As my bus made its way through the Loop, I realized that my father and my uncle knew very little about the City of the Big Shoulders. On that blustery afternoon in late February I became a free agent.

The schedule for putting me into the show was one that only a complete novice would agree to. I was to attend the performance that evening at the McVickers Theater, on Madison Street, and the next day report for duty, to be taught the dances by the dance captain and the music by the show's conductor. After mastering that, I would be directed through the dialogue scenes by two stage managers and fitted for costumes on my lunch break. By management's calculations this could all be accomplished by rehearsing for a full day on Tuesday, followed by a three-hour session before the matinee on Wednesday and another full day on Thursday before a brush-up rehearsal before my debut Friday evening. I would have to grow a beard as fast as possible so I could rid myself of the fake one I'd attach to my hairless face with spirit gum. Only a boy without a beard would agree to such an arrangement.

That Monday night I stopped by a coffee shop beside the theater to have a bite before watching the show that had so transfixed me three years before. Sitting at a center table were two bearded middle-aged gentlemen conversing in a highly theatrical manner. Gales of laughter issued from the taller one, who spoke loudly enough to be overheard by the entire restaurant. After asking what a Monte Cristo sandwich was, I shyly made my way over to the two and asked if they were actors in the show.

"I wouldn't say that Mister Finkel is an actor," said the shorter one, "but considering the time it takes for him to deliver his lines, he is definitely in the show."

"Mister Brenner," said the taller man, "is jealous because he knows that whenever the public sees Fyvush Finkel's name on the sign outside the theater, they recognize they are in the presence of a star!"

"A star from Orchard Street," said Brenner. "Mister Finkel neglects to tell you that at forty-five he is making his English-language debut. They don't sell knishes in the lobby when the actors are asked to speak their lines in English."

Finkel's baritone laugh ricocheted around the restaurant like cannon fire. He was a tall, angular man with two great pools for eyes and a nose of Semitic bravura.

"May we have the honor of knowing who we are speaking to?" Finkel's rich, musical voice was courteous and deliberate. Everything about him inspired laughter.

"My name's Lewis Stadlen," I told them. "I'll be joining the show on Friday. I'll be playing Mendel the rabbi's son and understudying Motel the tailor."

"Then you've come to the right table," said Maurice Brenner, whose curly, food-stained beard framed his baby face. He wore glasses with Coke-bottle lenses, but his most animated feature was an active, watery mouth.

"Lewie!" said Fyvush, offering me the seat beside him. "From now on you're one of the team. Just don't let Brenner give you any line readings. Only Mister Brenner can make a small part seem smaller."

"And only Mister Finkel a can take a semicolon and turn it into a monologue. That's what happens when English is your second language."

"I'm seeing the show tonight," I told them, whereupon Finkel and Brenner both turned reverent.

"Then you will be seeing a great actor tonight, Lewie. For my money, Luther Adler's performance is better than Zero Mostel's."

"Who was excellent," said Brenner. "We're not taking anything away from Zero Mostel."

"We're certainly not! But Luther Adler's performance is better. One of the greats. An actor's actor," said Finkel.

"Who also has an epicurean eye for a beautiful woman," added Brenner.

"That too. But we are not talking about beautiful women. We are talking great Tevyes, and tonight you're going to see a great Tevye!" Finkel exclaimed.

"Like a clinic!" said Brenner.

"Better even than Zero Mostel," repeated Finkel.

"Who was great!" said Brenner.

"But not as great as Luther," said Finkel.

"You're right. Not as great as Luther."

And with that I accompanied my new colleagues backstage to be introduced to the house manager, who escorted me and a hatchet-faced character actress named Helen Verbit, who was understudying the role of Tevye's wife, past some burly stagehands and out into the orchestra. As the lights began to dim I could barely contain my excitement. Turning To Helen Verbit I whispered, "I hear that Luther Adler is even better than Zero Mostel."

"Better than Zero Mostel?" she said incredulously. "That motherfucker couldn't kiss Zero Mostel's ass!"

From the moment the conductor lifted his baton, I realized that this incarnation of *Fiddler* suffered from a conspicuous lack of energy. I had listened to the Broadway cast recording enough times to know that in New York, Milton Green had conducted the music at a much brisker pace. When the curtain rose on Zero Mostel looking up to find a fiddler on his roof, Mostel had communicated the pride of an entire oppressed people. His elegance lay in his vulgarity; he was a peasant communing with God. When Luther Adler looked up to find a fiddler on his roof, he looked like a man who was pissed off that he was still playing the same part after replacing Zero for four months on Broadway.

Where Zero's body bent, Luther's body leaned. When Zero struggled to comprehend a simple issue, Luther was so smart he should have been made the leading rabbi of Minsk. But worst of all, Luther was committing the greatest sin in the Adler family playbook. His performance lacked size.

Not that one didn't recognize the man's talent. That's what was depressing. His performance was that of someone who thought he could turn it on and off. He was perversely refusing to recognize anything that Zero Mostel had discovered doing the part, and for that reason alone his performance as Tevye was distinctly unfunny.

"You see what I mean?" Helen Verbit hissed, sticking her elbow in my ribs. "He's missing every laugh. That miserable bastard thinks he wrote the book!"

A few of the supporting performances were actually superior to those in the original, and no one was funnier than my new friend Fyvush Finkel, who turned the inconsequential role of Reb Mordcha the innkeeper into a scene stealer. (He did take his sweet time when delivering a line.) No, the fault lay with Luther and his costar, Delores Wilson, an opera diva who insisted on singing brilliantly instead of playing the exhausted harridan that Maria Karnilova had so artfully created on Broadway.

What I found equally depressing was my temerity in entertaining these opinions. It was enough to make me hate myself.

My professional debut that Friday proceeded uneventfully, save that I caught my long gray coat in the door of the men's chorus dressing room while I was racing to make a costume change. As I attempted to wrestle the coat free I heard the jeering laughter of an actor who played the role of Fyedka, the Russian suitor. I found it astonishing that anyone would derive such pleasure from my difficulties. But hey, that's show business!

Then there was my first note session with Luther, who insisted that I report to his dressing room at every intermission so he could critique my performance line by agonizing line. I was unaware of it at the time, but my introduction to Luther had in fact been preceded by a letter from Stella, the substance of which was that she was sending him one of her students, a boy who was a little crazy but very nice, and that she realized what a complete bastard Luther could be to a young actor, and so in deference to their relationship, she was asking him to be gentle, or at least not unkind. Luther took her admonition as an excuse to torture me every day, until I grew balls big enough to fight back. It was a hazing ritual. He believed it was his responsibility to abuse me.

"Do you see my mustache, darling?" he said to me after I had been in the show for about a week. You knew you were in trouble when he called you darling. "Does your mustache look like mine?"

"Well, mine is false and yours is real," I pointed out.

"Besides that, darling," he said, spreading his own with his fingertips so that a microscopic separation appeared above his lip. "Every mustache has a separation in the middle, but yours does not." At which point he picked up his makeup scissors and cut mine in half. "Now go back to your dressing room and glue both pieces back onto your face, leaving a small separation in the middle." Thank you, Luther.

By the second week he was critiquing my line readings under his breath while I was performing. In the middle of a sentence I'd hear him muttering, "Well, at least he's doing that one better than last night," or "*Again* he doesn't understand what the hell he's talking about." It was enough to make one long for the halcyon days of Sanford Meisner.

Whatever my initial reservations had been about Luther's performance as Tevye, I was now completely in his thrall. Like it or not, Luther was our leader, and although he chose to give a minimum of effort seven performances out of eight (there was a lot of dog in Luther), he was a man of unquestioned authority. He seemed to be held in the highest esteem by the entire company, with the obvious exceptions of Helen Verbit and Harold Prince, who refused to speak to him.

An actor of large talent who had allowed his soul to become eroded by a lifetime of envy and professional disappointment, Luther had been a founding member of The Group Theater, a company that was to have a disproportionate influence on the American theater for the remainder of the twentieth century. During the 1930s he played most of the important roles presented by the Group, most notably Joe Bonaparte in Clifford Odets's *Golden Boy*.

The Group Theater's mission was to present plays of social conscience, but after half a decade of success the actors began to struggle against sublimating their personal ambitions for the good of the group. The first signs of unraveling came after Franchot Tone left for Hollywood in hopes of becoming a movie star. Not long after Luther's success in *Golden Boy*, John Garfield, a junior member of the company who believed the role of Joe Bonaparte had been written for him, also departed for Hollywood, where he became an immediate sensation at Warner Brothers. Unwilling to miss an opportunity to match Garfield's success, many in the Group Theater went on hiatus for a few years, and most of the company, including Luther and Stella Adler, headed west to be screen-tested.

John Garfield, an actor of unparalleled sex appeal, projected a tragic, everyman persona that sold millions of tickets. Luther may have been a magnet for the opposite sex when he walked out a stage door, but on film he projected an intellectual arrogance that made him appear sinister. The two men were raised on Manhattan's Lower East Side, but Garfield grew up in a tenement while Luther grew up as a member of Yiddish theater royalty. With John Garfield you could almost anticipate the tragedy that would kill him at the age of thirty-six. His appeal lay in his chiseled good looks and agonizing self-doubt. Luther was implacable. Like Luther, the characters he played knew better than everyone else. At bottom, the only person who believed that John Garfield's career was subtracting from his own was Luther.

During *Fiddler*'s Chicago run, there came a night in early summer when Lynn Fontanne and Alfred Lunt had driven down from their farm in Wisconsin to see Luther onstage. He'd been going through the motions for weeks, but now he had the incentive to perform; these were two people he deeply respected. When the time came, however, his performance was lifeless. He had allowed too much time to elapse after his last honest effort. I could see that he was enormously disappointed with himself. The next night, with the Lunts back home in Wisconsin, Luther performed the way he had wanted to the night before, but he had missed his opportunity to impress the Lunts.

I was a young man adrift in the city of Chicago. I would enter a restaurant, and order a shot of Jack Daniel's, the drink I had seen my grandfather order in countless restaurants. Then I would order a Chicago butt steak, because it was a local cut and reasonably priced. Everyone around me was older, as Albert Hague had intimated: the waiter, the desk clerk, Sammy Saddler, who played the piano at the Croyden Hotel bar. A young person walks around oblivious to the fact that he is surrounded by people who have been knocked about by life.

Mostly I traveled the streets alone. Tinkers to Evers to Chance. Hymie Weiss, gunned down on every street corner. I would stare down at my hands and hope that one day they would be lined with the deep blue veins I admired on more experienced men. I was lonely but secure, in that I had a place to go six days out of seven. Only on my day off would I begin to worry: would anyone care if I never returned?

By far my greatest pleasure lay in spending time with the character actors, on whose dressing-room door hung a sign proclaiming the Hebrew Actors' Union. Maurice Brenner sat closest to the door, and next to him, Fyvush Finkel. Beside him sat the senior citizen of the group, Baruch

Lumet, who played my father and whose real son was the distinguished film director Sidney Lumet. At a slight distance from the others was Clarence Hoffman, who played the role of the Russian constable. The constable appears once in the first act and late in the second act to evict the Jews from the village of Anatevka. The three men could barely stand Hoffman, whom they believed a compulsive liar. An imposing figure with a great shock of red hair and a thick, bristly mustache, he was a cross between a circus clown and Joseph Stalin.

The dressing room of the Hebrew Actors' Union was always abuzz with outrageous opinion. *Fiddler on the Roof* was the long running annuity they would ride into the sunset. It was a room that radiated warmth and confidence—with the exception of its *eminence noir*. Hoffman would pretend to be reading a dime novel until his colleagues' conversation subsided. He would then lower his book like the wise man he believed himself to be and volunteer a piece of information that would drive the others to distraction.

"Do you know how much it pains me to walk out onto the stage every night to throw my fellow Jews out of Anatevka?" he asked me shortly after I had joined the company.

"Who gives a shit?" said Brenner, who bristled at the very sound of his voice. "Just go out and do your job."

"One of these nights I'm going to walk out there and the words simply won't come out of my mouth" Clarence continued.

"The paying public doesn't give a damn that you're Jewish, Clarence!" said Finkel. "You're not being paid to be sympathetic."

"Have you ever heard the term emotional recall?" asked Clarence.

"What of it?" Brenner retorted.

"It's impossible for me to evict my fellow Jews without experiencing emotional recall. It was how I was trained as an actor."

"You were trained as an actor by Hiram Schlumputz!" screamed Fyvush. "What were you a member of, The Actor's Studio?"

"As a matter of fact, after the war Marlon Brando and I shared a cold-water flat above a synagogue."

"Was that before or after you dropped the atomic bomb on Japan?" asked Baruch Lumet.

"I never said I dropped the atomic bomb on Japan. I said I lifted the atomic bomb into the cargo hold before it took off from the Volcano Islands."

At this point Maurice Brenner would reach for a can of room deodorant he'd bought at a Chicago novelty shop, with a label featuring a squatting bull in the midst of a bowel movement and the words "Bullshit Repellent" prominently displayed, and begin spraying the room.

"Believe what you want," said Hoffman. "Marlon Brando, Dane Clark, and Monty Clift were all present at my son's briss."

"I wish I was present at *your* briss," said Brenner. "I'd have asked the rabbi to snip your head off." At that, Clarence Hoffman went back to his book.

One afternoon during a matinee, Fyvush turned to Brenner and inquired after the whereabouts of the elderly Russian actress Eugenie Leontovich.

"What a marvelous actress," said Fyvush. "I remember her as the queen mother in *Anastasia*."

"I haven't heard of her for years," Brenner said. "I wonder what's happened to her?"

"You wonder what's happened to her?" said Clarence, lowering his book. "What's happened is she happens to be dead!"

"She's dead?" said Fyvush dubiously. "I don't remember reading anything about Eugenie Leontovich being dead."

"Then you'll just have to take my word for it," said Clarence. "I know she's dead because I happened to attend her funeral."

"Was that before or after Merle Oberon gave you oral sex in Calcutta?" asked Baruch Lumet.

"I never said Merle Oberon gave me oral sex in Calcutta," Clarence whined. "What I said was that Merle Oberon was a high-class call girl I would sneak into General Stilwell's tent."

Brenner jumped to his feet and began spraying the room.

"You were at her funeral?" said Fyvush, the blood rushing to his nose. "I don't remember you telling us that story."

"That's because it was such a miserable day," Clarence explained. "When I got out of the limo at the cemetery, the rain was so torrential that my new shoes sank into a foot of mud. Fifty dollars I paid for those shoes. And where were all the people? Me, maybe five others, and a Russian Orthodox priest. I couldn't believe it. A distinguished actress like Eugenie Leontovich and no one shows up at her funeral? It must have been on account of the weather." He went back to his book.

A few days later I was sitting in my dressing room talking to Herb Corben, who played Reb Nachum, the beggar.

"Guess who lives on the same floor of my apartment building?" he asked me. "Do you remember the old Russian actress Eugenie Leontovich? Yesterday she knocks on our door and invites Joyce and me over to her apartment. All afternoon we're talking theater while she's serving tea out of a samovar. What a lovely woman."

I dragged Herb down the hallway to the Hebrew Actors' Union. "Herbie," I demanded, "tell them what you just told me."

"Just that this old Russian actress, Eugenie Leontovich, lives in our building and yesterday she was kind enough to invite my wife Joyce and me over for tea."

"Clarence!" I exclaimed with a prosecutor's zeal. "Last week you told us Eugenie Leontovich was dead!"

Clarence looked up from his novel and stared at us. "So," he said, "I could be wrong."

Chapter 9

I had always been the nervous type. While many of those in my profession seemed to hunger for the limelight, my personal goals were limited: I sought peace in the certainty of repetition. Public challenges always made me uneasy. Only the specter of invisibility motivated me to be ambitious. I was always more comfortable breaking even than I was at winning or losing. This is not to say that I was not my own favorite subject. I fascinated myself, but I carried the baggage of so much self-contempt that I was often depressed. Exceptional people were all around me and I did not consider myself one of them. My salvation lay in the fact that I preferred not to be boring. Stella was right. At twenty I was nice and a little crazy. I identified with the noble loser, but if anyone sought to take advantage of me, I could easily imagine myself smashing their skull against the pavement. I was a defensive egotist.

Part of my job was to understudy an actor named Stanley Soble, who played the role of Motel the tailor. Every Thursday afternoon I performed that role with all the other understudies on the stage of an empty McVickers Theater. Because it was too expensive to pay stagehands, we would indicate the scenery with folding chairs and were accompanied by a lone pianist. It was a dream of mine to one day take Stanley's place as Motel before a paying audience.

On a weekday evening several months into my Chicago engagement, the stage manager told me that Stanley was ill and I would be going on for him that evening. My body instantly grew numb as I visualized the very real possibility of failure. I arrived at the theater early to familiarize myself with a different dressing room and to put on clothes I had never worn before. (This may seem minor, but the business of shedding one's character for another can be undermined by a lack of familiarity. We are in many ways the product of our daily habits.) If I was going to succeed, I would need the encouragement of my colleagues—You're gonna be great! or Go out and kill the people!—age-old theatrical clichés conferred with fraternal generosity.

Five minutes before the start of the performance I was summoned to the Luther's dressing room to find him ashen-faced.

"Are you prepared to do this thing?" he asked me.

"I think I am."

"That's a big fucking relief. You know about closing the thingamajig?"

"What thingamajig?"

"The house! The house, for Christ's sake. At the end of the second scene you've got to grab hold of a fucking rope and pull the house together. Have they rehearsed you doing that?"

"I don't think so."

"*You don't think so?* Either you rehearsed it or you didn't. If you don't pull that fucking rope in time, every one of us is going to die." He began pacing the room. "Listen to me. You're a young man who doesn't have a clue. Whatever you do, *don't act*! Do you hear me? Say the lines and get the hell off the stage. You're a *pisher* from my sister's acting class. Just say the lines and pull that fucking rope and everything will be fine. You understand what I'm saying?"

"Yes." Although I wasn't quite sure what he meant about pulling the rope.

"Don't act!" He dropped to his knees. "*Please* don't act. Promise me you won't act!"

"I won't act," I assured him.

He threw up his arms in disgust and ascended the stairs to the stage.

There are several rules pertaining to a first performance—not that I was aware of any of them. Having no experience, I was little more than a deer in the headlights. Gene Saks, a fine director, once told a group of us on a pressure-filled opening night to throw out all the shit. He amplified this by saying that acting on the stage was no different from walking a tightrope. To succeed meant taking the risk that you might lose your balance and die. This was a wonderfully astute observation to a group of professionals who had at one time or another been too pumped up to do their best. What I needed to do was relax enough to allow my nervous energy to merge with my muscle memory, erasing all notions that this was to be my moment in the sun.

The first time understudies go on they're usually successful, because they're too nervous to think. It's in the midst of their second performance when they begin to realize they have parachuted into an alien world. For the first two scenes of my maiden performance I was doing just fine. The part of Motel was amusing and sympathetic, and all I had to do was display a certain nervousness in the presence of a patriarchal figure. But as the scene drew to a close, I became aware that I had the technical responsibility of yanking Tevye's house shut with a large rope in order to avoid an enormous set piece that was heading straight at us. Having only mimed the pulling of the rope at understudy rehearsal I was completely unprepared for the force it would take to close up the house. For ten horrifying seconds, as I pulled on the rope to no avail, I heard Luther screaming, *"This is it! We're all dead! He's killed us. The little fucker has killed us!"* Seconds before what would have been a career-ending collision, a stagehand named Frank Aronsky raced out and, grabbing the rope from my trembling hands, yanked the house shut.

Luther Adler's eyes resembled two pieces of gefilte fish as he pushed me aside to make his entrance for the next scene. It was one thing to be acting with an amateur and quite another to be sitting in the death seat while the amateur was driving the bus. From that day on he would regard me less as a nuisance than as a menace. That didn't mean Luther didn't like me. We had now shared an onstage moment he would never forget. My presence had come to symbolize all aspects of a cultural life he recognized to be in irreversible decline. Whenever we did our scenes together he leaned on me with such force that if I moved away, I knew he would fall on his face. Lessons such as these are not taught at university.

And then real life intervened, in the form of a call from my friend Rita Schwalb. She had been diagnosed with a form of cancer called melanoma. "Do you know what that means?" she asked me. "It means I'm going to die." I couldn't answer. A few weeks later I returned to New York to spend the day with the most talented and fearless of my friends. She was twenty-one years old. I walked around the city all afternoon. On the phone she'd told me she had developed cancerous cysts all over her body. I never made it closer to her apartment than a few blocks. Turning away at the last moment, I spent the day getting drunk at the bar of the Hotel Great Northern. The next morning I flew back to Chicago.

A letter arrived a few days later.

> Dear Lewis,
>   You are a no good friend.
>   It doesn't matter. I love you anyway.
>   Love,
>   Rita

Rita Ann Schwalb died on September 19, 1967. I flew back for the funeral, where I cried and cried and cried.

Chapter 10

There's a documentary about the Benny Goodman orchestra traveling the country on one of those art deco aluminum buses that resemble a rocket ship or a silver bullet. Goodman's name is painted on both sides of the bus in stylized script. The documentary has the faded color of someone's 8-millimeter home movie. It could be today, but a today faded by time. Most evocative are the images of the band members leaning against the bus during rest stops, loopy musicians smoking their Chesterfields and casually flirting with the female vocalist. This routine must have gone on for decades, since the Benny Goodman Orchestra was rarely idle. That bus with the cursive lettering went everyplace. It was a lifestyle on wheels in which everyone was taken care of as long as they could put up with Goodman's hectoring, a traveling musical circus in which all they had to think about was getting on and off the bus and playing their Big Band music. Boys and girls together. There are worse ways of earning a living.

The national touring company of *Fiddler* was about to pull up stakes after a nine-month run in Chicago and travel the Midwest for a series of one- and two-weekers in Minneapolis, St. Paul, Indianapolis, Dayton, Omaha, Des Moines, Kansas City, Oklahoma City, and then on to destinations unknown. We were a month away from boarding the bus when we learned that our most important member wasn't coming with us. Luther had pissed off the people who paid for the bus. They were tired of his contemptuous, lazy performances and uncooperative interviews in which he would rail against the current state of the theater and how he was being mistreated. When it had come time to renew his contract Harold Prince had taken a pass. Luther's final performance was to be the seventh of October. The next day we were all to assemble at Union Station and jump aboard the *Milwaukee Road* for the daylong trip to Minneapolis. Our flawed leader would be heading in the opposite direction, back to his farm in central Pennsylvania. There would be no more Luther.

Luther at the time was sixty-one, although according to my lights he might have been ten years older. The youngest child of the great Jacob and Sarah Adler, he had been tossed onto the stage of their Grand Street Theater before he could talk. It was assumed the theater would be his calling; he knew nothing else. To be the star of a play like *Fiddler on the Roof*, knowing in your heart that it's the play, not you, that sells the tickets, is a humbling reality for the actor forced to carry the main load. And sixty-one (or whatever it was) is a frightening time of life for an actor, who finds himself older than 90 percent of the people around him. We all remember the day when we were the youngest.

Furious as Luther was about slights real or imagined, he was a wounded warrior heading into the last month of the Chicago run. More than any of us, he required the emotional security of being needed, and he had blown it. One constant in the theater: When you overestimate your importance, it returns the favor by promptly biting you in the ass.

It was in this fraught atmosphere that Luther gave me my final lesson in onstage deportment. After that fateful day when I had nearly killed Tevye, Golda, and his five daughters by not pulling the rope hard enough to close the house, I had gone on a few times without major incident. As we were about to move on to a more strenuous road schedule, Stanley Soble put in for a one-week vacation, thereby giving me the opportunity to do the role for eight straight performances. I was so thrilled by this turn of events that I sneaked up to the company manager's office and, stealing a piece of McVickers Theater stationery, sent out my own press release to Chicago's foremost gossip columnist, Irving Kupcinet: "Paul Newman lookalike Lewis Stadlen begins performing the role of Motel the tailor beginning the third week of September." Amazingly enough it appeared in Kup's column.

Once again I was called into Luther's dressing room, and once again he implored me not to act. With only a few weeks to go, he was slowly divesting himself of the role of Tevye, but for Luther to show any compromise at this point would be an admission of death.

After the first performance he had two notes for me: I was to move farther downstage in the beginning of the scene in which Motel nervously asks for his daughter's hand. His second note was more substantive, an acting lesson I use to this day.

"When I say, 'Work hard, Motel. Come to us soon.' And you say, ' I will Reb Tevye. I'll work hard.' What's going on in that head of yours?" he asked me.

"I'm very sad to be leaving Anatevka," I told him. "We might never see each other again. I'm very upset."

"Wrong! Never play sad! Never play upset! What the hell is upset, anyway? Listen to me. It's almost the end of the goddamned play. Everybody wants to go home. They've been sitting on their asses for three hours. They want to have a drink. *I* want to have a drink."

"Am I talking too slowly?"

"Faster would be nice, but that's not the point. When the situation is sad, you say the line with *hope*. You summon up the courage to be *brave*. If you say that line hopefully, the audience will cry. If the audience sees you're the one who's crying, there won't be a wet eye in the house. Do you understand me? Let the audience cry. Play the line hopeful! Act like you're brave."

For the rest of the week I tried to move sufficiently downstage to satisfy Luther. I never did. "Downstage! Downstage!" he would mumble under his breath. After every performance he lectured me that I had gotten it wrong. But this was a mere bagatelle compared to my reading of the line "I will, Reb Tevye. I'll work hard." As hopeful as I tried to make it, I was never hopeful enough.

"Be brave, goddamn it," he would seethe after every performance. By the end of the week my dream of playing Motel had turned into an actor's nightmare. By the time Saturday night rolled around, I never wanted to run into Motel again. I would say the lines as quickly as possible and gratefully return to being Mendel, the rabbi's son. I could stand Luther's wrath no longer.

For the final time I raced onto the stage ahead of Luther. Still believing it was possible to avoid his fury, I headed as far downstage as possible without tossing myself into the orchestra pit. Luther entered, planted his feet stage center, and after shooting me a hateful glance, turned to the Saturday night audience and screamed, "Again he doesn't move downstage. We're in goddamned kindergarten here!" The audience stared back in confusion.

That was it! I had had enough! For the rest of the scene all I could think of was how I was going to grab Luther by his tzitzis and pummel his sixty-whatever-year-old body senseless. The scene played at such a fevered pitch that before I knew what was happening, Tevye had left the stage and I was standing alone in my spotlight singing "Miracle of Miracles." Only I wasn't concentrating on my lyrics, I was figuring out how I was going to confront Luther. I was so discombobulated with rage that I finished it all right, only to realize that I still had half the song to sing. So I sang the whole thing over again, to the bemusement of our conductor. Nothing quite like hitting a crescendo when the crescendo is yet to come.

By intermission I had gotten hold of my emotions and decided that if anything needed to be said to Luther, it could wait another twenty years. I slogged my wounded ego through the rest of the show until I reached that fateful moment when I picked up my carpetbag and, with the bravest of hopeful smiles, delivered the line "I will, Reb Tevye. I'll work hard." I could have just as well been singing "When there's a shine on your shoes, there's a melody in your heart." Then I retreated from the stage, not looking back, never to be Motel the tailor again.

As I stood in the wings thinking that the curtain couldn't come down fast enough, I was joined by the actress playing my wife. Looking out at Luther, she remarked "Boy, he sure is pissed off about something. I've never seen Luther this angry. He's practically foaming at the mouth!"

"Well, if he's foaming at the mouth," I told her, "it sure isn't because of me. I did that line exactly the way he wanted it."

"Oh, yeah?" she said. "Are you absolutely sure about that?"

"Absolutely."

"Good," she responded, "because I think the person he's looking to kill is you."

"Fuck him. He's been driving me nuts all week."

"Hey! You're swinging through an open door with me," she said. "I'm just telling you what you have to look forward to."

One of the magical moments in *Fiddler* is the staging of the curtain call. With the entire cast spread around the the edge of a revolving turntable, every cast member takes a single bow the moment they travel down stage center. Then the turntable continues its clockwise motion, returning the cast members to their places. After the entire cast has taken their bows the turntable stops and the actors part to reveal Tevye at center stage dancing with the fiddler, who represents the continuity of tradition. It's got to be the finest curtain call in the history of musical comedy.

As I stood on the turntable that night, moments before I was to take my bow, two hands reached out from a clump of bodies in the center of the stage and with maniacal intensity began pulling me back into the circle. About to lose my balance, I grabbed hold of an actor behind me, steadying myself enough to complete my bow. The turntable began moving me upstage while my unseen attacker continued to manhandle me. Only when it stopped was Luther revealed, apoplectic, hanging on to one of my arms.

To thunderous applause the cast formed a line to take our final bows. Luther smiled at the audience, but the moment the curtain hit the deck he began charging in my direction. The curtain rose a final time and Luther's demeanor turned warm and fuzzy, but as soon as it descended he plowed his way past several actors, screaming at me, "I told you to say that line hopeful! I told you to be brave! You're crying the goddamned line! Say the line *hopeful!*" He began to beat his fists against my chest.

"But I *said* the line hopeful!" I screamed back at him. "Jesus. I practically *sang* the line. I was afraid I was sending it up."

"You said it sad!" he said, choking with anger.

"I didn't."

"You did, goddamn it! You said the line sad!"

They say that the first eye contact you make with a lover contains an encrypted message telling you how it will all play out in the end. Perhaps I knew where Luther and I were headed the moment he cut my fake mustache in half. At any rate, I sucked in my gut and gave the old boy a piece of my twenty-year-old mind.

"All week I've been trying to do it your way," I told him in front of a group of actors who couldn't leave the stage fast enough. "I've tried to do it your way and I've never succeeded. So tonight, I did it my way! Is that what you want to hear? Tonight I did it my way."

"Then you are a *fucking amateur!*" he said, tears pouring down his cheeks. With that, my acting teacher's brother turned on his heel and exited the stage.

Luther refused to speak to me that final week in Chicago. The youngest member of a large family, he wasn't used to being challenged, and I had wounded him. Didn't I realize that his criticisms were our bond? I was an ingrate in his eyes, but as we silently passed each other in the bowels of the McVickers, I could tell he noticed something in me that reminded him of himself, and that couldn't be all bad. My time with Luther had been affirming in a way, because beneath his disdain for everything, Luther was just an old trouper who couldn't reform. In a profession full of fish eaters, he was the real deal.

During his final performance he went out true to himself, refusing to do cartwheels just because we were expecting him to give his "A" performance. His final message was that there was more to life than being approved of by Harold Prince. It was at the curtain call that he proved himself the consummate artist. After he'd taken his final bow, a group of ushers raced down the aisles and heaved two dozen roses at his feet. Luther picked them up slowly and acknowledged them before walking over to Paul Lipson, the actor who was replacing him. Kissing Paul on both cheeks, he handed him the flowers to signify the passing of the torch. Then he moved to the farthest end of the proscenium arch and took his final, measured walk from one side of the stage to the other.

Having made Luther ten years older than he actually was, and watching him take that slow walk into the theatrical unknown, I wondered if this was the last time the great Luther Adler would ever appear on the stage. In actuality, Luther was to appear in about ten more plays and half a dozen movies, but at that moment I saw myself as a fly on the wall of theatrical history. I began to cry.

Milking applause from an audience he despised, Luther looked up at me and for an instant appeared to be moved by my tears. As he was about to walk past me, he turned his large head a fraction to the side and, speaking out of the upstage corner of his mouth, remarked, "Look at Stadlen crying. Schmuck!"

I went to Luther's dressing room to ask him for an autographed picture. He obliged me.

> *To Lewis,*
> Walk down that lonesome road. It isn't easy.
> Good luck,
> *Luther*

That photograph, now framed, has hung on the wall of every dressing room I've occupied.

Chapter 11

For me the road represents more than freedom; it represents escape. Any number of psychiatrists, lovers, and wives have made a point of telling me this as I slog through one middle-age crisis after another.

"How could you possibly want to play Nathan Detroit in *Guys and Dolls* on the road when you could be doing *Crazy for You* on Broadway?" a well-meaning clinical social worker asked me on the eve of my forty-fifth birthday.

"It's the part, darling. It's the part."

When I mentioned that there was something comforting about the small, well-heated storage space we had rented off Route 6 in northeastern Pennsylvania, my wife, aware of my proclivity for escape, remarked, "I'd rather live in a home."

For whatever reason, I have always thought more clearly in transit. Nothing except reading baseball box scores over early morning coffee can compare with my first perusal of a road show itinerary of the American and Canadian cities that will be my home for a year. Who needs Broadway when you can pack a suitcase and head for a place that hardly knows you? Sure, there's always the problem of taking yourself along for the ride. St. Louis is cold in the winter and the downtown stinks, but I would rather experience the open road than the predictable monotony of the New York theater scene. Those who've never experienced the novel pleasures of Pittsburgh and Cleveland are strictly provincials.

The actor Sam Levene lived the last thirty years of his life at the St. Moritz Hotel on Central Park South. People thought he was crazy, but I've always felt there are worse compromises than retiring to the scent of clean sheets and warm bath towels. If I hadn't been an actor, I think I'd have made a hell of a bellman at the Ritz-Carlton—as long as I could move from one Ritz-Carlton to another.

Nothing and everything transpires on the road. Every day is significant. (Wasn't it Nashville where we celebrated your birthday last year?) Every day begins without despair. You don't have to self-start or reinvent yourself. The majority of people I meet don't understand this.

"Isn't it lonely being away from home all that time?" they ask.

"Oh, yes," is my dutiful reply.

"Don't you miss your family?"

"Well, we always make it a point to meet up every two or three weeks. You know, absence makes the heart grow fonder."

That's the obligatory response. You don't want to give the impression that you're having too good a time. But the bottom line is that those of us who relish life on the road are birds of a feather. Many actors disdain this life—I might add at their peril. Show me an actor who won't perform out of town and I'll show you a short career.

Unlike the banker, the lawyer, the shop clerk, the professional who has bought into the notion of a society that looks after you (of course that notion may now be dead), an actor's universe is more ephemeral. Too much regulation and we feel chained to a rock. The lifestyle of the traveling troupe is as regimented as a performer's life gets. Your decisions are basically limited to where you'll be staying; your day off is usually spent traveling to a different city. You're offered a limited range of options, and speaking for myself, that's great: too many options confuse me. Give me a remote control and a hundred television stations to choose among and I'll spend my time surfing in a state of disorientation. Give me two stations, and I'll either decide to watch one of them or turn the set off and read a book.

The road offers an endless variety of simple pleasures, and nobody much cares how you conduct yourself as long as you stay healthy and get to the theater on time. It's definitely not the lifestyle for obsessive corporate climbers, those bent on upward mobility, but the fewer of them the better, especially when you're spending hours together waiting around in airports.

Eventually I always drag myself back to New York to make a splash in some Broadway play that makes a profit, but I never feel truly liberated until I can stuff my momentum back into my suitcase and check out the best steakhouse in Kansas City. I suppose that's why I enjoy such a rarefied fame.

As for my first taste of touring after leaving Chicago, Fyvush Finkel and I became roommates. In Minneapolis we checked into the cheapest hotel on the housing list, which turned out to be a brothel. Five times a day a knock on the door would be followed by a query about whether we wanted a date. The rent was sixty dollars a week, thirty apiece. I still remember the first time we entered the room and realized the place was little more than a flophouse. Fyvush walked over to one of the beds and folded down the top sheet. He was putting two sons through the Mannes College of Music on a salary that could not have been more than three hundred dollars a week.

"Clean sheets! Plenty of fresh towels! What more can a man ask for, Lewie?"

The day before we left town, unable to resist temptation any longer, I opened my door and accepted a date with a scrawny black woman who couldn't have been much older than me. All I remember was her grabbing my hand as I reached for the light switch. "There ain't nothing that's done in the dark that can't be done in the light," she told me. It turned out to be a terribly disappointing experience, and the happiest day of my life.

Two weeks later we checked into a beautiful old relic, the Hotel St. Paul. It has since been renovated and is now one of the jewels of that fair city, but in 1967 it had seen better days, which was why Fyvush and I could afford to stay there. After unpacking we strolled down to an elegantly shabby dining room, where our waitress confided that she had never left the state of Minnesota though she was closing in on fifty. A few days later I bought my mother an ivory cameo for her forty-seventh birthday, which I mailed from the local post office. It was the first time I had ever sent anything through the mail, and one of the most intimate gestures I ever tendered her.

One evening after a performance, the entire cast was invited to the home of some St. Paul natives who were theater aficionados. We were bussed to a large Victorian house just outside the city and before the buffet dinner were paraded past a veritable glass menagerie, a vast collection of animal figurines that had been the lifelong project of the man who lived there with his elderly mother. The nontheatrical guests were middle-aged married couples. All the husbands were gay; their wives sat on the opposite side of the living room discussing the prospects of the Minnesota Twins, who had been to the World Series two years before. The husbands and wives never talked to each other. ("Blow out your candles, Laura. And so goodnight.")

In Dayton, Ohio, I went out with a lithe, long-legged stripper whose professional name was Linda Bennett, the Park Avenue Debutante. I was so nervous at dinner that I never touched my sirloin steak. Afterwards I escorted her back to the TraveLodge where she was staying and waited while she talked endlessly with her agent, who had called to tell her that her next booking, in Youngstown, had been canceled. I had never in my life heard a woman use such language. I waited around for an inordinate amount of time, hoping she might decide to spend her night off stripteasing for me, but she never got off the phone. All I could do was wave goodbye. Every *fuckin' this* and *fuckin' that* raised her pedestal higher, until she disappeared like a goddess into the gloomy Ohio firmament.

Indianapolis was so boring we never left the hotel. I've always thought Indianans are exceptionally prideful. This is the only state in the union that declines to participate in Daylight Saving Time. Ask Hoosiers for directions and they become suspicious and churlish. They vote Republican in every presidential election before the clock strikes seven. (Until Mr. Obama came along.) You'll find a lot of three-hundred-pound women in Indiana. It's the only place in the Western Hemisphere that makes me lonely for Los Angeles.

In Omaha I set out to find the perfect steak. (The stockyards were so close to our hotel that you could smell forever.) Omaha was the first city I visited where the local television news highlighted traffic accidents and the garroting of local citizens in their refurbished basements. What I failed to realize was that Omaha was ahead of the curve. In a few years every city's television news would highlight traffic accidents and the garroting of local citizens in refurbished basements. It portended the end of the Edward R. Murrow era. In the middle of the week many of our gay cast members got up at the ungodly hour of seven-thirty to spend the day at Boys' Town.

Kansas City was a blast. I've always found something evocative about the town that produced the Pendergast political machine and Harry S. Truman. It's a strange mixture of Midwest and cowboy culture, with an attractive skyline and beautiful architecture. That Kansas City identified with *Fiddler on the Roof* was a testament to the show's universal appeal. It wasn't just about Jews in Russia; people who lived in the dead center of the country recognized they had all migrated from someplace else.

As I got on the bus from Kansas City to Des Moines, I walked past our seventy-year-old company manager, Jim Miller. I was unaware of it at the time, but Miller represented a dying breed, a manager who actually took pride in representing a group of heathens to the outside world. A dead ringer for the actor Robert Keith, he was diminutive and soft spoken. He was always impeccably dressed, with a handkerchief in his breast pocket that matched his tie. He always wanted to look his best in anticipation of the day he would have to bail a cast member out of jail. As I stepped onto the bus I asked him what Des Moines was like.

"Des Moines?" said Miller with a wicked smile. "Des Moines is the devil."

Oklahoma City featured oil rigs right outside our downtown hotel window. The Tex-Mex food was excellent, the weather horrible. The December winds would sweep off the plains with such force that the trees along the highway were bent at grotesque angles. When Oscar Hammerstein wrote the lyrics to "Oh, What a Beautiful Morning!" (The corn is as high as an elephant's eye /And it looks like it's climbing clear up to the sky") he must have been drinking a pina colada in the Virgin Islands.

A sea change awaited us in Oklahoma City. The national company of *Fiddler* was going to transform itself into an hour-and-forty-five-minute tab vision that we would perform twice a night, seven days a week, at Caesar's Palace in Las Vegas. Theodore Bikel would be taking over the role of Tevye, and the show was booked for a six-month run. We arrived in Las Vegas on Christmas Day, and after a week's rehearsal had our gala premiere before an audience of tuxedo-clad Teamsters and some of the most glamorous call girls in the world. During the opening number I became so enamored with the cleavage of a woman in the front row that I lost my footing and fell flat on my ass.

A strange conversation ensued the moment I got offstage. One of our cast members was a moderately good-looking fellow in his mid-forties named Ralph Vucci, whose greatest talent was persuading women to go to bed with him. Whatever it took to be a master cocksman, Ralph had it. His sense of amour-propre depended on his picking up a woman every night. His technique was to be patient and to do a lot of listening. It was fun to watch him do his nightly dance around his prey. He came on touchy, boyish, naughty, and slightly lost. He projected need, but never a desperate need. He pretended to be the kind father, but the women who went with him knew deep in their hearts that he wasn't *that* kind. His resonant voice masked a basic hostility to women. In short, he was an endearing cad, and women love cads.

"You like that gal in the first row?" he asked me. "I'm taking her out after the show."

"I know her," I told him. "Her name is Greta. I went to acting school with her at Stella Adler's."

"You've got the wrong girl. Her name is Gloria. I met her last night at the craps table."

"I don't think so," I said. "If that's not Greta, she's got a twin sister."

"Baby, you got the wrong girl. I'm telling you, her name is Gloria."

For the rest of the performance I couldn't take my eyes off her. If this was Greta, she had absolutely transformed herself. It was amazing what shedding a few pounds could do. Once, after acting class, I had taken her out on a date and she had treated me with kindness and affection. I remember the moment I dropped her off at the Empire Hotel. Desperate to get laid but unable to figure out who to do it with, I kissed her politely on the cheek and left her at the elevator door. I just didn't find Greta's extra few pounds alluring enough to make me want to take her upstairs.

After the show I took a seat across the cocktail lounge from where Ralph and Gloria were getting acquainted. It would only be a matter of time before Ralph reduced her to putty. Suddenly their conversation grew heated, whereupon Ralph leaped to his feet, threw some money on the table, and left her. I waited a few minutes before walking over and presenting myself.

"Is it Gloria?" I asked her. She looked a little flushed. "You look like a girl I once knew in acting class."

"I wouldn't know who that girl is. What's your name?" she asked.

"Lewis," I said. "The girl I knew was named Greta." I had never had such an oblique conversation, but Las Vegas is an oblique kind of town.

"Ah, yes. I knew a Lewis!" With a flourish straight out of the movies she shook her platinum mane, then fished a cigarette out of an expensive gold case and lit it.

"How long has it been, Lewis?" she said wearily.

"Maybe a year," I answered. "If it's you I'm talking to."

"You mean the girl from acting class?"

"You look beautiful."

"You mean sexy. Let's face it, I have always been sexy."

Who the hell was I talking to?

"So. Gloria." She immediately grew agitated and stubbed out her cigarette.

"It's Greta, Greta, Greta!" she said. "I hate this." She grew red in the face. "Would you buy me a drink?"

"I was talking to Ralph during the show."

"Yes, Ralph. Ralph is very upset with me." She laughed. Suddenly she softened. "Lewis, Ralph is very upset with me because like any self-respecting call girl I had to tell him my price."

"You're a call girl?"

"Yes, I'm a call girl. That is, six months of the year I'm a call girl. I make a ton of money and then I run back to Stella's class and study to be an actress. Do you hate me because I'm a call girl?"

"No," I said. All I wanted to do was kick myself for ever leaving her by the elevator at the Empire Hotel. I wanted to tell her that if she wanted me I was hers. I was swamped with feeling. She wasn't a pudgy little girl anymore. She seemed so mature, so in charge, and just pissed off enough to flood me with tenderness. We spent another hour together walking around the casino. Everybody knew her and treated her with a kind of leering reverence. She was a woman who could sell her body once for about what I was making in a week. I wondered if it would be terribly bad form if I offered to buy her.

"I'm not really a bad girl," she assured me. "I'm having a pretty good time."

A bad girl! This was the first time a woman had referred to herself as a bad girl in my presence. My romantic heart skipped a beat and sent a signal to my brain that we were at last exploring some higher level of human behavior. Admitting to being bad seemed so much more aboveboard than pretending to be good. I was desperate to make a pass, but something told me I would find little success circulating between her two lives. She had already revealed as much to me as she was going to. She was just killing time as she waited for the coded announcement over the casino's PA system: "Oh Princess Lativa. Princess Lativa. Will you report to the front desk, please."

I stayed in Las Vegas for eight more weeks. When my contract year ended I left for New York without the slightest idea what I was going to do next. Playing Mendel the rabbi's son hardly qualified me as an actor. If it hadn't been for my father's shrewdness I probably wouldn't have gotten the part in the first place. I would turn twenty-one in another week. The war in Vietnam raged on. Perhaps I would live on a goat farm in St. Croix and write the great American novel. About what? I was so green I had rejected a high-priced call girl when she was willing to give it to me for free. Luther Adler was right. I was a fucking amateur.

Photo Section A

Rita Schwalb as Ado Annie & me as Will Parker in *Oklahoma* at the Gray Gables Theater Workshop. (1961.) One of the few times I would be cast as someone really dumb. We were both fourteen.

The National Touring Company of *Fiddler On The Roof*. (1969) I'm on the left wearing a false beard as I await my real one. Baruch Lumet, (Sidney Lumet's father) is the rabbi to the right of the bride.

The incomparably brilliant, Zero Mostel in the film version of *A Funny Thing Happened On The Way To The Forum*. I was later to be nominated for a Tony Award in the 1996 revival of that play.

My Glorious Brothers & Shelly. *Top left going clockwise.* Alvin Kupperman (Zeppo), Irwin Pearl (Chico), Danny Fortus (Harpo), Shelly Winters (Minnie), and me as Groucho. (1970)

The one & only Julius Henry Marx and your's truly walking across the stage of the Imperial Theater on opening night. Mort Marshall is to our right.

Minnie's Boys. (1970) A rare peaceful moment with Shelly Winters.

The opening night curtain call. My unique friendship with Groucho was to last until his death.

Alvin Kupperman (Zeppo) Kaye Ballard (Minnie) and me in the Pittsburgh Civil Light Opera version of *Minnie's Boys*. (1972) By far the best prodction that ill fated show ever received. Thanks to Kaye.

The Sunshine Boys (1973) The Broadhurst Theater. Sam Levene is sitting. Jack Albertson is behind the curtain and I'm in the middle.

A dapper Jack Albertson in a publicity shot. *The Sunshine Boys.*

Playing Ben Silverman in *The Sunshine Boys*.

"Candide". The Broadway Theater (1974) Before half hour.

Chapter 12

About the time I was stepping off the plane from Las Vegas, the film *The Graduate* had taken America by storm. It concerned a college graduate (portrayed by an unknown Dustin Hoffman) who, returning to his parents' upper middle class home, becomes paralyzed by his unsettled future. Pressured by a menagerie of materialistic adults, he is drawn into an adulterous affair with Mrs. Robinson, the wife of his father's law partner. The film immediately captured the public imagination and integrated itself into the American psyche. Here was a young man whose parents were demanding to see the fruits of their financial and emotional support. I took in the film a few blocks from my father's Fifty-seventh Street apartment, and as much as I delighted in its artistry, I also shuddered at the catatonic look in Dustin Hoffman's eyes.

Fortunately for me, the year was 1968. There would never be a better time to throw myself into the black-and-white world of American politics. A few weeks before leaving Las Vegas I had read a column in *Newsweek* by Kenneth Crawford in which he predicted a serious challenge to Lyndon Baines Johnson's presidency. A scholarly Minnesota senator named Eugene McCarthy and an army of youthful recruits were planning to challenge the president in state primaries across the country to gauge the full extent of opposition to the war. A decade later, President Jimmy Carter was asked how he felt about his daughter, Amy, protesting the influence of the CIA on world affairs. Carter, the most intellectually honest of presidents, remarked that it made perfect sense for young people to protest the inequities of society before they had acquired too much of a financial stake in it, such as a thirty-year mortgage and a two-car garage. He was pilloried in the press for suggesting such a thing, but a few years later there would be a scarcity of paunchy middle-aged men confronting Chinese tanks in Tiananmen Square.

I don't mean to disparage the social outrage that accompanied my generation's participation in the events of 1968. The political oligarchy in this country was flexing its muscles to the point of obscenity.; political opposition leaders were getting assassinated left and right. But speaking for myself, as one who committed himself to Eugene McCarthy with missionary zeal, it was also a great way to mark time while I figured out what to do with the rest of my life. And it was a great opportunity to meet some really good looking girls.

In 1968 my political views were the by-product of my grandfather's liberal Democratic views and, on my father's side of the family, a decided sympathy toward all regimes on the Left. The intellectual arguments promoted by Joseph Stalin's Popular Front in the 1930s had definitely found their way into the version of history I'd been weaned on as a child. An example of this mindset: Stalin had signed the Nonaggression Pact with Hitler only to stall for time, wisely recognizing that the capitalist democracies were licking their chops at Hitler's imminent invasion of Russia. Why not knock off two birds with one stone? Of course the truth was more complicated. There was the unmentioned Franco-Russian pact for one thing, and nobody talked about Stalin lying drunk on the Kremlin floor for six days after his only true friend in the world, Adolf Hitler, had betrayed him and invaded his country. Not much gratitude there, after Stalin had upheld his part of the bargain by liquidating most of the Polish intelligentsia.

The line I had been raised on was that the Soviet Union had been corrupted by the unremittiing belligerence of the West. Had it just been left alone after the Bolshevik Revolution, Lenin and Trotsky would have chopped down the cherry tree and never told the Russian people a lie. George Orwell was a revisionist stooge for exposing Soviet complicity in the Spanish Civil War. The main reason the United States had dropped two atomic bombs on Japan was to keep the Red Army as far away from the Pacific rim as possible. (As if a Soviet postwar presence in Japan would have been a good thing.) These were the opinions I was raised with, voiced by the most well meaning people, humanists who quite clearly saw the manifest inequities of our own system but were blinded to the systematic horrors in the Soviet Union. Granted, Hitler presented himself as a raving maniac while Stalin imitated everybody's kindly Uncle Joe, but you didn't exactly have to look under a rock to figure out that the Soviet Union was an unconscionable tyranny.

In 1968, I'm embarrassed to say, I still rooted for the Russians during the Olympics, and more than anything I wanted Lyndon Baines Johnson out of office. My liberal Democratic grandfather David Chassler did not agree. He remained a passionate fan of Hubert Humphrey. (Oh Lyndon! Where have you been keeping yourself all these years?)

I worked at the Speakers Bureau for Eugene McCarthy right up to the tumultuous Democratic Convention in Chicago. I gave serious thought to driving there and being part of the street demonstrations but decided instead to spend the weekend with my new girlfriend at a B-and-B on Martha's Vineyard. As it turned out, getting hit over the head by one of Mayor Daley's cops would have hurt a lot less. My new flame checked us into the same room she'd once shared with her history professor at Barnard College and spent the entire weekend weeping into her pillow. I was too dumb to figure out what was going on.

It was not that I lacked seriousness, but the longer I watched Gene McCarthy perform on the campaign trail, especially after his rival Bobby Kennedy's assassination, the more I believed that he didn't want to be president. McCarthy represented the people who believed they were too good for American politics. (They may have been right.) He aspired to be the honorable loser.

In 1973 I saw him in the audience of *Candide*, a musical I was starring in. Never having met him, I asked the house manager to bring him backstage. He was a tall, handsome, erudite fellow who had given up his Senate seat to teach a course in poetry at the New School. I asked him if he enjoyed teaching.

"I can't grade," he told me. *I can't grade?* This from the guy who had once run for the most powerful office in the world? It would still be a few years before I decided not to offer my political support to the guy who most reminded me of myself.

In the early part of 1969 I began to read: Norman Mailer, Sinclair Lewis, Theodore Dreiser, Hunter Thompson, F. Scott Fitzgerald. Not a big deal, but since I had previously resisted formal education, becoming an autodidact was a step forward—especially since I was failing miserably at everything else. I had been fired a number of times for being a horrible waiter (I kept telling the customers that I really wasn't a waiter, I was an actor). I had been axed as a counterman at Zabar's after slicing off the tip of my index finger while cutting cheese. Then, in late summer, I was asked to take my second draft physical.

When I had taken my first physical, shortly after returning from Las Vegas, I had gone down to Chambers Street with a psychiatrist's letter in one hand and a weathered asthma inhaler in the other. I was quickly shuffled off to a large rectangular room on the second floor where I waited patiently to present the letter from my family doctor advising the army that I was far too unstable to serve (which I was). That was in March 1968. Now it was August 1969, and both the military and the Draft Resisters League were no longer fooling around. The antiwar movement smelled weakness. Walter Cronkite and CBS were reporting American war atrocities, and there was a sense that public opinion was shifting dramatically against the war. Vice President Spiro Agnew had become the point man for the Nixon administration, and he was a bilious, polarizing figure. The war was increasingly being perceived as unwinnable.

In 1969 I showed up at the appointed time, psychiatrist's letter in hand, having no vision of the future other than that I didn't want to die for Richard Nixon. I was extremely confused. My life was going nowhere. The five thousand dollars I had saved from the *Fiddler* tour had evaporated. I was in one of those depressed states in which having chosen a restaurant, I would immediately change my mind, figuring that if I had decided to eat there, it had to be a lousy idea. Sooner or later I was going to have make a decision about my life, but first I had to get through this physical.

The sign on the door of the orientation room read "You are here to protect the world from the Communist menace." No sooner had an officer with a thick southern accent addressed us as soldiers than a representative from the Draft Resisters League jumped to his feet and informed us that we were civilians, operating under a civilian code. The first time I had been through this drill it had been a painless procedure, a matter of sitting in that second-floor waiting room, staring at one another for a few hours, wondering what kind of man would be so cowardly as to avoid military service by claiming he was mentally unfit. All of us were Caucasian and seemed to come from middle- to upper-class backgrounds. When my name was called, I remember sitting before an army psychiatrist who opened my letter, looked at me with a disgust that implied I was a lying dog, stamped something on a piece of paper, handed me back the letter, and told me to report to the uniformed personnel at the back door. I was out of there by noon.

This time was different. We were told to remove our clothes, whereupon another soldier with a heavy southern accent and a flashlight started examining the area between our butt cheeks. Then we were lined up and after an an army doctor had extracted blood, we spent the next two hours being put through tests to check our eyesight and hearing, both of which I did my very best to fail. Nothing I did seemed to deter the desk soldiers, who kept stamping my papers and sending me farther down the line, at the end of which, I was sure, a bus awaited to drive me to the transport to Southeast Asia. In three hours not a single soldier had asked if I had brought a letter from my psychiatrist.

As much as I dislike authority, I've never been rebellious enough to disrespect the law. In fact, I rather revere the law, assuming it mostly protects me while enforcing a sensible set of guidelines that provide social order. Should a policeman stop me on the street for an infraction, I would never think of doing anything other than obliging him. But now I was afraid my life was endangered. I was operating under a heightened state of fearful awareness. Like a dog who can smell a man's evil intentions, I decided it was time to put my clothes back on and take an unscheduled visit to the room on the second floor where the army psychiatrist hung out. He was sitting alone, eating a tunafish sandwich.

"What are you doing here?" he asked me. "Can't you see I'm eating my lunch?"

I handed him the sealed letter from my psychiatrist whose contents I was never to learn. And I remember my father telling me not to be afraid to behave like an idiot. "They'll try to sucker you into making you feel a part of something. Don't let them. Act like a nut! You're never going to see these people again." Standing in that empty room in front of the army psychiatrist, a flake of tuna stuck on his lip, I did my best to act like a nut.

His glance was withering. I had never been observed with such contempt, yet all it made me want to do was kiss him. He stamped my letter, handed it back, and continued eating his sandwich. I raced downstairs to the cracker who had told us to remove our clothing and handed him my stamped letter.

"But you haven't completed the physical," he told me with a big smile.

"No, I haven't," I said, "but I did complete most of it before I realized I was supposed to give this letter to the psychiatrist."

"Well, I can see that," he said, looking at me as if I were a worm he intended to impale on a hook. "But you haven't completed the physical."

"That's very true," I responded, "but since you already have the recommendation from the psychiatrist—"

He conferred his most sadistic smile and repeated, "But you haven't completed the physical. So what I want you to do is take off your clothes and join that group over there and start over again. That way, you'll have completed the physical." And for good measure he grabbed the seat of my pants and gave my ass an affectionate squeeze.

For the next three hours I stood behind a tall, bearded fellow who told me he was studying architecture at Cooper Union. His left arm was covered by a navy peacoat, the sleeve empty by his side. At every step of the physical a desk soldier demanded to see his arm.

"Fuck you!" he kept telling them.

"I'm going to ask you one more time. I want you to show me your left arm!"

"Fuck you!" the man would reply. "You want to see my left arm? You get one of your fucking superiors to come out and make me." Every time he said that, an intimidated desk soldier would pass him down the line until he had completed the entire physical without showing anyone his arm. His act of civil disobedience completely disrupted the army's chain of command. Nobody knew what to do with him, so they passed him straight through.

When I had finally completed the physical, I was handed two subway tokens and was thanked for serving my country. Having witnessed the outrageous behavior of my one-armed friend, and realizing the road to freedom stood only a few feet beyond the door, I righteously refused the tokens.

"Those are the rules," said the soldier. "Everyone who comes down here receives two tokens."

"If you give me these tokens I'm just going to throw them in the air," I told him.

"You can do anything you want with them," the soldier remarked politely. "But the army says you're entitled to two tokens."

"Even if I tell you I'm going to throw them away?"

"Even if you tell me you're going to throw them away."

With that I walked out the door, inhaled the pungent smell of salt air from the Hudson River, and with the spirit of the Boston Tea Party coursing through my veins, tossed the tokens into the air. It was time to admit to myself that there were more excruciating dilemmas than starting from the beginning.

Chapter 13

What if you've presented yourself to the world as one thing when you're nothing of the kind? It's easy to buy a ticket to a play and criticize it at intermission, and quite another to step forward and sell yourself as the guy who deserves to be up there, the guy who could do it better. That's why the acting business is not for everybody. If a strong breeze comes along and inflates your sails with confidence, just go along for the ride. It's best not to be overly contemplative.

During the summer of 1969, New York city was abuzz with the improbable play of the New York Mets. Our lovable baseball team, which had never finished higher than ninth place, was somehow battling another perennial loser, the Chicago Cubs, for first place in the division. A friend from Gray Gables, Michael Denbo, and I were attending games and allowing ourselves to believe that our boys could do it. If the Mets could pull this off, maybe there was hope for us. On a sunny weekend in August, Michael and I drove down to his parents' home in the Philadelphia suburb of Moorstown, New Jersey. I didn't realize it, but the curtain was about to ring down on my youth.

I define the end of my youth as that indeterminate moment when certain circumstances align and your destiny is decided for you. I could no longer hide behind the illusion that I was a student, although I had everything to learn. I had my own apartment on West End Avenue but my bankroll was shrinking. I had asked my father a few months earlier how much money I stood to inherit now that I was down to my last thousand, and his brusque reply was "Nothing."

After engaging Michael in a spirited game of whiffleball in his parents' backyard, I began searching the Philadelphia newspapers and discovered that my old *Fiddler* road company was opening that evening at the

Shubert Theater on Broad Street. Looking for an excuse to bum around downtown Philadelphia, we decided to crash the opening night party where, much to my delight, I was greeted with the warmth of a returning hero.

I had walked through the right door at the perfect moment. The actor who had replaced the actor who had replaced me as Mendel the rabbi's son had just given his notice, and I was asked to consider rejoining the company in my old position. The stage manager was particularly effusive, since he wouldn't have to teach the part to someone new. Everywhere I turned I was surrounded by adorable female faces. I had chopped off enough of my finger at Zabar's to realize there were worse jobs than the one I was being offered. To return to the stage without any illusions about who I was, twenty-two and in need of a paying job, was a no-brainer. So what if I wasn't really an actor? I wasn't much of a cheese cutter either.

Dancing the night away with a delightful dumpling by the name of Elizabeth Hale, I took leave of Michael Denbo knowing that when I returned to Philadelphia I would have not only a job but possibly a female roommate. I decided to take the initiative and not do something stupid. Yes, I said, yes, I will yes.

In the theater, work begets work. I hadn't unpacked my bags before the cast's talk began to center around auditions for a new musical called *Minnie's Boys* about the Marx Brothers. With *Fiddler* I had blundered into the perfect fit: a life without stress, an adorable girlfriend. Philadelphia was just far enough from New York that no one would bother me. And now I was being exhorted to give it all up and entertain the notion of moving on to something new. I didn't want new, I wanted old. I wanted happy. I wanted to be invisible.

"You *have* to audition," said my new girlfriend. "When people look at you they think of Groucho Marx."

"They do not."

"They do. You're always imitating Groucho Marx."

"I do not."

"Oh, don't be ridiculous. You love Groucho Marx, and now you're telling me you're too lazy to take the train to New York to audition?"

"I don't have an agent."

"You don't need one. They're holding an open call this Friday. They need to discover people to play the Marx Brothers. They're looking for unknowns. You've got to go in!"

I knew that if I did, I would ruin everything. (Which is not a bad starting point if you're auditioning for the role of Groucho Marx.)

Let me make this perfectly clear. I was not always imitating Groucho Marx. As a matter of fact, my appreciation for Groucho Marx had come at a cost. When I was fourteen, my father had ruined our perfect weekends together by remarrying. This didn't sit well with me because I was no longer the center of attention; there would be no more weekends of endless hot dogs and bowling. I refused to go to their wedding. My mother was devastated. (It was probably the one issue she and I could agree on.) Lenore, my new stepmother, did everything in her power to overlook my ill temper, but I wasn't having any. I wanted her to return to the tenement from whence she'd come.

It was in the heat of this limitless fury that I was introduced to the Marx Brothers. My father wanted the three of us to go to the Thalia Theater, at Ninety-fifth and Broadway, to see a double feature, *A Night at the Opera* and *A Day at the Races*. Naturally, I refused to go. For the second time in my life, my father dealt with my intransigence by delivering a crisp, well-timed slap across my face. When the three of us arrived at the Thalia the line stretched around the block. Still smarting, I stood a few couples behind the young marrieds, refusing to speak.

The Thalia looked less like a movie theater than a superintendent's basement apartment. It sat about two hundred people, and its sight lines were marred by four columns that made you strain to see the tiny screen. Redolent of popcorn and perspiration, it was the anti-movie palace, and much as I wanted to hate it, there was no denying that the space felt cozy and inviting. Soon *A Night at the Opera* flashed on the screen.

Who were these guys? It was a blessing that I was sitting alone, because I couldn't have shared the experience with another human being. The audience was going nuts. The year was 1961, and the tradition of reviving old movies was new. (Even the old movies weren't that old.) Two hundred people in an oversized sardine can were screaming with laughter. In the middle of the screen was this tortured, muscular little man who had the perfect comment to make about everything. If he wanted something from you, he insulted you. When he got what he wanted, he raised his eyebrows to the heavens and insinuated that the sky was about to fall in. The women he desired were superficial sexpots who were only using him, and the more he realized he was being used, the more his ardor increased. Just when he believed he had the world by the short hairs, a menial would kick him down a flight of stairs. Groucho Marx was a genius! He bore the world's pain on his shoulders. There was no separation in his greasepaint mustache.

When the two films were over I met my father and Lenore in the lobby. "How did you like it?" my father asked.

"It was all right," I told him. Thus my introduction to Julius Henry Marx.

The open-call audition for *Minnie's Boys* stipulated that actors auditioning for the roles of the five Marx Brothers should be prepared to sing an up-tempo musical number and a ballad. Important roles were seldom cast through open calls, but as Liz Hale had insisted, the audition was a talent search to find actors uniquely qualified to *impersonate* the Marx Brothers. I decided I would forgo preparing two songs. Every guy and his brother would be doing that. Instead I wrote a comic sketch in which I would sing like Groucho and interrupt the song with sarcastic patter. I would create the illusion that the producers were actually watching Groucho doing his thing.

After a couple of days I decided not to audition at all. I was convinced I could never find an accompanist who would be willing to work with me in Philadelphia and then take the train to Manhattan and play for my audition. Fyvush Finkel then volunteered his sixteen-year-old son, Elliot, who was studying to be a classical pianist at the Mannes conservatory. Elliot stood six foot six. I immediately worked him into the routine by referring to him as Emily, as if he were Groucho Marx's usual foil, Margaret Dumont. This made little sense, but it captured the anarchic flavor of Groucho's relationship with authority. The song I chose was "It's Only a Shanty in Old Shantytown," which Gladys George had rendered vividly in one of my favorite films, *The Roaring Twenties*. It was an overly sentimental number, and Groucho's comic point of view mocked all sentimentality. Then, to familiarize myself with Groucho's speech patterns, I wrote my own jokes in a rhythmic cadence.

I'd begin the song:

> *It's only a shanty in old shantytown,*
> With a roof that's so slanty it touches the ground.
> Just a tumbledown shack
> By an old railroad track,
> Like a millionaire's mansion
> It's calling me back...

(Then, speaking to Elliot) "And I'm glad you called me back, Emily. I'm only sorry my checks came back before I did. But listen here, my good lady. Just because I have a sunny disposition doesn't mean you can dispose of me at any time. I may handle your business end, but I can still withdraw!" It would go on that way ad nauseam, until someone demanded I stop.

On an autumnal Friday morning, Elliot Finkel and I disembarked from the train at Penn Station and headed toward Shubert Alley. It was a mob scene. In front of the Shubert's stage door hundreds of unknown actors dressed up like the Marx Brothers were milling around, dozens of Harpos in trenchcoats lifting their legs to any passersby who would take them. The sound of silverware spilling onto the sidewalk was continuous. Fifty Chicos in green Italian peasant hats were tearing up opera contracts. It was depressing.

But where were the Grouchos? Were they holding the Groucho auditions at some secret location? A few moments later I spotted a tall, heavyset fellow with hideously applied eyebrows and a cork mustache clumping around the alley with a long plastic cigar hanging from his mouth. He was the only one. I was competing against one other Groucho.

My audition was a triumph. You could immediately hear muffled sounds of self-congratulation coming from the back of the orchestra. I've experienced only a few such auditions, where the powers that be converge out of the darkness and toss bouquets in your direction. You've solved their problem, and they race down the aisles on little businessmen's feet, applauding themselves for having found you.

Within moments I found myself in the suffocating embrace of the director, Larry Kornfeld, a large, fleshy gentleman in his mid-thirties dressed in an orange-and-brown dashiki. Beside him was the diminutive choreographer, Pat Birch, as taut and washboard trim as Larry Kornfeld wasn't. Standing next to them was Arthur Whitelaw, the superconfident producer of *Minnie's Boys*. Everything about Arthur bespoke success. Here was a young man who had elbowed his way onto Broadway and in a few years had made it all look easy. A theatrical wunderkind, he had introduced the young Liza Minnelli to the world in an Off Broadway revival of *Best Foot Forward*, which he followed with *You're a Good Man, Charley Brown* and then his latest Broadway sleeper hit, *Butterflies Are Free*. People on the street were mentioning his name in the same breath as Harold Prince.

I was immediately escorted across Eighth Avenue to Arthur's theatrical offices, where I was given a soft drink and grilled by the play's general manager, Marvin Krauss. What had I done? Where had I come from? How come I didn't have an agent? I shouldn't worry about a thing; they'd make sure I was well taken care of. Only one obstacle remained before they could officially offer a young unknown the part of a lifetime. I would have to prove I could dance well enough to perform the role of the young Groucho.

The real Groucho Marx had a brilliant, eccentric dancing style that was so idiosyncratic I wondered if I could replicate it. Would I be able to pick up a dance combination quickly enough to seal the deal? If I had confidence in any part of my talent, it was in my ability to move. Joe Vilane had given me a vocabulary of dance, but would that vocabulary be adequate for a Broadway choreographer? I told myself to stay calm.

I was taken back to the stage of the Shubert, where Pat Birch directed me to extend my arms and do a tango step so rudimentary that the only way I could screw it up was if one of my legs fell asleep. I was asked to do Groucho's bent-knee glide a few times without even a variation. Then Pat announced to the brain trust that she could state unequivocally that I would be able to perform the routines she was working out at the Jerome Robbins Theater Lab on West Nineteenth Street. I'd passed the Broadway dancing litmus test without ever having to perform a choreographed step. Either Pat Birch was really rooting for me to get the part or she was holding back on the hard stuff.

Staring out at broken factory windows as my train limped past North Philadelphia, I mused at how much my life had changed since I'd taken the same train in the opposite direction that morning. All I could think of was how excited my mother was going to be when I told her I was actually going to meet Groucho Marx.

Chapter 14

Being cast in *Minnie's Boys* made everyone who knew me think I was destiny's child, but several problems with the show were apparent from the outset. Arthur Whitelaw hadn't raised all the needed capital, so the show's official starting date kept getting pushed back. This meant I could continue touring with *Fiddler* indefinitely, which suited me fine. Second, they were having difficulty casting the role of Zeppo, which meant that I was called back to New York from Wilmington, Delaware, so that Danny Fortus, who had been cast as Harpo, Irwin Pearl, cast as Chico, and I could see whether brotherly chemistry existed between us and whoever they chose for Zeppo. On meeting for the first time we all agreed we were the three luckiest young people in Actor's Equity and that we should watch as many Marx Brothers movies as humanly possible before starting rehearsal. Also, a rumor was flying around that two-time Oscar winner Shelley Winters was about to be signed for the part of Minnie. Arthur badly needed a star to raise the remaining capital for the show.

Just before the audition began, our illustrious director, sporting the same dashiki, called the three of us together to give us the game plan.

"When an actor we really like is singing a number, I'll give you boys the signal, and I want you to jump up on the stage and do your crazy Marx Brothers thing."

"What do you mean?" I asked him.

"You know, that crazy Marx Brothers shtick that got you the jobs in the first place. Buzz around the guy and drive him crazy."

This was a bad sign. Didn't our director realize that the Marx Brothers had honed their material over a thirty-year period, that they had begun performing as children on the lowest rung of vaudeville, polishing their act by trial and error before emerging as their recognizable selves?

Their genius lay in giving the impression that every bit of wordplay, every piece of physical comedy, was being improvised in the moment, but the reality was that the words were being furnished by the likes of George S. Kaufman, Morrie Ryskind, S. J. Perelman, and Harry Ruby. The Marx Brothers may have been inspired improvisational wits at a cocktail party, but their comic personas had been as painstakingly crafted as any in the history of show business. "Go out there and do your crazy Marx Brothers shtick?" Hmmmm.

Of course we tried. Whenever Larry gave us the signal we would run around some poor uncomprehending bastard and start licking his face or pick him up and carry him around the stage. There was a real whiff of the amateur to these proceedings. It was as if our director was hoping we might evolve into the Marx Brothers by osmosis. He seemed to believe that W. C. Fields had made himself into the world's greatest juggler not by practicing but by being born with a dozen duck pins in his diaper.

Larry Kornfeld had never directed a Broadway musical or play in his life. He was a licensed psychologist who had directed several Off Broadway musicals at the Judson Church in Greenwich Village, all of them written by a brilliantly undisciplined composer-minister by the name of Al Carmines. Carmines's pieces were decidedly avant-garde, although his melodies were reminiscent of Tin Pan Alley. Because his shows lacked the discipline of the Broadway musical, Arthur Whitelaw decided that Kornfeld would be the perfect person to direct the anarchic lunacy personified by the Marx Brothers. Instead of hiring a director whose creative life had evolved with a vaudeville sensibility, Arthur hired a counterculture academic. If Larry Kornfeld had ever seen a Marx Brothers movie, he never got the joke.

Another bad omen presented itself a few weeks before we were to begin rehearsals. Shelley Winters had indeed been signed to play the title role of Minnie, and one night after a performance of *Fiddler* in Boston, I raced over to Liz Hale's Beacon Hill apartment to catch her appearance on Johnny Carson's show. The word on Shelley was that she was great but extremely difficult to work with. That night she burst onto the set and immediately began a fight with Carson's first guest, the producer David Susskind. Susskind was famous for being abrasive and opinionated, and apparently he had once said something that Shelley had taken umbrage at. For twenty minutes they fought like hyenas. Shelley appeared to be drunk, and no matter how many times Susskind attempted to disengage, she kept coming at him. Finally, looking more sympathetic than he had any right to feel, Susskind stared at her as if she was a damp hair clinging to a glass. "Oh, Shelley," he said with a sigh. "You're every man's first wife."

In mid-December the cast of *Minnie's Boys* assembled for the first time at a rehearsal studio at the YMCA on Eighth Avenue and Fiftieth Street. The company was a mix of such solid musical theater veterans as Arne Freeman, Mort Marshall, and Roland Winters and a few lesser-known character actors, a group of high-kicking chorus girls and boys, and the five of us who were to play the Marx Brothers. After many auditions, Alvin Kupperman and Gary Raucher had been cast to play Zeppo and Gummo. The day's schedule began with a meet and greet. Arthur Whitelaw invited the show's composer-lyricist team, Larry Grossman and Hal Hackady, to perform the musical's title song, and after bagels and coffee we awaited the arrival of Ms. Winters, who as the headliner was exercising her prerogative by showing up a half hour late.

There is nothing quite like the optimism that pervades a room when show people meet for the first time. Their smiles could not be broader. Everyone in the room is desperate to believe the best about everyone else. Those who have shared history convene in an amiable cluster while everyone else eyes the room for a future lover or friend. What distinguishes these people from all others is their courage, the courage it takes to walk around a room in tights, showing the world the unmediated shape of their physiques. An inordinate physical attractiveness is evident in these people. Their teeth are straighter and whiter than the average person's, their legs longer, their asses higher. They've been waiting months for this day, and the room has a whiff of the history of all Broadway hits. *My Fair Lady* started this way. So did Gene Kelly and Fred Astaire.

At last the door swung open and Shelley Winters entered, followed by her female secretary, who already appeared exhausted by her employer's star power. Everyone stopped what they were doing and turned their attention on this large, blond woman whose responsibility it would be to lead us into the creative unknown.

"I haven't stopped working on the new song." she positively chirped to our composer. "Do you think we could, you know, take it down a few octaves? Hello, everybody." She paused, clearly winded. "I'm Shelley! Who are you?" Everyone in the room broke up. Arthur Whitelaw raced over and smothered her with kisses. Hi's and hello's cascaded through the hall. She filled the room with a boundless, disconnected energy that we all recognized as her celebrity trademark. Her every thought was punctuated with a burst of nervous laughter. "She's adorable." "She's perfect." "My mother's in love with her." "She's the spitting image of the real Minnie" were comments heard above the rustle of chairs as our stage manager, Frank Hamilton, told us to seat ourselves around an oblong table for the first reading.

Just then the show's press agent, Max Eisen, entered with a TV reporter who was scheduled to interview Shelley for a segment on the evening news.

"Excuse me!" said Shelley. *"Excuse me!"* Suddenly she was on her feet, script in hand, and with a sound not unlike that of a bawling infant in a crowded restaurant, she released an adenoidal whine that shook the studio's rafters. *"Nobody said anything to me about TV cameras and interviews! Look it up in my contract! I want them out of here! Get them the hell out of here!"*

Pandemonium ensued. Shelley was led screaming from the room. The rest of us could do nothing but seek solace in the silence that descended. It was an outburst without provocation. Certainly a little publicity on the evening news could not have been objectionable to someone addicted to being the center of attention. This was not a person who *could* be difficult. This was a person who demanded to be difficult, as a means of exhausting the world around her.

"There are two kinds of pain in the asses," quipped Mort Marshall, who had been hired to play our uncle, Al Shean. "There's the interesting pain in the ass, and the great big fucking waste of time pain in the ass. I wonder which one she is?"

Shelley returned a half hour later, having relented and done the interview. We were now an hour behind schedule.

Larry Kornfeld sat at the head of the table and addressed the five of us playing the Marx Brothers. Since *Minnie's Boys* traced the evolution of Julius, Leonard, Adolph, and Herbie Marx until they evolved into Groucho, Chico, Harpo, and Zeppo, our director wanted to be certain everyone was on the same page.

"When the play begins," he asked the assembled, "exactly how old are the Marx Brothers?"

"Chico was the oldest," said Irwin Pearl.

"So what age does that make you?"

"Eighteen?" ventured Irwin. At this point everyone was anxious to dive in and start rehearsing the play. Kornfeld extended his lower lip.

"How about seventeen and a half."

A faint murmur ran around the room. "Now, who's the second oldest Marx brother?"

"Harpo," said Danny Fortus. "He was two years younger than Chico, so I guess that makes me sixteen." Once again we all turned to Larry, who appeared to be wrestling with a difficut thought.

"How about sixteen and a half."

I looked over at Arne Freeman, Mort Marshall, and Roland Winters. All three appeared to have swallowed the same canary.

"Listen," I said, "since Groucho is the least childlike of the four, why not make me the oldest?"

"Lewis makes an interesting point," Larry allowed. "So, when the play begins, how old is Groucho?"

"Fifty-seven and a half!" said Mort Marshall. "Listen, I don't mean to be a wet blanket, but don't we still have to elect an Equity deputy? Besides, Minnie may have a pot roast in the oven, and we haven't even figured out how old I am yet."

"Mort makes an interesting point," said Larry.

"Jesus!" said Arne Freeman. "He was making a joke. I'm sorry; I just had a distressing conversation with my stockbroker, who reminded me that I'm not as young as I used to be. Do you think we could get around to reading the play?"

"Of course we can, Arne. How many of us want to start reading the play?"

"That would be very nice," said Roland Winters.

"Then let's get at it."

Sitting in Thanos coffee shop three hours later, Danny Fortus, who really was fifteen and a half and had been acting professionally since he was seven, took a bite of his egg salad sandwich and remarked, "I don't know about you guys, but I smell a bomb."

Minnie's Boys faced yet another problem. Instead of it being a story about the Marx Brothers, it was really a story about the Marx Brothers' mother. The musical *Gypsy* was also about a famous entertainer and a mother, but that mother was the center of the play's conflict. *Gypsy* was the story of a mother using her children to achieve the fame she desired for herself. So when Jule Styne and Stephen Sondheim composed an evening's worth of songs for Ethel Merman, those songs dramatized the conflict of the play. *Gypsy* was the story of Madame Rose, not Gypsy Rose Lee. Minnie Marx was the opposite of Madame Rose. Everybody loved Minnie, especially her sons, so the only conflict in our play was whether Minnie would put her lovable foot in her mouth and destroy her sons' careers—which everyone knew was never going to happen.

The original libretto had been written by the comedian David Steinberg, but the real Groucho Marx didn't like it and insisted that his son Arthur and Arthur's writing partner, Robert Fisher, rewrite the book. Arthur had been a nationally ranked tennis player, but he wasn't much of a writer. Groucho and Arthur shared a painful father-son relationship; it probably wouldn't have been a bad idea to write a musical about them.

Worse, a paranoid perception was developing that a paying audience might be offended by the spectacle of four actors pretending to be the Marx Brothers, even though we were putting on a million-dollar musical about them. As soon as the five of us signed our contracts we had to promise Larry Kornfeld and Pat Birch that we would watch no more Marx Brothers movies as long as we were in rehearsal. (If they weren't going to watch one, why should we?) All this was a shame, because they had hired a talented cast, and Grossman and Hackady had written a charming score that really did channel the spirit of the Marx Brothers.

Until this point my only experience had been with *Fiddler*, which may have been a little tired after playing on the road for three years but was so brilliantly conceived that it stood as a monument to those in the American theater who actually knew what they were doing. As a child watching what appeared to be seamless musicals, it never occurred to me not to sink luxuriously into my velvet seat and accept even an imperfect musical as part of some comforting and harmonious universe. As I watched the poker players sing "A Little Tin Box" in *Fiorello!*, I recall my father gently clasping my hand and above the din of tumultuous applause whispering, "They won't do an encore, because this is a George Abbott Production." *A George Abbott Production!* The perfect bromide for a world in chaos.

By the second day of rehearsal it was obvious that this wasn't going to be a George Abbott Production. Shelley Winters showed up with an elastic bandage around one ankle that she would wear until the day we closed. Pat Birch would rehearse a musical number by assuming a dancer's pose and standing motionless until one of us jumped to our feet and said, "What if I do a little shuffle off to Buffalo here?" To which she would enthusiastically shake her head and say, "Absolutely! So Margie is going to do a shuffle step." Then she would assume another pose until someone else popped up and suggested another step.

I was having problems of my own. I couldn't remember what I had done to replicate the essence of Groucho's voice and body movement. Everyone was telling me not to be Groucho Marx. Who were these people, and why were they giving me such bad direction? I even found myself imploring God. Why was life so inequitable? Why was this production such a sham? Why was Shelley Winters playing my mother? I deserved a better mother. The whole mess made my back arch, my hands break at the wrist, and my voice rise to the timbre of an aggrieved lemming. Fuck them if they were too scared to take a joke. They had hired me to play Groucho Marx! This was my great opportunity, and I resolved to be mighty selective about who I listened to.

Rehearsing in this confusing environment was actually proving a boon to the four of us playing the Marx Brothers. Absurdity sharpened our perspective. It wasn't terribly difficult to walk with a slouch when you knew the woman playing your mother was going to mess up half the lyrics in every song. Shelley could remember every song she had sung in a 1940s garment workers' revue, but she couldn't recall much of anything else. Part of her problem was the specter of Katharine Hepburn and Lauren Bacall, who were also making their musical comedy debuts that season in *Coco* and *Applause*. Shelley thought she was in a three-way beauty contest. With a few exceptions, those like Shelley who aspire to stardom see themselves as symbols with their own constituencies. If they decide to have a well-publicized affair with another celebrity, they essentially take their fan base along with them. When Barbra Streisand started sleeping with Ryan O'Neal, they were fucking for the multitudes. Fame is a full-time job. It takes more than talent to convince the world you deserve your own orbit around the sun.

Shelley Winters considered herself a star. She had labored tirelessly to present an image of herself not simply as a two-time Academy Award winner but also as a great humanitarian. A buxom little Jewish girl from St. Louis, she positioned herself at the forefront of every liberal cause. She had been around long enough for the public to watch her make the transition from sexpot to matron. (To quote Broadway producer

Alexander H. Cohen, "Thirty years ago, that girl had the greatest body I ever saw!") Like Marilyn Monroe, she projected a vulnerability women especially seemed to admire.

"Why don't you look at me more lovingly?" she would ask me after we had rehearsed a scene.

"Because I'm playing Groucho Marx. I'm working on a character here."

"Danny Fortus looks at me lovingly."

"Danny Fortus is playing Harpo. Harpo loved everybody and everybody loved Harpo."

"I'm having a hard time remembering my lines because you're looking at me with hatred in your eyes."

"I'm not looking at you with hatred in my eyes. Groucho's a skeptic. That's what makes him funny."

"Listen, I happen to know a little something about acting myself. Can I make a small suggestion as to how to play the scene?"

"How should I play the scene?"

"You see the way you're looking at me with such hatred? Why don't you listen to me for a second? I'm not such a bad actress. Would you like me to bring in my *three* Academy Awards?" (She had won two.)

"How would you like me to play the scene?"

"I want you to play the scene—just this once—like you're Motel the tailor."

"You want me to play Groucho Marx like I'm Motel the tailor?"

"Just this once. Just for the hell of it."

"You want me to stutter?"

"Just this once."

She was right. I was looking at her with hatred.

Then there was the case of Arne Freeman. Seventy-year-old Arne had signed on to play the thankless role of our father. He had one lovely song to sing at the conclusion of the first scene, and there was a persistent rumor that it was about to be cut. All of Arne's scenes were with Shelley, who had shown up on the second day of rehearsal with a head cold to go along with the Ace bandage on her ankle. At one point Arne's had to share a closet with her during a scene in which we were hiding from the landlord, who was demanding the rent. Shelley got into the habit of leaving her used Kleenex around the set, and it wasn't long before Arne walked into the studio with a bad cold.

"Don't come near me with that cold," demanded Shelley. "I just got over one myself."

"How the hell do you think I got mine?" said Arne. "You've been spitting in my fucking face for three weeks!"

We were one big happy family.

On a sunny Saturday afternoon after we'd been rehearsing for three full weeks, Arthur Whitelaw, several associate producers, and assorted friends took their seats along one wall of the studio to watch the first formal run-through of *Minnie's Boys*. Larry Kornfeld made a brief speech advising the audience that our efforts represented more of a stumble-through than an actual run-through, but if they liked what they saw, they could hoot and holler nonetheless. "We want to see how the whole thing fits together."

For the next three and a half hours we more than stumbled, we crashed. Shelley couldn't remember much of anything, and the show came off as an energetic train wreck set to music. Nobody seemed to care about the domestic woes of the Marx Brothers' parents, but the piece occasionally came to life when the four of us were forced into farcical situations that brought to mind scenes from actual Marx Brothers movies. Danny Fortus drew enthusiastic applause for his beautiful ballad, "Mama, a Rainbow," and Julie Kurnitz, playing a Margaret Dumont type, and I brought down the house with the comic duet "You Remind Me of You." As the afternoon progressed the four of us began to inhabit our characters rather than doing stock impersonations. It was becoming obvious to everyone present that the strength of the show, if it had one, had to do with the story of the boys.

At the end of the day everyone but me was excused. My mind began to race with excitement. They were prepared to rip up my contract! (I was being paid four hundred dollars a week.) They were going to put my name above the title directly across from Shelley's! When I'd changed into my street clothes I was called into the darkened studio to meet with Arthur Whitelaw and Pat Birch. Larry Kornfeld was conspicuously absent.

"We have a big problem with the show," said Arthur, looking down at his Gucci loafers. "Do you know what that problem is?" They had to be talking about Shelley's performance or Larry's incompetent direction, but being twenty-three and considering this was my first Broadway show, I decided to let them tell me.

"Patty," said Arthur, "why don't you tell him?"

"The problem is *you*," said Pat. "You're playing the role too much like Groucho Marx."

"But I'm *playing* Groucho Marx."

"Nonono!" they yelled in unison. "We want you to play Lewis Stadlen! Trust us. Nobody wants to see an actor impersonating Groucho Marx."

"But I'm not! I'm starting off with my voice in a higher register, and as the plot unfolds I'm finding ways to incorporate his mannerisms."

"Leeewwwwiiissss," said Pat, drawing out my name to indicate that she was willing to be patient. "We watched you all afternoon. Your performance is distorting the balance of the show."

"And Shelley?" I asked them.

"Shelley is going to be *wonderful*," said Arthur, "as soon as she gets a better handle on the lines."

"Shelley's going to be *marvelous*," said Pat. "The audience is gonna eat her up."

"And the direction?"

"Let us handle that," Pat snapped, like a Latin American general on the way to a coup.

"We're very pleased with how everything is going," said Arthur. "You just have to put the idea of Groucho Marx out of your head."

"You don't want me to play Groucho Marx?"

"*Never!*" they cried in unison, grateful there was still time to save the show.

"Never in the whole play?" I asked.

"Only once," said Pat Birch.

"And when is that?"

She put her arms on my shoulders and looked soulfully into my eyes. "You can be Groucho the last minute of the play."

"The last minute of the play?"

"*If that!*" said Arthur.

"Trust us," said Pat. "We're only looking out for the welfare of the show."

A few moments later I found myself in the twilight of Eighth Avenue. It had been a long and exhilarating day. In the back of my mind I knew I had it in me to carry the show on my back. I decided to take a leisurely stroll downtown to look at the show's logo, which had just gone up on the Imperial Theater marquee. It was a colorful, warmhearted logo, closer to the spirit of the show than the show itself. On an off-white background in pastel lettering were the words *MINNIE'S BOYS!* Just above the capital *M* was an amusing rendering of gentleman with frizzy hair, raised eyebrows, and a ridiculous greasepaint mustache. If I hadn't known better, I would have sworn it was Groucho Marx.

Chapter 15

Larry Kornfeld was fired after the first preview and replaced by a witty, kind-hearted gentleman named Stanley Prager. Stanley didn't claim to be Jerome Robbins, but he was a thorough professional who had been hired six weeks too late. Pat Birch talked a good game as long as she was juxtaposed with Larry Kornfeld, but she couldn't bullshit Prager. She was fired at the end of the first week and replaced by another honest professional, Marc Breaux. Shelley Winters came down with a bad case of the flu and missed two performances while her recently hired understudy was sent on to play the role with a script in her hand. During the first scene, both of her contact lenses managed to slip out and she was unable to read. For the rest of the act she would sidle off to the wings where stage manager Frank Hamilton screamed out the lyrics to a half dozen songs. The rest of us ad-libbed her remaining dialogue. She was fired as soon as they could find another understudy.

Arthur Whitelaw decided to replace Arthur Marx and Bob Fisher with S. J. Perelman, who had written the original screenplay for two Marx Brothers movies, *Monkey Business* and *Horse Feathers*. Perelman immediately informed Arthur that he hated the real Groucho Marx and wasn't about to rewrite a musical based on his life. But Arthur persisted and persuaded Perelman that he needed only commit to being picked up at his Bucks County farm and driven to the show and back in Arthur's chauffeured Rolls-Royce. After watching a Tuesday night performance, Perelman left the theater and, without saying a word to anyone, was driven back to Bucks County. As he stepped out of the Rolls, Arthur's chauffeur inquired, "Is there any message for Mister Whitelaw?"

"Yes," said Perelman. "Tell Mister Whitelaw to close the show and fix the clock."

From its first preview performance, *Minnie's Boys* was a good-natured, well-intentioned mess. Awful as some of it was, most of the audiences seemed to want a musical about the life of the Marx Brothers to succeed. Even the most cold-hearted theater professionals seemed willing to award it a pass. If only we could improve it just enough to mask its more egregious faults.

There was little disagreement that Shelley had been a big mistake. Although she closely resembled the real Minnie Marx, the public didn't know what Minnie looked like, nor did they care. What they did care about was her halting comic delivery and her barely adequate singing voice. On the stage of the Imperial Theater you couldn't keep messing up takes the way you did in the movies, until you had exhausted the actor playing opposite you. Shelley Winters cared only about Shelley Winters, but unlike some of the legendary monsters of the stage who knew how to co-opt the best material for themselves, Shelley hadn't a clue as to how to make her performance better. By the fourth week of previews they were looking around for a replacement.

As for me, I was being paraded around the city as Broadway's flavor of the month. I remember being pressed up against a wall by some souped-up Broadway character who asked me, "Is there a special responsibility that comes with genius?" He was one of a small army of familiar faces that were suddenly pulling their chairs up next to mine. Everyone was interested in my opinions. I began to wonder, Wouldn't it be amazing if I had actually been a genius all these years without ever knowing it?

This avalanche of attention is indicative of the power that accrues from a great role. My salvation had been to place myself in the audience at the Imperial Theater and imagine what it would be like to watch some jerk give a superficial rendering of Groucho Marx. What I had discovered about Groucho Marx was that he wasn't simply Otis P. Driftwood. The real Julius Henry Marx had paid a steep price for his comic philosophy. Forever pissed off that his mother found him charmless and unattractive and that his first sexual encounter with a woman had resulted in a case of the clap, he saw the world through a prism of inequity. At twenty-three, with only a rudimentary understanding of who I was, I was being asked to play a man as fully formed as anyone I would ever know. It was one of those rare instances in which being an actor becomes a noble calling.

Alvin Kupperman and I were leaving Sardi's restaurant when Arthur Whitelaw accosted us and steered us back into the dining room. Heading straight for us, clutching the arm of Arthur's well-stacked assistant, Susan

Bell, was an elderly gentleman of sallow complexion who wore a blue gabardine blazer, a baby blue turtleneck, and a rakish beret.

"Boys, meet Groucho Marx."

"Don't go anywhere," Groucho commanded Susan. "I've grown very fond of her. You know, you're only as old as the woman you feel." He waited for the laughter to subside before turning his attention to me. "Who are you?"

"My name is Lewis Stadlen."

"And who do you play?"

"I play you, Groucho."

"And who are you?" he said, turning to Alvin.

"I'm Alvin Kupperman. I play Zeppo."

"Well, you look as untalented as Zeppo." His attention shifted to the exit. "When does what's-her-name get here? Or is she still eating?"

"Shelley?" said Arthur. "I don't believe the lady has arrived yet."

"Is that what you call her? In Hollywood we used to call her something else." He began looking me up and down. "How does it feel to be me?"

"I love it!"

"Well, don't get used to it. It's hard enough for me to be me without you being me. Do you think we can get out of here before what's-her-name arrives? She's the only woman I miss more when she's here than when she's not here." And with Susan in tow he retreated out the door.

Groucho went to the show that evening, and whatever he later communicated to Shelley couldn't have been complimentary, because the next night Stanley Prager and I were summoned to her dressing room.

"He's looking at me with hatred in his eyes," she told Stanley in a disturbingly high-pitched quaver. "As long as he keeps doing that I won't be able to do the scene."

"I don't hate you!" I told her. "We're marooned in Nacogdoches, Texas, without any money. The situation seems hopeless. It's the first time I walk away from you doing the Groucho walk. It's nothing personal."

"Stop treating me like your real mother," she said, wiping a glob of cold cream off her face.

"Why don't I look at it tomorrow?" said Stanley, who suffered from a rheumatic heart that would stop two years later.

Shelley stood up in her dressing robe and began pacing the room. "Let me point something out to you," she said, looking over at the two of us. "When this show closes, I go back to Hollywood and get paid two hundred and fifty thousand dollars a picture. When this show closes, he goes back to the unemployment line."

Stanley Prager grabbed my wrist and pulled me off the couch.

"How dare you say something like that to him!" he told her. "What an awful thing to say to anyone. Come on, Lewis," he said, leading me out of her room. "I told my oldest daughter this was a terrible business; she just won't listen to me."

He walked me out the stage door and leaned me up against the wall of the theater. "Lewis, there's something I have to say to you. That woman? This show?" He stared down at his feet, which were surprisingly small. "This show is never going to be what you want it to be."

I had listened to my father tell Stanley Prager stories since I was a kid. How they had performed together at Chester Zumbar's, in the Catskills. How Stanley had taught him about sketch comedy and how to behave around women. I had listened to him sing "Her Is!" on the cast album of *The Pajama Game* (a George Abbott Production) a thousand times, and now he was counseling me to give up.

"Why not?" I asked him.

The decision was made to fire Shelley and replace her with Dorothy Loudon, Kaye Ballard, or Totie Fields. Nothing was official, but all of us were hoping they'd make the move as quickly and seamlessly as possible. I was praying they'd cast either Ballard or Loudon, two bona fide musical comedy talents who could kill in the part. A stand-up comedian, Fields had never performed in a play before.

Webster's New World Dictionary defines *hubris* as "Arrogance caused by excessive pride." Arthur Whitelaw was either going to admit to himself that hiring Shelley Winters had been a huge booboo or he was going to let himself off the hook and blame the fates. Instead of hiring either Kaye Ballard or Dorothy Loudon, who might have turned the show around, Arthur offered the role to Totie Fields, whose health problems were so severe that one of her legs would be amputated the following year.

It didn't matter. Shelley Winters wasn't going anywhere.

They fired her, but she wouldn't leave. Backed by her personal manager and theatrical agent, Shelley refused to budge. Arthur could fire her, but he'd have to pay her full salary until the end of her contract. Certain that little could be accomplished if she remained in the show but with his finances overextended, Arthur did an about-face and welcomed her back.

I don't mean to portray myself as an innocent in all of this. As Groucho's personality intertwined with my own, I began expressing how I felt about things. For the first time in my life my opinions seemed to carry weight. I may have been a novice, but in this crowd I believed I had a clearer vision of Marx Brothers comedy than those calling the shots. This temporary sense of power transformed itself into an overheated yearning for the fairer sex. After a day of throwing my weight around, I felt the need to cuddle with something soft.

There was this tall blonde I'd seen walking through an alley in Chicago while I was doing *Fiddler*. She was appearing in *On a Clear Day You Can See Forever* at the Shubert. I had tried to interest her, but at the time I was just another rabbi's son walking around State and Madison. Three years later she showed up as one of the dancer-singers in *Minnie's Boys*. Margie Edson lived in a fourth-floor walkup at Ninth and Forty-sixth, and the moment I laid eyes on the bathtub in her kitchen I fell in love. Her choice of attire was demurely chorus girl, and she had a tough-girl vulnerability that simply drove me mad. Put a tall, blond, curvaceous woman in an overcoat with fake fur on the collar and I'm crawling on my belly like a baby turtle scrambling toward the ocean. She was a lovely girl who I believed my mother would never approve of, and that made me want her all the more.

I shared many things with my mother, but physical intimacy was not one of them. The closest we ever came to touching was when we bumped into each other. So at thirteen, when I was loaned a copy of *Sex in the French Cinema* by my father's commercial artist friend Burton Wink, I raced to my bedroom and devoured it page by startling page. Midway through the book was a photograph of a tall, dark-haired woman who was unapologetically fleshy. She was standing in front of a bed with a powerfully disputatious look on her face, dressed only in a black brassiere, matching G-string, garter belt, black stockings, and a pair of spike heels. Her hair was as full-bodied as her sumptuous breasts and Olympian ass. This was the woman I wanted to be *my* mother. I also found myself romantically aroused (though slightly less so) by Leslie Caron's interpretation of Cinderella in the MGM musical *The Glass Slipper*. My prepubescent sensibilities were deeply affected by the film's tag line: And they all lived happily ever after!

Minnie's Boys trudged on in previews for eighty-four performances, our opening night repeatedly delayed until every clinker had been rearranged and polished. The process reminded me of a *New Yorker* cartoon I came upon thirty years later showing a theatrical agent sitting at a desk with a telephone in his hand. The caption reads "To tell you the truth, Lance, I think you've reinvented yourself so many times we're right back where we started from." If *Minnie's Boys* had followed its original blueprint and opened at the Erlanger Theater in Philadelphia, it most certainly would have closed out of town. As it was, Arthur Whitelaw's funds were almost depleted by the time we stopped tinkering and opened on March 26, 1970. Rearranging deck chairs on the *Titanic* was the cast's attitude whenever the brain trust decided to revise the one musical number that worked. In the ten weeks leading up to our official opening, we had gone so far as to take the musical number that opened the second act and use it to close the first.

Arthur Marx and Bob Fisher were fired and replaced by two television writers none of us were ever introduced to. By the fourth week of previews we were playing a first act that bore no relation to the second. For a few performances yours truly was sent out as Groucho Marx to tell the audience what had transpired during the intermission so they wouldn't be completely mystified by the second act. When the new first act played no better than the old one, we went back to the old one. Eventually we scrapped most of the new second act. Within a month the new television writers hired to replace Marx and Fisher were fired and the old television writers rehired. The only thing that stayed the same was that Ace bandage on Shelley Winters's ankle.

Perhaps it's fruitless to analyze a moment of lunacy that may ultimately have been the show's undoing. After all, the production's laundry was being aired in full view of the Broadway community. A few wise guys were actually taking book on which troubled musical would run longer in previews, *Minnie's Boys* or an adaptation of Sinclair Lewis's *Elmer Gantry*, which was faring even worse than we were without half our advance. It had finally become clear to our decision makers that the show's strength involved anything to do with the Marx Brothers. Fears that the audience would be turned off by our interpretations proved unfounded, and as the weeks turned into months Shelley's character had practically disappeared, especially in the reconfigured second act.

It was decided to reintroduce her by making her the center of a large group number, without allowing her to do much of anything. For five minutes the entire cast performed cartwheels, shlepping Shelley from one side of the stage to the other while sparing her the necessity to sing, dance, or act. Within those five indescribable minutes of nondeception, *Minnie's Boys* seemed to lose whatever sympathy it had worked so hard to engender.

Chapter 16

On the day before a New York opening, a company moves within a solar system of its own. It is a planet in outer space, detached from the moon and stars, and its orbit is the stairway from the dressing rooms to the stage. Each actor sits at his make-up table, staring into the brilliantly lit mirror at his own image, making the prescribed movements that will detach him still further from the world of reality and allow him to achieve the anonymity of complete disguise. The more he becomes at one with the part he is to play, the less of himself that peeps through it, the further he sinks into the atmosphere of make-believe and unreality, the safer he feels. He is seeking a judgment from the real world, not of himself but of the hidden image he carries within him that is both his goal and his refuge. The general conception that all actors are born exhibitionists is far from the truth. They are quite the opposite. They are shy frightened people in hiding from themselves—people who have found a way of concealing their secret by footlights, make-up and the parts they play.

Their own self-rejection is what has made most of them actors. What better way to solve the problem or to evade it than to be someone other than the self one has rejected, and to be accepted and applauded for it every night. They have solved the problem, but not its torment.

– Moss Hart, *Act One*

The day of our opening I walked the streets in search of the muse I had ridden in on. Whatever good fortune I had envisioned for myself was being subverted by a vengeful thirst for recognition from those who had ever done me ill. By the time the curtain went up that evening, I was tight as a drum. There's a misconception among actors that they are the best critics of their own work. Sometimes you feel in communion with the gods; at other times you want to race to the wings in despair. Often the reason for these states is undetectable. With talent and craft you can give a performance that is representative of your vision, whether you are totally in the moment or dreaming of the restaurant you want to take your date to after the show. A good stage actor dedicates himself equally to the performance he is not in the mood to give as to the performance he believes will solidify his reputation. It's usually the former effort that's worth the price of admission.

Doing the first act of our opening night was misery. I spent most of my time worrying that Danny Fortus's performance as Harpo was eclipsing my work. Midway through the act he sang the most endearing song in the show, "Mama, a Rainbow," magnificently and brought down the house. For the next ten minutes I fretted, convinced that I was blowing the opportunity of a lifetime. Not until after the intermission did I calm down and decide to be part of the play. Stella Adler's voice resonated in my head: "What is it you wish to be, darling? An actor or a star?"

At the curtain call, Groucho appeared onstage and graciously remarked that I was better than he was and a good deal younger. Then he took me aside and with surprising tenderness asked me to do the Groucho walk across the stage with him. Photographs show the two of us walking side by side, the arch of our backs perfectly matched.

The reviews were mostly scathing. Clive Barnes, then writing for the *New York Times*, mentioned Groucho's generous remark about me but added that the possibility of anyone writing a musical based on the life of Lewis J. Stadlen was highly unlikely. Enlisting his genius for punning, he referred to Grossman and Hackady's score as "Gross and Hack." Totally unfair: It was one of the more likable scores of the season. John Simon wrote in *New York Magazine*: "Miss Winters is a disaster—or, to be more exact, a disaster area. Along with Groucho, Chico and Harpo, we now have a Zero Marx." As the ten-week run of *Minnie's Boys* drew to a close, audiences declined precipitously and management was forced on many occasions to paper the house.

On the afternoon of May 20, the day we were to close, Shelley's understudy, Thelma Lee, our beleaguered stage manager, Frank Hamilton, and I were walking across the stage when we were confronted by a breathless Shelley Winters.

"Selma," said Shelly, "I'm so sorry you never got a chance to play Minnie Marx. I begged the producers to let you on, but they said Shelley, you're the star. You are what the public is paying to see."

Thelma took a delicious dramatic pause.

"Miss Winters, you don't have to apologize to me. I realize that if Frank got on the biscuit and announced that at this performance the role of Minnie Marx would be played by Thelma Lee, the entire audience would storm the box office and demand their paper back."

Chapter 17

Since childhood I had assumed that Broadway shows were professional undertakings because they were performed between Forty-first Street and Sixth Avenue and Fifty-fourth and Eighth. My experience with *Minnie's Boys* was an eye opener. Obviously, quality wasn't a matter of real estate but of talent and creative vision. Those responsible for *Minnie's Boys* had made every mistake in the book, and still they had come within a silly millimeter of pulling it off. There lies the implausibility of the American theater.

It's interesting (at least to me) how the institutional forces behind the lively arts can mistake an incompetent for a genius. Few other professions offer such latitude in their definition of excellence. If a musician hired to play a musical score finds it impossible to hit the right notes, he's promptly replaced by someone who can. If a professional baseball player finds it impossible to get at least two hits in ten at-bats, no sportswriter will claim that his deficiency is a sign of brilliance. The notes and numbers will paint a reasonably accurate picture of the individual's competence or lack thereof. Not so in the theater.

The perception of an actor has a lot to do with his or her personal charm, especially the first few times they appear before the public. There are those an audience imagines having sex with, and those an audience would rather hear tell a joke. Gene Kelly makes you feel one way, Phil Silvers another. On the other hand, George C. Scott may not be as gorgeous as Tab Hunter, but talent has a way of blunting the edges. Sex appeal is surely subjective, but that doesn't mean that any actor can play *King Lear*.

Every few seasons an actor will cause a momentary sensation by arousing a sexual response in a drama critic, and it may be years before that critic stops referring to him or her as the next Sir Laurence Olivier or Gwen Verdon. "He's the finest actor of his generation" is another bouquet based largely on the equivalent of a teenage crush. It's not unusual for actors on the receiving end of these encomiums to develop a sense of superior personal hygiene. Very thin women with miniscule breasts who never appear to perspire are particularly susceptible to extravagant praise. Young men with sculptured pectorals who can simulate a midatlantic accent and who have enough hair to cover the scalps of a dozen balding character actors are likely to attract multiple acting awards. This would be harmless enough if the praise did not encourage them to appear the next season as Macbeth, Major Barbara, or Hedda Gabler. Eventually, the critic who lionized them will turn treacherous or, even worse, praise them anew, so that an unsuspecting public will begin to wonder whether Jessica Tandy and Hume Cronyn were actually as great as they remembered them to be.

My performance as Groucho Marx in *Minnie's Boys* was the only occasion in my long career when I was treated as a phenomenon. If I needed a corrective, several of the critical elite insinuated that I was not an actor at all but merely a fellow who'd been dug up from under a rock to perform an uncanny impersonation of a famous man. The most perceptive compliment I received came from a cameraman on the *Dick Cavett Show*. "I loved your performance," he told me, "but I couldn't decide whether you sounded more like Groucho Marx or Phil Rizzuto."

What I had accomplished with *Minnie's Boys* was to integrate myself into the theatrical community. I also proved to myself that, at least in this instance, I was capable of coming up with the goods. This was more than I'd ever given myself credit for, although I was careful to remind myself that that and a token would get me into the subway. Nevertheless, I was momentarily perceived as an actor of *some* repute. My only plan for the future was to play a character as far from Groucho Marx as was humanly possible. But could I?

One of the first things you're told as an aspiring performer is that it's nearly impossible to succeed in major league show business without an agent or a personal manager. After *Minnie's Boys* a bunch of them were banging on my door. When I was a kid my father, an uncanny mimic, had convulsed me with his reenactment of the phone conversation he had the day his agents, Marty Baum and Abe Newborn, canceled a full week of nightclub bookings and stranded him penniless in Montreal.

Marty, who later became a successful Hollywood producer, was the aggressive go-getter, while Abe presented himself as the Jewish intellectual.

"How can you do this to me, you unprincipled fuck!" my father would scream into an imaginary phone.

"But Ira," he said, perfectly rendering the Talmudic cadences of Abe Newborn's speech, "the club owner told me you bombed. You didn't get a single laugh the entire Saturday night show."

"You booked me into a nightclub where they don't speak *English*, shithead! And now you're canceling the rest of my week because I don't speak French?"

Now Marty Baum would take the phone and say, "Ira? What did you say to Abe? He's crying. Abe Newborn is crying in the office. What on earth did you say to Abe?"

Six agents tried to sign me after *Minnie's Boys*. So which one did I choose? Abe Newborn. For a solid year I'd been mesmerized by my father's version of Abe piling on the bullshit with a trowel. The real Abe wasn't as funny as my father's imitation. By now I've had many agents: big agents and medium-sized agents, short and tall, gregarious and soft-spoken. At some point during human evolution, when the wolf decided to cozy up and become a dog, somebody came up with the idea of taking 10 percent from the superstar who could fart the loudest.

Chapter 18

The project I chose to appear in after *Minnie's Boys* was a melodrama at New York's Public Theater entitled *The Happiness Cage*. There isn't much to tell about this effort except that I was lousy in it and that an enormous favor was done to me by the director, a favor I didn't find out about for twenty years.

The Public Theater was the invention of its charismatic producer, Joseph Papp, who infused the place with his insatiable ego and ambition. The Public saw itself as a social theater with a mission to explore contemporary political themes. In 1970 the overriding issue was the war in Vietnam. *The Happiness Cage*, by Dennis Reardon, was set in the psycho ward of a veterans' hospital, where a group of incorrigibles led by yours truly was being experimented on by a malevolent U.S. military with massive doses of psychedelic drugs. A silly morality fable with a strong antiwar bias, it appealed to Papp and his associate, Bernard Gerstein.

The play had been developed in a workshop production the year before, with my part played by Martin Sheen, who was on location shooting a film. This meant that along with two other actors, I was being parachuted into a production that had already been rehearsed and performed. The part of Reese was a far cry from Mendel the rabbi's son or Groucho Marx, and from the beginning I felt out of place. I was a twenty-four-year-old actor without any chops. The situation wasn't made any easier by the numbing arrogance of the Public, which perceived itself more as a social movement than as a purveyor of entertainment.

From day one I felt little affinity for the atmosphere of the place. There was not a single esthetic that reminded me of Judy Garland or Mickey Rooney. I had entered the business because I wanted to be in *The Pajama Game*, where I could be seduced by a dozen chorus girls. The

Public Theater, formerly the Astor Library, reminded me of exactly that: a library. Some of my fellow actors made it clear that they wouldn't deign to perform on Broadway even if asked. (A notable exception to this culture of superiority was Charlie Durning, who couldn't have been more supportive even though I was quite undeserving of his praise.) And hovering above the entire enterprise was the half-benevolent, half-demonic Joseph Papp, who inspired a cultlike loyalty reminiscent of another autocrat named Joe.

We opened to surprisingly favorable reviews, but only the subscribers liked it, and we closed in five weeks. I missed the final performance after stepping on a rusty nail backstage, an event that vexed Mr. Papp, who accused me of dogging it.

The believability of my performance was illuminated during one of our Sunday matinees. The character I was playing, half Italian and half Puerto Rican, was slipped some LSD by a sadistic intern (Charlie Durning) during the second act. For the next five minutes I wandered around the stage in a drug-induced delirium, intermittently reciting my lines in Spanish. As my monologue hit its crescendo, a woman in the second row turned to her companion and remarked, "He's supposed to be Spanish? I thought he was Jewish!"

There was a good reason why my performance was so unconvincing. I didn't know how to act. I had performed acceptably as Groucho by using the tools I'd been given by Stella Adler. I also had an actual personality I could study. Now I was being asked to create a rounded character based on nothing more than my interpretive skills. Stella had taught me to look for the part of the political equation my character represented and to create a subtext beneath the playwright's words. But because I was part of a plot I scarcely believed in myself, my performance was reduced to playing a quality.

The worst kind of acting is playing a quality, because it lacks specificity, and if the actor doesn't understand why he's doing certain things, the audience will lose interest. An example: You can't simply say the character you're playing is sad or neurotic, because "sad" or "neurotic" can't really be represented. To play a quality for an entire evening is to say a character is unhappy, but "unhappy" isn't playable, because it's a feeling rather than an action. To reach the root of unhappiness, you must discover something active that an unhappy person *does*. The actor who knows his craft will make a choice, will say to himself, "The character I'm playing is so initially trusting of everything he's told that, midway through every conversation he experiences a breach of faith and decides that what he's being told is really an insidious lie." To strip yourself of the confidence that people are telling you the truth is an active symptom of neurotic behavior. Listening and disbelieving is active; being neurotic is inactive. Another example: A character defines himself as being close to God. How does one convey being close to God without actually talking about it? The actor with craft decides, I'm close to God because I'm continually searching for those who need my help; the less a person shares my conviction, the more I'll dedicate myself to understanding him. To play a quality is to affect a general notion of piety, but piety isn't active; searching for a way to help a person is.

At twenty-four I understood none of this. I spent the entire rehearsal process trying to figure out how to play a man who was half Italian, half Puerto Rican, and very angry. The experience left me feeling stymied and uncomfortable, and I was enormously relieved when I was told the play would close. I wrote off my failure to the environment I was performing in and Joe Papp's hovering presence.

As for the favor, a week before we had started rehearsal, our director, the talented actor Tom Aldredge, had driven me to the Jersey Shore, where Joe Papp was vacationing, to get his final approval before casting me. Joe was charming, in his authoritative way, and in the middle of lunch mentioned that he had seen the movie *Patton*, which he considered one of the great antiwar films. Oblivious to the fact that Joe hadn't gotten where he was by being contradicted, I took issue with his characterization and suggested that because of George C. Scott's charismatic performance the film actually glorified war. Joe listened politely, but I'm certain he considered me an upstart. Twenty years later I ran into Tom Aldredge at a Broadway coffee shop and asked why he'd never directed at the Public Theater again.

"You," he said gently. "A couple of weeks into rehearsal Dennis and I were called into Joe's office. 'I hear this Stadlen fellow isn't cutting it,' he told us. 'I want you to fire him.' 'That's not true,' I said. 'Besides, you haven't seen a single rehearsal. Who's been telling you he isn't cutting it?' Joe admitted it was the assistant director he had assigned to me so he could have eyes and ears in the room. Dennis and I were deeply offended, and we told him we'd quit if you were fired. I also demanded that the assistant be taken off the project. It was probably the only time in the history of the Public Theater that Joe Papp couldn't fire someone. I never intended to tell you this, but since you asked…"

If Tom Aldredge hadn't refused and if Joe Papp had fired me, my confidence would have been badly shaken, and who knows what turn my professional life would have taken. Tom Aldredge sacrificed his own fledgling directing career to stand on principle. I wish I'd been better in the part.

Chapter 19

Many young actors have asked me about the best way to get started. The answer I give them is to positively visualize who you would someday like to become. What kink in your personality would make you feel like a success? Perhaps it's the fantasy that every Friday night you, Al Pacino, Robert De Niro, and Martin Scorsese get together at your favorite restaurant in Little Italy and discuss the meaning of life. Perhaps you see yourself playing Hamlet at the same local theater where you saw your first play, or closing in a Broadway show that everyone agrees deserved a better fate. How you visualize your future will say a great deal about how you perceive yourself in relation to an indifferent world.

Part of my attraction to the acting profession has had to do with a sense of martyrdom I believed would cast me in a sympathetic light. I never dreamed of becoming a household word; instead, I visualized a rarefied fame that would appeal to those not easily seduced by the lure of popular culture. I inherited this cultural snobbery from my mother, and it has always played handsomely to my desire to feel underappreciated.

In 1970 I walked into the Vivian Beaumont Theater and watched a performance of William Saroyan's *The Time of Your Life*. Saroyan had written the play in 1939. Legend had it he had checked into the Hotel Great Northern, on West Fifty-seventh Street, with a case of booze and a Remington typewriter and had written the whole thing in less than a week. Almost every tale associated with Saroyan concerned his epic capriciousness. A self-destructive self-mythologist who had basically pissed off everyone he had ever come in contact with, his literary reputation by 1970 had been reduced from boy genius to sophomoric wiseguy, a self-promoter who had run out of intellectual gas.

The Time of Your Life takes place at Nick's Pacific Saloon, a watering hole underneath the Golden Gate Bridge in San Francisco. For three transporting hours every form of human grotesque enters through the door of Saroyan's imagination. The whole thing is held together by a philosopher-drunk named Joe who prefers to observe humanity through an alcoholic haze. Joe never leaves the bar. He employs Tom, an enormously large, mentally slow disciple, to run errands for him. The play consists of little more than the interactions of the bar's customers: an unhappy married woman who drinks, a philosophical dockworker, a cop, a talented dancer who wants to be comedian, a restless young man anxiously awaiting the arrival of his blind date, a two-dollar hooker who is being threatened by a vice cop, a penniless black family man who plays a mean piano, an octogenarian Arab with a one-track mind, a man who may or may not be Kit Carson, a monomaniac who has dedicated his life to hitting the jackpot on the pinball machine, a slumming middle-aged couple from Nob Hill, assorted streetwalkers, the blind date, and the taciturn barkeep, who pours the booze and provides the refuge.

The Lincoln Center production was anchored by the marvelous ruddy-faced Irishman James Broderick, who played Joe. Broderick was an actor's actor, the father of future star Matthew Broderick. The rest of the cast was fair to middling, but *The Time of Your Life* touched my heart. I promised myself I would one day perform the role of Harry the hoofer, the incompetent comedian with the gift of dance (a role originated on Broadway by Gene Kelly). The problem was that the play, along with Saroyan's reputation, was going through a period of critical disparagement. It was three hours long, had a large cast, and was considered too fanciful to have much contemporary relevance. I remember telling my mother how delighted I was to have seen it.

"My goodness. William Saroyan," she said. "Years ago we thought he was the cat's pajamas. He was so handsome. He turned out to be a terrible human being."

By 1971 the idea of starting a national theater to rival the British model had become something of a preoccupation among the cultural elite. The idea had been floated decades before but had always withered. The United States seemed too large geographically to be represented by a single national theater. Where would the theater be headquartered? How would it bear the expense of traveling from city to city? An even thornier problem was the matter of who would administer it. New York remained the hub of theater production, but it was now competing with a not-for-profit regional theater movement that had spread across the country. In Washington, D.C., Zelda Fichandler, the artistic director of Arena Stage, who along with Margo Jones at the Ally Theatre in Houston, had reimagined what is now the regional theater movement, believed she was the most qualified person to head a national theater. In New York it was Joseph Papp. In Los Angeles, Gordon Davidson, who controlled the Mark Taper Forum, thought he was best suited for the job. Others were convinced that a producer of commercial theater, a David Merrick or a Robert Whitehead, would be better qualified to run things. This rivalry remained an impediment to both planning and fund raising.

Back in Los Angeles a group headed by Henry Fonda and the actress Martha Scott joined the competition by creating Plumstead Productions, an entity dedicated to presenting classic American plays. With the assistance of Broadway producer Alfred DeLiagre, they found financing to tour nationally after a limited engagement in New York. The group had mounted *The Front Page* at a theater in Mineola, Long Island, in the late 1960s with Robert Ryan and a cast of established, mostly Los Angeles-based actors. The following year Plumstead presented Thornton Wilder's *Our Town,* with Henry Fonda playing the stage manager and Martha Scott, who had performed as Emily in the original production, now appearing as Emily's mother. The two productions had been financially successful enough to allow Plumstead to raise money for a third.

Say what you will about the vulgarity of the profit motive when it comes to producing theater, the difference between those who've made a financial killing and those who have had to raise an annual budget only to liquidate whatever excess exists at the end of the year is the difference between dealing with a Henry Fonda or a Robert Brustein. No one in the commercial theater is trying to prove their moral superiority to Yale Rep; they're too busy going about their own hectic business. The opposite can't be said for those who ply their trade in noncommercial theater. The regional theater movement spends an endless amount of energy trying to justify lousy wages by indulging in a dialectic that no one really cares about except themselves. Beware of those who dedicate themselves to the purity of anything.

In the fall of 1971 Plumstead Productions decided to present a national tour of *The Time of Your Life,* starring Henry Fonda as Joe. It would open at the new Kennedy Center in Washington, D.C., then play successive three- and four-week engagements at the Locust Street Theater in Philadelphia and the Studebaker Theater in Chicago before concluding its run at the Huntington Hartford Theater in Los Angeles. Plumstead was presenting a model for a touring national theater that could conceivably be run at a profit.

As soon as I heard this thrilling news I contacted my new agent, Eddie Bondy, at the William Morris Agency. (I had recently managed to extricate myself from the embrace of Abe Newborn.) Eddie had told me the day before that I had been cast in a new Broadway musical based on Joe McGuinness's bestseller *The Selling of the President*. I had auditioned without being allowed to read a script (never a good sign). It was a Saturday, but I had gotten Eddie's home number from information. When he found out who was calling, he was livid.

"Don't you ever—and I mean ever—call me at my home on a weekend! Do you know why?"

"No, Eddie."

"Because by calling me at my home on a weekend," he said, his high-pitched voice infused with rage, "you're treating me like a nigger!"

When I told him I'd sell my soul to play Harry in the touring version of *The Time of Your Life*, he exploded anew.

"What is wrong with you fucking people!" he screamed. "Five minutes ago Julie Harris calls to tell me she's leaving for Oshkosh to do some fucking one-woman show about some cunt poet only my Uncle Schlumputz has ever heard of, and now you're telling me you're going to turn down a big Broadway musical to do some *facocta* play they just discovered up Carol Channing's ass! You and Julie Harris should be buried together! And don't you ever call me on my home phone again."

Eddie died of a heart attack a few years later. He was without question the best agent I ever had.

Chapter 20

Rehearsals for *The Time of Your Life* began in Los Angeles in December of 1971. I had successfully auditioned at the ANTA Theater in New York a few weeks before, choosing to sing an obscure Gershwin tune, "Blah, Blah, Blah!" although I wasn't auditioning for a musical. As in my *Minnie's Boys* audition, I threw in some jokes to showcase my comedic talents. When I finished, the director Ed Sherin deadpanned "Is that all you've got?"

It's fashionable these days for casting directors to give courses in the art of auditioning. I hereby pass on a few modest tips that have worked for me, whether I'm auditioning or on the other side of the table auditioning others.

1. Decide who you're playing. In the case of Harry the hoofer, I chose material to dramatize his lack of guile.
2. Any way you can differentiate yourself from everybody else is a plus. Singing a song when one hasn't been requested is a way of doing that. Use your imagination.
3. If you're a woman, always wear high heels (unless you're auditioning for the role of a Bavarian peasant, and even then it's not such a bad idea).
4. If you're a woman, make physical contact with the director, especially if the director is heterosexual (a touch on the wrist will suffice). You thereby become more than a photograph and a resume after you've left the room.
5. Don't give off negative attitude. Everybody wants to think you'll be a dream to work with.
6. No matter how well you know the material, never audition

without the script in your hand, or your audition will be confused with a performance.
7. Whatever you do, do it with *size*.
8. If you want the job badly enough, visualize your audition as a way of getting to a destination. It's no different from renting a car to get where you need to go. Spend a little money to make a little money (for example, hire your own accompanist). None of this means you're going to succeed; it just means you're giving yourself the best chance to succeed.
9. If you're male, go out and buy a five-dollar cigar. Take a look at yourself in the mirror and start screaming, *"I'm a star!"*
10. Keep reminding yourself that this business is not for everyone.

The Time of Your Life began rehearsing in a large room above a cafeteria on Hollywood and Vine. The first person I saw was Henry Fonda, a man in perfect harmony with his own body, with a smile emblematic of all smiles that originate in sadness. Our director, Ed Sherin, an articulate fellow with the demeanor of an Ivy League quarterback, had put together a stock company that looked like a Hollywood back lot. The assembled cast was spectacular: Gloria Grahame, the perfect movie bad girl, then in her late forties, cast as the lonely housewife, Mary L.; Strother Martin, the wildly idiosyncratic purveyor of prairie scum, playing Kit Carson; Jane Alexander as Kitty Duval, the grieving two-dollar whore; Bert Freed as the malignant vice cop, Blick; a burly bear of an actor named Victor French as Nick; Lou Gilbert as the Arab; barrel-chested John Crawford as the longshoreman, McCarthy; a red-faced Irishman, Richard J. Slattery, as the cop; a massive former Canadian football player, Pepper Martin, as the slow-witted Tom; and two young actors, a delicate, almost feline-looking man, Ronnie Thompson, playing Pinball Willie, and Richard Dreyfuss in the role of the anxious suitor, Dudley Bostwick.

I had some history with Dreyfuss, but we'd never met. The year before, I'd auditioned for a film whose plot involved a group of Vietnam deserters. After auditioning for the director twice, I was told that the role had been offered to another actor who couldn't make up his mind whether to accept the role or go to New York to appear in an Off Broadway play. That same day I had a call from a director named Jimmy Hammerstein, who told me that he had directed a play called *Line,* by Israel Horowitz, that was being transferred from Los Angeles to New York without its leading actor, who had dropped out to appear in a film. Would I consider taking his place? If I accepted, he'd rehearse me alone for two weeks before reassembling the cast and opening in New York. He couldn't make me an official offer, however, until the other actor finished negotiations for the film. A few days later an apologetic Hammerstein called to tell me that the actor in question had decided to turn down the film and rejoin the play. Five minutes after he hung up I got a call from the film's casting director telling me the other actor had turned them down to appear in a play, so the film role was now officially mine. Dreyfuss was the actor who had been the first choice on both projects. I had never heard of him, but I gratefully accepted his sloppy seconds.

Moments before we were to do the first table reading of *The Time of Your Life*, I introduced myself to Richard, telling him the story of how he had bested me on the two other jobs. His manner, though not unfriendly, suggested that the situation couldn't conceivably have resolved itself any differently. The gleam in his eye suggested absolute confidence. (If he'd been Al Jolson, he might have added, "And you ain't seen nothin yet!")

First table readings are showcases for the hellish insecurities of actors and bear little resemblance to the production's eventual form. No one wants to be seen as the director's big mistake. The collective anxiety is palpable, and finally one brave soul signals that he has the courage to raise his voice above a whisper and set a healthy pace. When in doubt, *talk loud*. It's very freeing.

After lunch our director asked us to read the play again, this time with an attempt at greater clarity. Dreyfuss performed his role to perfection. He would always be terrific as Dudley Bostwick, but he was never better than in that second reading above the cafeteria. When the session was over there was a collective exhalation of relief. A knot of people formed around Richard, who had exceeded even his own lofty opinion of his abilities (or maybe not). Smelling what might be a wounded animal, he sidled up to me and said, "Listen. I think I'm gonna get pretty bored playing this part. Why don't we learn each other's roles so that during the run we can switch parts?" I wasn't sure I could perform my own part, and now this cocky little bastard was finished with his and moving on to mine.

By the third week of rehearsals the role I had convinced myself I was born to play had become an utter mystery. Harry was a gentle grotesque, oblivious to the fact that his true talent lay in his body and not in his mind. His personal challenge was to overcome his delusion. I've known many dancers and actors who cannot accept the burden of their gift. Harry's problem isn't that he subverts himself with crippling self-criticism—he isn't bright enough for that. He just wants to be a comedian, but because he's incapable of making anyone laugh, he must slowly recognize that his usefulness as a human being is as a dancer. Without the dance, he's out the door. Saroyan gave Harry three horrendously unfunny comic monologues that have to be performed with the expectation that they will bring down the house. Ed Sherin had instructed all the patrons of Nick's Saloon to keep a straight face and never throw me a bone. Everything I said was met with total silence. The funny part was that I was dying the worst kind of stand-up comedian's death. What I had to figure out for myself was what to make of it.

Almost every rehearsal process goes through the same maddening cycle. The first three weeks are a discovery period that begins to disintegrate the closer you get to leaving the studio and moving into the space where the play will be performed. Suddenly the inexperienced actor begins distrusting all his instincts, and even the sturdiest pro may lose confidence. A few days before we were to fly to the Kennedy Center, I began the backward descent of a man desperately searching for a characterization. One of my colleagues, Lee Debroux, was doing a brilliant job playing a falling-down drunk. Every half hour he'd enter the bar without any lines and stumble from one side of the stage to the other. His dedication to an inherently thankless role filled me with such admiration that I begged him for his eleventh-hour advice.

"Do the first comic monologue like you're reciting Marc Anthony's big speech from *Julius Caesar*," he suggested. "Interpose your lines with the lines 'Friends, Romans, and countrymen, lend me your ears. I have come to bury Caesar, not to praise him.'"

Later that day, just before our last run-through, I began assiduously transposing the intent of Harry's comic monologues with Marc Anthony's orations. When the session was over, Ed Sherin asked if he could speak with me privately.

"May I ask you a personal question?" he inquired sympathetically. "Are you fucking nuts?"

I rediscovered the part later that evening over a second glass of Jack Daniel's.

The beauty part was that I was acting with people who knew more than me. After we arrived in Washington, the entire cast was invited to a screening sponsored by the American Film Institute of one of Fonda's early films, *Young Abe Lincoln*. The first of Henry's many collaborations with director John Ford, throughout the film he wore a prosthetic nose, mole, and wig that altered his appearance completely, making him the very image of Lincoln. The film had a haunting musical score composed by Alfred Newman. John Ford's direction captured an America bursting with pride, a young nation in which every man's ambitions were achievable in a climate charged with raw energy. Ford juxtaposed Lincoln's personality and intellect against the virulence of the mob, a prelude to the country's drift into civil war.

Henry's performance stressed the storyteller in Lincoln, a man who could calm the multitudes with self-deprecating humor and a serene temperament. Wherever he was—on the porch of a log cabin, staring out at a winding river that reminded him of a past love, or in a courtroom defending a client accused of murder—he would uncoil his lanky body and nonjudgmentally slow the proceedings just enough to defuse the malignant atmosphere that seemed seconds away from erupting. Casting Fonda as Abe Lincoln was brilliant, because Henry had a gift for somehow expanding time and endowing it with grace. Actors who are able to dominate the large screen do so by projecting thoughts that reveal their souls. This gift can't be taught. Here, Henry Fonda's physical attractiveness had been transformed into homeliness, yet his understanding of goodness (something Henry possessed in large measure) allowed us to comprehend Lincoln's greatness.

For much of his adult life, Fonda's favorite hobby involved sitting on his bedroom floor with his best friend, Jimmy Stewart, building model airplanes. There had been much tragedy in Henry's life. Two wives had committed suicide. The traits that so endeared him to an audience were outgrowths of his natural reticence, his inability to communicate his deepest feelings. It was ironic that this combination of grace and inhibition, when set before a camera, translated into a unique kind of introverted dignity. I've always thought that, compared to Henry Fonda, the rest of us look like monkeys.

He was also a talented artist who painted in the style of Andrew Wyeth—or perhaps Andrew Wyeth painted with the sensibility of Henry Fonda. By the time I caught up with him he was sixty-eight and a fully evolved man, generous and funny and, on those rare occasions when his wife Shirle left his side, capable of some very un-Henry Fonda-like mischief. With a drink in him he was fond of knocking on hotel doors at three in the morning. Nobody minded, because when they opened the door, there stood Henry Fonda! He was also given to getting down on his hands and knees and imitating an elephant being shot on safari. To know him even a little was a distinct honor.

Richard Dreyfuss was a revelation of a different sort. Most actors hide behind the masks of their characters, and Richard seemed to be hiding more effectively than most. There was no doubt, however, that he was a precocious talent. His self-possession could be as annoying as it was compelling. The annoying part was his conviction that he walked alone in the garden of human experience. When he spoke of his undying love for his high school sweetheart, Julie Cobb, he implied that this passion lay beyond another human being's ken. The suggestion that we were not competing with each other, which we surely were, was met with a declaration that he was no more in competition with me than he was with a legend like Henry Fonda. (I found this incredible, knowing that both of us had sat through Henry's portrayal of Abraham Lincoln.) It was difficult to argue with a contemporary who had such undeniable self-confidence. He had already planned out his future; he was to be his generation's equivalent of Spencer Tracy, an actor he felt towered above the rest. In his own mind he had already transcended his contemporaries. When you went to the movies with him he refused to sit next to you, because your presence disturbed his concentration.

As an actor he seemed to have all the self-esteem I lacked. Not that I didn't believe myself capable of succeeding, but unlike Richard, who already saw himself in a tuxedo accepting the first of many Academy Awards, I was still searching for a personality I could approve of.

The colleague who helped me most was Victor French, who played the role of Nick. Victor had an aggrieved personality that I found most endearing. He took himself seriously as an actor and not nearly seriously enough as a man. A big old bear carting the weight of the world on his shoulders, he was later to appear on two highly successful TV series playing Michael Landon's sidekick. He died in his late forties of lung cancer.

Victor did a wonderful thing in the play that intrigued me. As a bartender he was never without his dishtowel, which he manipulated as artfully as Cyrano manipulated his foil. The action of the play was interrupted several times by the ringing of a telephone on a wall, downstage left. Every time Victor had to answer the phone he would throw his towel down on the bar, his mien registering somewhere between annoyance and rage. Nowhere did the stage directions say "Nick angrily answers the phone." When I asked him why the phone made him react that way, Victor, who also taught an acting class in Los Angeles, introduced me to the concept of stage territory, a technique invaluable in breaking down a role.

All actors have their own way of doing things. Intuitive geniuses like Marlon Brando, Judy Garland, and Mickey Rooney do everything impulsively and probably couldn't care less about translating their technique into words. However, most of us aren't geniuses, and a bit of clear thinking can go a long way. "As Nick," Victor told me, "I hate that damned telephone. Listen, I never wanted the bloody thing in my saloon in the first place. Some fast-talking salesman convinced me I was losing twenty percent of my business to a joint up the street because my customers needed to be reached by telephone. So I've only had the damn thing in here for two months and I hate everything about it."

"Why do you hate it?" I asked.

"What year is it, for God's sake?"

"I don't know."

"Well, you gotta know. It's nineteen thirty-nine, and the world is on the verge of committing suicide. Mussolini. The Japs in China. Hitler and the Nazis invading Poland. Everything on the other side of that door is unwelcome except the people who seek refuge here. The phone brings in the world, and I want nothing to do with it. Every time it rings it reminds me of that slick little salesman who made me buy it. Let the bum up the street take my business. I hate that phone!"

Victor lit up another of the Luckies that would eventually kill him. "That's the meaning of stage territory. It's about making decisions about everything. If I don't like the phone, I don't walk to that part of the stage unless I'm absolutely forced to. You like a person, you walk toward them. You don't like a person, you stay away. This is my favorite barstool. This one keeps breaking, so it's my enemy. I hate that barstool. Stuff like that."

"What if the director tells you to move where you don't want to?"

"You tell him Sorry, I don't like it over there. Listen, any director who makes you go where you don't want to go isn't much of a director anyhow. The good ones will edit your moves two weeks into rehearsal. They'll bless you for it. Stage territory, my young friend. Nobody ever gave a lousy performance because he knew what he was doing."

In other words, use your imagination to define a character beyond what even the playwright has envisioned.

After we'd performed a number of previews at the Kennedy Center, Ed Sherin felt the play was running long and decided to make some cuts. They were smart cuts, lines that seemed redundant. Everyone respected the play, but it was running over three hours, and whether we liked it or not, the viewing habits of a theater audience had altered in the thirty-three years since the play had first been produced.

Jane Alexander was playing the role of the whore, Kitty Duval. A young woman who had migrated from a farm in the Midwest and had turned to prostitution as a means of surviving urban life, Kitty, the unprotected child of European immigrants, was vulnerable and harassed by a morally unforgiving society. Jane had garnered critical acclaim for her role as black boxing champion Jack Jefferson's white mistress in both the Broadway production and the film of *The Great White Hope*. She came from an affluent New England family and could project an aura of nobility that made many a drama critic swoon. Whether nobility and feminist determination best exemplified a San Francisco streetwalker was debatable. Hers was an interpretation calculated to leave no doubt that you were watching an important actress.

"As long as you're cutting dialogue," Jane said toward the end of the note session, "would you mind terribly if you cut the line about me being a two-dollar whore? Make me a twenty-dollar whore and I'll go home happy." Twenty-dollar whore indeed.

When I was fourteen, my Gray Gables buddy Michael Aptner and I went out on a double date. Both girls lived in the West Seventies, and when we took the subway to pick them up, we mistakenly boarded an express train that bypassed every station between Fifty-ninth and 125th Street. We watched helplessly as eight stations flashed by. Would the train never stop? Our mistake left us frantic but also somehow exhilarated. Our innocence was bliss. I had that same feeling when I stepped up on the tiny stage of Nick's Saloon and improvised a dance to Benny Goodman's recording of "Goodbye," and, later, "The Tennessee Waltz." I was enmeshed in the uncertainty of the ride. William Saroyan's world might never stop, and that was fine with me.

Throughout the run Richard Dreyfuss kept up a drumbeat about the play's deficiencies and how bored he had become. He was planning his great escape to bigger things while the rest of us basked in the protection the play afforded us.

Clive Barnes, writing in the *New York Times*, suggested that if anyone was serious about forming a national theater, a nucleus could be found in the Plumstead Playhouse production of *The Time of Your Life*. It would never happen: Henry Fonda and Martha Scott were in it for the joy of the work. They had neither the stomach nor the years ahead of them to dedicate their lives to bureaucratic warfare.

Midway through the tour, a British producer signaled his intention to mount the production in the West End. We were packing our bags for London when we learned that Henry had decided against it. He had been offered a role in what turned out to be an insignificant film. (At sixty-eight he was petrified that no one would ever offer him another movie role.)

In Washington, D.C., I told Richard Dreyfuss an anecdote about something that had happened in my life. "That's a great story," he said. "Would you mind if I steal it and tell people it happened to me?"

"What the hell do I care?" I said. It was just the kind of request that made Dreyfuss the kind of hockey puck he was.

That evening, in a restaurant called Eddie Morocco's, Dreyfuss told my anecdote in front of me and several members of the cast as if it had happened to him. It occurred to me that if I were to take many more gulps from the river of life, I should probably look in all directions or I might end up looking like a wildebeest.

Chapter 21

Twenty-five is a muddled age. All your baggage is relatively new. There are the aspirations you have for yourself, and those others have for you. You do a lot of waking up in the morning and telling yourself, "I'll show those bastards who's talented around here!" You're no longer young, but you're not quite old enough to be taken seriously.

Early into the run of *The Time of Your Life* I met Kathy Gray, who'd ridden the train down to Washington to visit her old pal Richard Dreyfuss. They'd gone to Beverly Hills High School together. After attending a performance at the Kennedy Center, she came back a second time and handed me a bouquet of pussy willows. I wasn't exactly sure what that meant, but something about the gesture made me uncomfortable. A few weeks later she visited again, in Chicago, only this time she shared herself with another cast member. Suddenly I found myself taking her more seriously. I was impressed by her good taste in men and her independence.

A serious female overture can be as offhand as a scrap of paper pressed into an unsuspecting palm or a one-night affair that shows she can take you or leave you. Before I knew what was happening, Kathy and I had become a serious item. I was introduced to her mother, her mother's boyfriend, and her grandmother, who was the publisher of the *New York Post*. The grandmother, who had been married three times, asked me if I was in love with her granddaughter, and suddenly I felt like a Hasidic Jew in a Noel Coward play. (Coward was Jewish and so were these people, but they were German Jews who behaved like Episcopalians, or what I thought Episcopalians behaved like.)

"Yes, I love her," I told the Yiddishkite-Episcopalian grandmother, who glided around the twelve-room East Side apartment on slender ankles like the queen of Romania. I was stepping up a class. I had found a Jewish woman who wasn't really that Jewish. I was attaching myself to a family of liberal Democrats who comported themselves like Wall Street Republicans.

On entering my future mother-in-law's home I would be handed my favorite drink in a crystal glass the size of a malted container. Within minutes of the booze kicking in, I'd find myself in a haze, laughing at a flood of banter. This was the way the very wealthy socialized. Everything was amusing in a disagreeable way until you got down to the weighty political issues of the day. This segment was accompanied by champagne, and once everyone clarified their political affiliations, out came the brussels sprouts and a very fancy French stew. These Jews wouldn't be caught dead eating a corn beef sandwich.

Kathy would gaze at me lovingly as I interjected my Eastern European sensibility into the conversation, but there was no denying I was a worthless, know-nothing fraud betraying every pipefitter and United Auto Worker I would never break bread with. I had fallen in love with someone who dreamed of being a Marxist rebel as long as her trust fund held out. She was warm and loving and wanted children, and she hoped I would one day become a big star like her friend Richard Dreyfuss was destined to become. As for me, I was looking for a good argument.

Chapter 22

The Broadway theater was still plugging away in the fall of 1972, but like an overpopulated Europe in 1910, the street was heading for big changes. The artistic wizards of the day were growing older. George Abbott, Paddy Chayefsky, Arthur Miller, Jerome Robbins, and Ethel Merman were giving way to Liza Minnelli and kitsch. Alan Jay Lerner was on the decline. Brain drain was settling in. Television was swallowing up the entertainment industry.

There is no sweeter sensation than being cast in a play a few months prior to the start of rehearsals, especially when the play has all the earmarks of a huge commercial hit. In the summer of 1972 I found myself competing against half a dozen young actors for a juicy supporting role in Neil Simon's *The Sunshine Boys*. A hilarious read off the page, it would take the worst kind of incompetence to transform this play into a flop. I was competing for the role of Ben Silverman, the nephew and William Morris agent of Willie Clark, an irascible, slightly insane member of a famous retired comedy team called Lewis and Clark. It's Ben Silverman's thankless task to persuade the two retired comedians to reprise their act one more time for a TV special honoring great comics of the past, his dilemma being that the two men loathe each other. The day I auditioned for the role I couldn't help but be reminded of the day I'd stood in Shubert Alley watching a hundred young actors rushing around like the Marx Brothers.

The way I looked at it, there were two keys to interpreting the role of Ben Silverman. He was a loving nephew and a long-suffering agent. (William Morris was the preeminent theatrical agency in New York at the time.) The character has to play straight to Willie Clark's insanity, until his courteous, well-intentioned partner, Al Lewis, shows up and the heart of *The Sunshine Boys* is revealed. The role was not a tremendous stretch for me. Neil Simon's urban Jewish argot fell trippingly off my tongue. My choice involved whether to accentuate the persona of the nephew or that of the agent. Being a nephew was a function of the plot; being an agent meant I could actively be both a benefactor and a bullshit artist. I decided to focus on the agent. Being a loving bullshit artist was a lot funnier. ("Ira? What did you say to Abe? He's crying in the office.") I imagine that decision was why the director, Alan Arkin, and Neil Simon cast me in the role.

By the time we began rehearsals for *The Sunshine Boys*, two significant changes had occurred in Neil Simon's world. Saint Subber, who had produced every one of his plays except his first (the one by Mike Ellis), had been bypassed in favor of the general management team of Emmanuel Azenberg and Eugene Wolsk. Neil's writing had become such a reliable franchise that he decided to function as his own producer and hire two general managers who would receive producer credit while he received the lion's share of the profits. Such an arrangement was a potential windfall for the Azenberg, Wolsk office, and both men were ready to prove to Simon that his decision would be a cost-effective one.

The second major change concerned a parting of the ways between Neil and the brilliant director Mike Nichols, who had been associated with all of Neil's greatest hits. Nichols had demanded a larger percentage of the weekly gross, a request that prompted Neil to suggest that Nichols and his agent take a walk. Instead, the comic actor Alan Arkin was hired to direct *The Sunshine Boys*, which seemed an inspired choice if you couldn't have Mike Nichols. Looming above the proceedings was the uncertainty of an unproven collaboration between author, director, and producer as well as the unknown chemistry of the two elderly gentlemen who had been cast to play the leading roles, Jack Albertson and Sam Levene.

The advance word on Jack and Sam went like this: Jack was a great guy, a lighthearted second banana who knew his place, a gangly old hoofer with the sensibility of a Jewish leprechaun. A pleasure to work with. As for Sam? Hold on to your testicles. This guy is murder!

"So he's directing my wife in the road company of *The Impossible Years*," said MacIntire Dixon, an actor I trusted. "He's working with the actor Abe Vigoda, who he absolutely hates. The second week of rehearsal, Sam says to Vigoda in that wonderfully contemptuous way of his, 'I want you to walk across the stage, say the line, and then sit down on the couch. Do you think you could do that for me?' Abe Vigoda says, 'I believe I can do that for you. The last role I played was King Lear.' So Sam says, 'The guy just played King Lear but he can't walk through a fucking door!' "

Everything I heard about Sam Levene was that he was the most difficult actor in show business. Whatever you do, watch out for Sam Levene!

The day I had auditioned, Alan Arkin's laughter had encouraged me to be bold. He laughed in a series of staccato explosions, rooted as much in pain as in mirth. I'd been a huge fan of his ever since the day I'd bought a matinee balcony seat at the Henry Miller Theater, where he was appearing in *Enter Laughing*. There was a scene in which he'd trapped himself in a lie while attempting to explain to his boss, Irving Jacobson, why he hadn't showed up for work. The two men performed in perfect rhythm as if connected at the hip. It was the first time I'd witnessed Alan Arkin's enraged comic earnestness, the nasal delivery of a man drowning in his own discontent. He was hilarious and moving at the same time.

From day one of rehearsals everyone was girding themselves for Sam Levene's first emotional outburst. The first time he asked Alan for an explanation of a line, I remember everyone's eye's darting around the room, waiting for the ax to fall. (Here it comes! The madman is about to destroy what we'd hoped would be a sane and peaceful process.) It was a strange cast assembled that morning in the dank and mournful Longacre Theater. Most plays are rehearsed in an antiseptic rehearsal space, but because this play concerned the ghosts of show business past, the powers had decided to rehearse on a vacant Broadway stage. It was an excellent decision. Besides the three of us, the cast included the most voluptuous blond baby-doll actress in the English-speaking world, Lee Meredith. She had played the role of the Swedish secretary, Ulla, in the film of *The Producers*. Her mere presence turned all the men connected with the production into slack-jawed idiots. Our patronizing remarks aside, every one of us would have shot a toe off for the opportunity to see her naked.

Then there was an elderly black actress, Minnie Gentry, cast as Jack Albertson's nurse, and an octogenarian ex-vaudevillian named Joe Young, who played the perfect sight gag. Well over four feet tall, he had drooping, deadpan eyes. The final performer would be my understudy and play a small role at the beginning of the second act. His name was John Batiste, and he had been cast primarily because he was Alan Arkin's guru and spiritual adviser. We were a roster of individuals with little in common. During the first three days I was petrified I'd be fired. I would dash out of the theater at the lunch break and eat alone. Not until I began rehearsing the third scene with Sam Levene did I begin to relax and rediscover my character.

Sam Levene had an enormous forehead. He was the first one off book because he was afraid his memory might betray him, so he initially slowed up the process by fumbling for words before he actually knew them. Jack seemed less concerned about the lines. They had been cast against type. Given Sam's reputation, one would have thought he would be playing the temperamental Willie Clark, but he had been cast instead as the reasonable Al Lewis.

From the start it was clear that Alan was discovering that much of the humor of the play lay in its characters' contradictions. He directed counterclockwise. If an actor's line referred to someone standing up, Alan would have the person sitting down. The play was about two old men whose lives had had meaning because they had been a team, albeit a team that couldn't agree on anything, including whether it was day or night. So Jack Albertson, the sane one, was cast as the maniac, while the maniac was cast as the sane one. Perhaps Alan's intuition was that both men's personalities lay somewhere in between.

If Alan Arkin's laughter emanated from pain, Sam Levene's entire demeanor radiated the conviction that he was about to be fucked. Within days it became apparent that he was incapable of dissembling about anything. The only currency he valued was honesty. Not for no reason had Hollywood snatched him up during the late thirties and made him the quintessential New York Jewish character actor, and it was for the same reason that he had earned his reputation for being a pain in the ass. If he thought you were a bullshit artist he would tell you right to your face. Sam Levene was the lonely Jewish boy from the Lower East Side grown old, who found it more tolerable to be alone than to deal with those who could adapt to anything. If a person was a frog, he raised a scornful eyebrow that read You're a frog! He was especially given to behaving contemptuously toward theatrical producers, and Manny Azenberg was to be no exception.

For his own maladjusted reasons he had refused to sign a standard one-year contract, even though he was destined to stay with the play longer than anyone else in the cast. For this reason alone, Manny had gotten him to sign for much less money than he would normally have commanded. He had fought for some senseless principle but kept his integrity intact by holding out for a bad idea. It was one of Sam's more lovable qualities, and as I was soon to find out, those who loved Sam Levene truly loved him. Those who didn't must have had their reasons.

Jack Albertson inhabited the opposite side of the emotional spectrum. Deft, charming, and elusive, he had survived sixty years of show business while saving the best part of his career for the later part of his life. If Sam presented himself to the world as dubious, Jack seduced you with a ready smile, but the truth was that both men recognized the capriciousness of the world they operated in, Sam always pushing back, Jack putting on an affable front while he politicked on the side. They were the perfect Sunshine Boys.

Alan approached me as if I were the part of himself he didn't particularly care for. I remember our having a cup of coffee and my launching into a story on how I had extricated myself from a tight situation by displaying a certain edge. "What is this thing about having an *edge*?" he said, practically screaming. He thought I was a philistine, which I was. I was soon to learn that Alan and his entire family had entered into a spiritual covenant with the man he had hired to be my understudy. John Batiste was some kind of Zen master, so while I was mouthing off to Alan about maintaining an edge, Alan was attempting to spiritually balance his direction of *The Sunshine Boys* with preparing a bowl of organic rice. Not until years later, when I reread J. D. Salinger's *Franny and Zooey*, did I realize how the conflict between East and West can turn a well-intentioned midwestern Buddhist into a freak (Salinger's words, not mine). Alan has always ratcheted up his creative juices by denying that his main purpose in life is to be a brilliant performer. It was this conflict fought within himself that made him so ferociously funny.

Chapter 23

After a month of rehearsal we boarded a bus in midtown and headed up I-95 to New Haven, where *The Sunshine Boys* was to play the first of two out-of-town engagements. We'd have one week at the Shubert Theater, then on to Washington, D.C., where we would play for three weeks at the National. Spirits were relatively high, although no one could be certain of what we had until we performed in front of a paying audience.

A specter of tragedy hung over the production. Neil Simon's wife, Joan, the mother of his two daughters, was dying of bone cancer. This was the real reason John Batiste had been hired to be my understudy. Alan's guru exerted a kindly, soothing influence over the near-hysterical energy that surrounded the whole enterprise.

The sun for our solar system was Neil Simon, whose burden was to maintain his reputation while perpetuating his legacy. He was supported by a team of courtiers (his two titular producers), whose job it was to legitimize his every whim. Since this was Manny Azenberg and Gene Wolsk's first shot at this job, they comported themselves as men with much to prove. To be fair, it was Manny who had the high profile in this regard. Gene was a numbers guy who went about his business with a minimum of fanfare. Manny was everywhere, and whenever you wanted to gauge Neil's state of mind, you needed only strike up a conversation with Manny to figure out which way the wind was blowing.

Early on I had attached myself to Sam Levene. I remember sitting by his knee on the bus ride up to Connecticut as he regaled me with stories about his favorite stage directors, George Abbott and Sir Tyrone Guthrie, whom he referred to as Mr. Abbott and Mr. Guthrie. Those he respected were accorded a tone of reverence.

"Mister Guthrie has an apartment in London—a flat," he corrected himself. "This flat's got no furniture except a table to eat on and a bed. There's no lock on the door. He keeps it open for all his friends who might need a place to stay." Then, as we pulled into downtown New Haven, "There's a restaurant across the street from the theater, Casey's. It's like the Sardi's of New Haven. Very good lamb chops. I'll take you there." A few days later, between shows, I saw Sam sitting alone in a booth at Casey's. Remembering our conversation, I asked if I might join him.

"Get out of here," he said, not unkindly. "If I wanted you to join me, I'd have asked you."

New Haven was the moment I'd envisioned when I walked out onto the wooden deck of our barn theater at Gray Gables, dreaming I would one day be an actor performing in the out-of-town tryout of an important Broadway play. When we arrived I dragged my suitcases into the lobby of the Taft Hotel, the very same one where George Sanders had set Anne Baxter straight: "Don't, Eve. You're too short for that gesture. It went out with Mrs. Fisk."

After our first preview Neil Simon cut a good ten minutes out of the play. Jack Albertson begged for another chance to perform some of the cuts, but Neil insisted.

"That line is a three-hundred-person laugh," said Doc Simon.

"Cut it out and the next line will make a thousand people laugh." Unsparing with his own work, Neil operated on the assumption that he could always come up with something better.

Then the New Haven reviews came out, the gist being that Neil Simon had written far funnier and more socially redeeming plays than *The Sunshine Boys*. By the following day the mood had changed completely. There was much grousing that Jack Albertson didn't know his lines well enough. Although it was true that Jack was guilty of the occasional slip, he was a man close to seventy, and the role was a comic actor's version of *King Lear*. Lots and lots of dialogue was being edited and rewritten every day. The more displeasure Jack sensed around him, the less secure he became. Called on the carpet a few days later, he blamed me for his troubles.

"If you'd only hired my friend Bert Convy to play the nephew, none of this would be happening. I can't act with this kid!" (I found this out a year after I left the show.) The whole thing was ridiculous. Jack was great in the part, but such is the power of the damaged egos that keep us all in stitches. To quote the brilliant scenic designer Boris Aronson: There are two rules in every production. Rule one, every production has a victim. Rule two, never be the victim.

To the surprise if not the delight of everyone, it was the melancholy presence of Sam Levene that proved to be our anchor. (Delight rarely reared its head during these proceedings. Making people laugh was a serious business.) Everyone involved in the project was grateful for Sam. His performance was eloquently rock solid. He had fashioned a characterization that matched his inclination to doubt the validity of everything. In his long career Sam had encountered the best directors the industry had to offer as well as the worst, and because he approached every situation fearing the latter, his admiration and respect for Alan Arkin's direction made him malleable. Yes, his role was a third as large as Jack's, but this meant he would enter and leave the stage without trying an audience's patience. It was one of those blessings in a long and distinguished career in which the part plays to the actor's talent and the actor becomes transcendent in the role. By the final performance in New Haven, Sam Levene was being lauded by the very people who had second-guessed themselves for hiring him.

Mindful that every dollar saved would find its way into Neil's pocket, our producers were becoming adept at cutting corners. Instead of flying the cast to Washington (we hadn't had a day off in two weeks), we were bused from New Haven to the nation's capital on Thanksgiving weekend. A trip that would normally have taken two hours by plane and six hours by bus took twelve, and Jack Albertson and Sam Levene were seventy. But the changes made in New Haven paid off. The Washington reviews were glowing. The *Washington Post* called it Neil Simon's funniest play since *The Odd Couple*. We had a full three weeks to settle back and revel in Neil's success anxiety.

Neil would sit in the back row of the National Theater and fixate on the two people in a sold-out audience who weren't laughing. His dissatisfaction with Jack Albertson's performance was being conveyed to me on a daily basis by Manny Azenberg, who would hang his coat in my dressing room before every show.

"If he'd learn his fucking lines instead of watching every goddamned football game, we'd have a hit on our hands!"

"He's exhausted."

"Learn the lines! We're in the big time now. Thank God for you and Sam."

As we entered our final week Neil concluded there weren't enough laughs in the show and began rewriting scenes with stale-food jokes. In the middle of the first scene I was to discover several half-eaten corned beef sandwiches left to mildew in Willie's underwear drawer. I went to Alan and pleaded to have the new material removed.

"So subvert the material," he said in his nasal delivery.

"What do you mean, subvert the material?"

"Subvert the material. Do it lousy. Deliver the line haphazardly. Fuck up the joke."

"You want me to fuck up the joke?"

"I thought you didn't like it."

"I don't."

"Then subvert the material. I give you my permission."

That night I subverted the material. The next day it was out.

On our final Saturday night in Washington, Alan walked into my dressing room and announced, "I'm sick of this fucking show. I'm taking my kid to the movies." It was the only out-of-town performance he would miss. That night, with Neil Simon and Manny Azenberg straddling a banquette in the rear of the orchestra, an exhausted Jack Albertson ran out of gas during a scene in the second act and jumped two pages of dialogue. Moments after the curtain came down, a near-apoplectic Neil, with Manny in tow, announced there would be a note session in Sam Levene's dressing room as quickly as we could get into our street clothes.

Throughout our time together the only person who had given notes to the cast was Alan Arkin. None of us doubted who had the final say, but Alan had established a sense of order and trust that had been responsible for the cast's equilibrium. To alter the chain of command at the eleventh hour was like the owner of the Yankees informing his players that he himself would be pitching the seventh game of the World Series. There was nothing to be done. Arkin was sitting in a darkened movie theater somewhere in the capital eating organic popcorn with his ten-year-old son.

As I climbed the stairs to Sam's dressing room, an aura of malevolent egocentrism hung in the air. I'm certain there wasn't a cast member who believed that whatever lay before us would prove beneficial to the show. A classic rule of theatrical comportment was being violated because of the bosses' frenzy. If notes are to be given to an exhausted band of players, a star's dressing room is not the place to give them. An actor's dressing room is the dividing line between his privacy and the pressures of the outside world. (The decision was probably made to avoid paying the stagehands.) It didn't take a genius to recognize that no one valued his privacy more than Sam Levene, who had been performing leading roles in, to mention just a few, such theatrical classics as *Guys and Dolls, Room Service, Light Up the Sky, The Matchmaker, Three Men on a Horse,* and *Dinner at Eight.*

The pretext for this harried note session was to allow Neil to vent his displeasure with Jack Albertson, who he believed was lollygagging his way through the play. Here was a perfect opportunity for Manny Azenberg to calm Neil down and remind him that everything was actually going very well. If the production hadn't been in excellent shape, Alan Arkin would not have felt confident enough to have taken the evening off. In all probability we were five days away from a major artistic and commercial success, but instead of soothing Neil's furrowed brow (a talent Manny would perform artfully during their subsequent collaborations), he supported Neil's contention that Albertson's performance was careening us down a slippery slope.

Because the play began with a long exposition scene between Jack and me that was followed by a lengthy second scene before Sam made his entrance, the first twenty minutes of Neil's note session consisted of a laundry list of withering criticism directed mostly at Jack. In a halfhearted effort to appear evenhanded, he directed a few critical barbs at me. Neil didn't address Sam, but even the least observant among us was aware of a whiff of petulance coming from Sam's direction. Then Simon, as sensitive as any guy whose living involved the ebbs and flows of conversation, turned toward the quintessential Jewish character actor of the age and leveled him with a directorial note that bore little relevance to the matter at hand. We all waited for the explosion.

"Who are *you*?" asked Sam, drawing out each word with maximum contempt.

"Who am I?" responded Simon, taken aback by Sam's insolence.

"That's right. Who are you?"

One glance at Albertson revealed that he was the most relieved person in the room. He must have felt like he had stepped out of his coffin and joined his nemesis on the winning side of the room.

"My name is Neil Simon, and I'm beginning to get your drift."

"And what is it that you do?" said Sam, now thoroughly engaged in his dance of self-destruction.

"I do a lot of things," said Neil. (Nothing is more caustic than the fury of an introverted man.) "Not only have I written the play you're appearing in, but I also wear a few other hats around here. I've invested some of my own money in this show."

"Are you the director?" said Sam, unbowed.

"No, I'm not."

"That's too bad. Because I only take notes from the director!"

For the next forty minutes Neil gave Sam notes while Sam pretended Neil didn't exist. Eventually Sam retreated into frozen silence, a posture that had allowed him to survive the rigors of his sixty-nine years while, paradoxically, making his life all the more impossible. In retrospect, I wish Sam Levene had had the capacity to understand how the system worked: shut up and recognize that your insolence has compelled powerful and vindictive people to hate you. I was only a kid, aware that a less aggrieved man could have handled the situation very differently. But to me, Sam Levene had taken a bullet for his partner—a partner who most certainly would not have done the same for him. Perhaps someone almost seventy should have recognized he had options besides falling on his sword, but to a young man who had insisted on playing death scenes as a ten-year-old, Sam Levene stood as an inspiration in a world of baloney.

Chapter 24

The Sunshine Boys played its first New York preview on a Monday at the Broadhurst Theater. Word on the street was so positive that Jack and I could hear the muffled sounds of hysterical laughter a full five minutes before the curtain went up. On Wednesday morning, the day before our official opening, *Variety* ran a front-page story stating that Neil Simon was holding up the sale of *The Sunshine Boys* to 20th Century Fox because there was no clause stipulating that Jack Albertson would re-create his role in the movie. The article was nonsense, calculated to cause Sam Levene the maximum amount of public humiliation. (Walter Matthau played the role in the movie.)

Within a four-day period there had been a complete reversal of management loyalties toward our two stars. For weeks they had threatened Jack with replacement while Sam had established himself as the bedrock of the production. But after Sam and Neil's pissing contest, management decided to drum home who was in control. A temperamental actor would be tolerated only beneath the proscenium arch. Sam, not unsurprisingly, had made himself persona non grata. Everyone connected with management stalked around the bowels of the theater as if they'd been betrayed. Hadn't they been warned that Sam Levene was impossible to work with? Even so, they'd ignored the buzz and engaged him to play the juiciest role he'd been offered in years. And this was how their trust had been rewarded: disrespected by an ungrateful misanthrope. For that Wednesday at least, the *Variety* article had the desired effect. Sam moped around, wallowing in self-pity. It was the perennial war between talent and management, complicated in this instance because management was the talented Neil Simon. Another actor might have taken his public flogging twenty-four hours before our opening to heart, but Sam Levene was made of sterner stuff.

In 1973 a Broadway opening night was different than it is now. The various media critics weren't invited to an early performance so they could ponder their reaction before their deadline. Back then, opening night was the show's one shot to get it right. Screw up and (you'd think) you'd pay the consequences. (I say this because after years of experience I'm not certain critics can recognize when you've screwed up.)

With success beckoning, *The Sunshine Boys* opened that Thursday evening to an expectant throng of admirers, pundits, and friends of the family. Opening nights are mostly nerve-racking affairs for actors and audiences alike. Many of the patrons sitting in the orchestra seats have invested in the play and are seeing the show for only the second or third time. It's the critics' solemn responsibility to sit stone-faced; the actors, familiar with this ritual, damp down their nerves by anticipating a canned and uptight response. The performance requires intense concentration and a healthy mental adjustment. You don't want to make the evening too much about you, or you'll suck the lemon dry. What you're really looking forward to is the show's aftermath, those luxurious minutes before your family and friends come stampeding down the hallway to your dressing room, when you sit, cold cream in hand, visualizing your first stiff drink.

When the curtain went up that night, Jack was fighting his nerves. Who could blame him? Within a week he had been transformed from the play's weak link to the production's savior. As for me, I was too stupid and inexperienced to feel much pressure. My character's function was mostly to react to Willie Clark's paranoid ravings about his ex-partner and later to act as a conciliator when the courtly, albeit dubious, Al Lewis shows up on Willie's doorstep. My greatest challenge, and it was a significant obstacle for me, was to embrace a character that was not terribly different from myself. This time there was no hiding behind an assumed voice and unnatural physical carriage. From the first day of rehearsal, Alan Arkin had challenged me to be more like Lewis Stadlen and less like Abe Newborn.

The dressing room setup at the Broadhurst had Jack on the stage level, Sam's and my dressing rooms down a flight of stairs in the basement, and the rest of the cast up various stairways on the stage-right side of the theater. After I had exited midway through the second scene, I returned to my dressing room, which was separated from Sam's by a plywood wall. Feeling that I'd acquitted myself satisfactorily, I settled back in a hardwood chair to listen over the intercom to the funniest scene in this very funny play, which remains to this day some of Neil Simon's most inspired comic writing. The former partners are bringing each other up to date, sharing what has transpired since Al Lewis decided to retire and break up the act. Sam's character explains to Willie how happy he's been, living with his married daughter and grandchildren in a New Jersey suburb, while Willie paints a picture of utter contentment, living alone and remaining active in show business. It's obvious that neither man believes a word of what the other is saying.

The scene concludes with their attempt to rehearse their signature comic routine, the doctor sketch, with neither man able to agree on anything, even the placement of a chair. Their aborted reconciliation ends in chaos, and each man resolves never to speak to the other again. Neil Simon had written one of the most inspired comic explorations of male incompatibility ever created for the theater. Now it was up to Jack and Sam to sell it to the critics.

Five minutes into the scene Jack became disoriented and couldn't figure out where he was. Over the intercom I could hear a long, desperate pause. When an actor "goes up" on his lines, his mental rhythm is disrupted and a second seems to last a minute as he attempts to recover his bearings. Time shudders to a crawl as adrenaline takes its circuitous route to your brain. Most of the time the actor who forgets his lines is suffering from some form of mental fatigue. It's common in the course of a long run to experience a loss of mental muscle memory similar to that of someone on an assembly line who zones out while performing an endlessly repetitive task. Since memorized words are merely symbols of an underlying action, the actor usually shifts back into the logic of what he's doing by inventing a close approximation of the words he's momentarily forgotten. But sometimes, and this was the state Jack found himself in, a wave of fear and self-loathing takes you to another planet, and you can't remember what play you're in, let alone what happens next. It's absolutely the worst feeling an actor can have, a complete loss of self-possession that's quickly replaced by a primal need to escape from the building.

I imagined Neil Simon and Manny Azenberg somewhere in the back of the theater, having a stroke. But in the time it took the two of them to burst a collective blood vessel, Sam, who had only days before done the unforgivable by challenging the celestial order of our tin-hat oligarchy, reeled in the lost Jack, taking him back to the place where the scene had come to a screeching halt. When Jack was still unable to respond with any of his lines, Sam recited them for him, and continued on with a few of his own until Jack, holding fast to the life preserver he had been thrown, picked up the dialogue.

Saved, but not quite. Jack was so badly thrown by the experience that halfway through the second part of the scene he went up again, this time more seriously. Once again Sam penetrated Jack's state of mental incoherence and rescued the enterprise. The rest of the evening was free of surprises.

The Sunshine Boys became the comedy success of the season. Our troupe's ten-week conspiracy against the rest of the world had concluded with a successful verdict. We were now actors trapped in a hit, with nowhere to go and nothing to do but serve out the terms of our contract.

Sam's performance was a model of consistency. He had waited close to two decades for a bona fide smash. At sixty-nine he would ride this one out to the end of the run, unless some personality conflict made it impossible for him to continue. Jack was the more ambitious of the two. Sam had long ago experienced the exultation of stardom; Jack had not. He had been a busy working actor for most of his long career, but up until *The Sunshine Boys,* his reputation was as a talented second or third banana. At sixty-nine he realized his competition had substantially diminished, and he meant to capitalize on this success and move on.

I was living in a fool's paradise, finding it hard to believe that life on the Broadway stage was not my birthright. I was hungry for challenges. A couple of months into the run I discovered a neat little trick in a scene I had with Sam that coaxed an unexpected laugh from the audience. Sam said something that was meant to be funny, and just as his laugh was beginning to subside, I'd comment on his laugh with a raised eyebrow, a knowing smirk, that made the laughter rise up again. Surprised by my success, I kept repeating it until one day, I looked over at Sam and thought I caught a look of disapproval. I'll admit that after doing it the second or third time a dim bulb went on in my brain under the heading of "cheap," but the audience laughed like clockwork every time, so I rationalized keeping it in. The next time I did it, Sam's countenance turned to ice. "I'll say the lines, but I'll no longer act with you" was the message his eyes conveyed. When I got back to my dressing room, Sam was standing on a chair nailing a hand-lettered sign to a ceiling beam: "Lewis Stadlen's dressing room is to the left, and Sam Levene's is to the right. Don't knock on my goddamned door."

I asked what he was so angry about, although in my heart I knew.

"You know what I'm angry about!'

"No, I don't."

"Yes you do. Just tell your friends not to knock on my door."

"What did I do?"

"You know what you did."

"I don't."

"You know what you did, because I told him to tell you not to do it and you did it anyway!"

"What did I do?"

"Go to the stage manager and ask him what you did. He knows, because he told you not to do it! And don't knock on my door!" Hammer in hand, he turned on his heel and slammed the dressing room door behind him.

I went to the stage manager and said that Sam seemed to be slightly upset.

"Oh, dear," he said, looking at me as if he had swallowed a canary. "He doesn't want you to do that thing. You know, that thing you do behind his back when you're both standing near the table. He asked me to tell you a few days ago, but I forgot."

Sam refused to speak to me for a week. Finally I barged into his dressing room with a bouquet of flowers and practically prostrated myself on the floor. "I love you. You know that. The stage manager never told me to stop. If he told me I would never have continued doing it."

"You don't *do* stuff like that," he said, embarrassed by the depth of my contrition. "Didn't Stella Adler teach you anything? You don't slow down the machinery to go for a bad laugh. This is good material. Any jerk can get a laugh with good material." He thought for a moment. "Well, practically any jerk. Be a good boy. Get your own fucking laughs."

Four months into the run, oppressed by his workload and convinced that every important person had already seen the show, Jack decided to exert minimum effort during a midweek performance ("doing a walk" is the term applied to a performer who consciously underachieves). At intermission, he became aware that Shelley Winters (of all people), who had recently been nominated for an Academy Award for playing Jack's wife in the disaster movie *The Poseidon Adventure*, was at the show that night. Jack, who played the nice guy with everyone, was bent out of shape because he hadn't been nominated himself, but instead of being honest and acknowledging his envy, he did what he always did, which was to say the opposite of how he actually felt. That Shelley had achieved something Jack desired for himself elevated her in his estimation, although he had confided to me months before that she had practically given him a nervous breakdown during the filming.

Every night, five minutes before the second act, Jack, Sam, and I would sit down on three folding chairs set up for us in the wings. During the course of a long run, backstage rituals calm the nerves, and those five minutes afforded us a certain intimacy. Nothing of great importance was ever discussed, but our closeness was special. That evening, Jack was in a state. Had he known of Shelley's presence, he would certainly have tried harder in the first act.

"Is there something wrong with this audience tonight?" Jack said. Sam remained silent.

"I don't think so," I ventured. "I mean, they're certainly not the best audience we've ever had."

"No, no. It's like fifteen hundred people with a bug up their ass. They're not an audience, they're an oil painting! Maybe it's the sound system. Have you noticed anything different about the sound system?"

I looked over at Sam, who seemed content to simply stare into space.

"Sometimes when you're not completely concentrated, the sound seems to come back a little differently," I suggested.

"Well, something's not the way it usually is, I can tell you that for a fact," said Jack.

"There's nothing wrong with the sound system and there's nothing wrong with the audience," Sam finally said, gently caressing the top of his gold-plated walking stick. "You stink tonight!"

It was a testament to Jack's unconfrontational nature that he threw his head back and laughed.

Sam was never shy about letting you know what he thought. Six months into the run he walked into my dressing room and began talking about the troubled presidency of Richard Nixon, a man he loathed. "They'll never get the bastard," he said.

"I'm not so sure."

"They'll never get him." Then he got around to the real reason for his pre-show visit. "A lot of new line readings," he said without the slightest hint of judgment.

"Well, we've been doing this turkey for six months now," I said. "I'm just trying to keep the show fresh."

He turned back to me in the doorway. "Go back to the old line readings. The new ones stink!"

I've always been attracted to men and women who aren't afraid to do the real thing. Mickey Rooney threw his mother-in-law's luggage out a hotel window in Palm Beach. (Well, someone has to do it!) A few chorines who shall remain nameless have knocked on my hotel door at two in the morning and offered themselves on a freezing wintry night or a blistering summer one. I love someone who's unafraid to state a controversial opinion, even if he's behaving like a lunatic. Such people stand in contrast to the small army of opportunists who package themselves as wild and crazy guys even while they're sucking up to those in power. I'm a fan of everyone willing to get in the face of the big cheese, even if this has consequences somewhere down the line. Sam Levene was that kind of man. When friends and colleagues came to visit him after a performance, they sometimes stayed for two hours or more. I know, because I was listening on the other side of the wall. No one loved and hated with greater purity. He never won a Tony, but he drove a thousand producers crazy before he died reaching for a cigarette in his apartment at the St. Moritz Hotel.

Chapter 25

The following season, 1974, I appeared on Broadway in a revival of Leonard Bernstein's musical *Candide*. Unlike the original production, which was directed by Sir Tyrone Guthrie and failed at the box office, this significantly revised version, produced and directed by Harold Prince, became a critical success, though it too lost a ton of money because it was ineptly produced. Prince, who was responsible for casting me in *Fiddler on the Roof* (something I'll always be grateful for), directed the play in a way that reminded me of how an aunt of mine played the guitar (although in fairness to my aunt, none of us believed that if we disliked her playing she would have us flogged). In it I played a variety of roles, including Voltaire and the philosophically myopic Dr. Pangloss. The experience was so unpleasant that it was a full decade before I could again listen to Leonard Bernstein's magnificent score. In fact, Bernstein wasn't allowed to have anything to do with the production. His encouraged absence was symptomatic of the atmosphere that pervaded the entire enterprise. Mister Prince's talent for self mythology seemed all consuming. The contributions of the cast, if publicized at all, were attributed to a collective lack of inhabition. We were not actors capable of performing Leonard Bernstein's demanding and intricate musical score, but street urchins plucked out of some Dickensian fantasy to be molded by the *genius* of Hal Prince. The final straw being the publication of an expensive coffee table book in which our character's names were listed beneath our photographs, but never our names. I was eventually handed my head after a knee injury and shown the door, but looking back I'm glad I didn't take the matter lying down.

From our first day of rehearsal we performed on an environmental set made up of a dozen platforms surrounded by wooden bleachers. Several hundred stools were scattered beneath a series of walkways that connected each of the performing areas. The entire set was built of unfinished wood. An abbreviated orchestra played on separate wooden balconies at each side of a miniature proscenium stage. Prince's concept was to present Voltaire's satiric vision of an insane world in the setting of an environmental circus. Patrons were encouraged to write graffiti on the walls. Giant burlap bags holding free peanuts were distributed around the playing area.

Bernstein showed up for a final dress rehearsal, and afterward he was enormously gracious, telling us it was the first time the show actually worked. But when he returned several days later in front of a paying audience the pain in his eyes was unmistakable. The production's youthful exuberance had come at the expense of his great musical score. Our cast was for the most part professional and winning, but the original Hershy Kay orchestrations had been scaled down for an ensemble a third the size of the original. Our *Candide* was a kind of relentless adolescent cartoon. It was fun, but it reduced a work of genius to a happening. Bernstein's music, as well as many of the score's original lyrics, matched the texture and erudition of Voltaire's brilliance, but they were replaced by inferior ones because Lillian Hellman wanted more money than management was willing to pay. Our production was not re-conceived as a work of art, it was designed as an ambitious individual's latest accomplishment, and in that it succeeded.

Twenty years later, while touring the country in Jerry Zaks's production of *Guys and Dolls*, I turned on the TV to see Harold Prince addressing a symposium of Cambridge students. Because it had been many years since our relationship turned acrimonious (in case you hadn't guessed) and I had enjoyed any number of his directorial efforts in the interval, and because I knew that as a twenty-eight-year-old I'd been somewhat out of control, I forced myself to listen intently to what he had to say. Never have I heard an individual speak at such length and say less.

The playwright John Guare once quipped that we are never older than when we are twenty-eight. Certainly that sentiment applied to me. For nine years I traveled an upwardly mobile path that distorted my perception of how things worked. My ethos was not unlike that of the Arab who revels in a glorious defeat. Too often I had become the mouthpiece for others' discontent. However, arrogant missteps aside, the most accurate forecast of what the future had in store for me came from an election volunteer when I handed him my voter registration card.

"Lewis J. Stadlen!" he said, looking up at me. "You know there's a very talented character actor named Lewis J. Stadlen?"

"That's me," I gasped, delighted to be recognized.

"No, no, that's not you," he assured me. "The guy I'm talking about is at least sixty-five."

PART TWO

the opposite of brilliance

Chapter 26

Anton Chekhov, my favorite playwright, has become fashionable, the patron saint of American actors. Whenever an actor is about to sign a six- or seven-year contract to appear on a TV series, they'll often say they're doing it to make enough money and accumulate enough fame so they can return from the West Coast and do Chekhov. My response is, Why don't you leave Chekhov out of it?

I love Chekhov because his writing explores the failure in all of us. His characters suffer from too much beauty, too much idleness, too much vanity, too much alcohol, too much artistic and intellectual pretension, too much lust, and too much incapacity to change. Chekhov believes that we are born what we are, and that we're essentially unable to be something we're not. We can put up a good front and invent a public persona, but our true nature will always prevail, and that will ultimately depress the hell out of us.

That Chekhov refers to his plays as comedies tends to confuse those who direct and perform them, because the characters complain relentlessly about their feelings of loss. The plots have much to do with dislocation. I think the author sees them as comedies because his characters go through their lives unable to recognize the transparency of their motives. A successful middle-aged writer's seduction of a teenage actress is conducted as an exploration of the creative process. An infirm man frightened of his mortality attempts to calm his oversensitive nephew, who is obsessed with pleasing his mother by putting on a play that will insult the meaning of her life. All the human contradictions of pettiness and generosity are cooked up in a stew of confusion and unrequited love.

To play Chekhov is to learn the lines like a jazz musician learns his notes, and then give yourself over to improvisation. You are forced to confront at every moment the melancholy act of living. ("The main thing is not the glory, not the glitter, no, not any of those things I dreamed of, it's having the strength to endure. The strength to bear your cross, to have faith. I have faith, and it's not so painful for me anymore, and when I think about my calling, I'm not so afraid of life. I'm not." That's Nina's final speech in *The Seagull*, about becoming a real actress.)

After concluding my run in *Candide*, I was facing not a loss of faith—faith had no definition for me—but uncertainty over whether I possessed the strength to endure. I had accomplished what I had initially set out to do. I had put myself on one of those framed Broadway posters that hung on the wall of the barn at Gray Gables. I was now part of the professional theater, and some of what I saw disgusted me. I had made a powerful enemy of Hal Prince, and no matter how much I protested his treatment, my explanations mattered only to my friends. Prince did to me what he had done to Zero Mostel. (After Zero had ended that contentious relationship, he famously remarked, "That Hal Prick is a Prince!")

Now, partly because of my big mouth and partly because few in the business (myself included) could figure out how old I was, I had consigned myself to the ranks of journeymen actors. Much as I had always taken pleasure in being perceived as an underdog, a journeyman was nothing I ever wanted to be. For the next decade and a half I would be a man in search of himself.

Chapter 27

In the summer of [1977] my good friends Ed Sherin and his wife, Jane Alexander, invited Kathy and me (we were now married) up to their home in Carmel, New York, for a barbecue. Many of the guests were show business people we knew. Since I'd just bought my first car, we were enlisted to drive some other guests up the Taconic Parkway to Ed and Jane's. I mistakenly got on the New York State Thruway and had to double back, which made us three quarters of an hour late. When I told Ed about my mistake, he gave me one of his contemptuous grins and remarked, "What are you, a moron? I told you to take the Taconic!" This was the nature of our relationship. He was the gruff older brother whose barbs delighted me. I suppose it was because I considered him a damn fine director, and after my most recent experience, *The Time of Your Life* seemed a beacon of lost innocence. I've never minded someone who wasn't particularly nice, as long as they had talent. Strangely enough, it's those who aren't particularly talented who pretend to be nice.

Ed and Jane's house was situated on a beautiful piece of rolling property not far from my grandparents' house in Mahopac. After an afternoon cocktail, Ed led me down to a badminton court, handed me a racket, and asked about my plans. I told him I was about to start shooting a film, *Between the Lines*, that would last about eight weeks.

"I have a play I'd like you to read," he said, lofting the birdie over the net. After several volleys his return went out of bounds and I was awarded the first point. "It's a play called *Semmelweis*. It's written by my friend Howard Sackler. He wrote *The Great White Hope*."

"What role do you want me to play?" I asked him.

"What are you, an idiot?" he said, smashing my service back at me with such ferocity that he nearly took my head off. "Read the fucking play and tell me what you think of it."

"Well, I usually like to know in advance what part you want me to play."

"Listen, jerkoff, that's exactly why I want you to read the play as a whole. Forget about which part you may or may not want to play."

For the next few minutes he mercilessly smashed the birdie back at me, always aiming for an identical spot, an exercise in psychological domination. How often could he exploit my weakness before I found the means to make a tactical adjustment? After he'd reeled off ten straight points, the two of us glared at each other. Either I was going to throw away my racket in frustration and walk off the court or he was going to ease up and let me return service. Neither of us gave in. I was both disheartened and perversely impressed by his survival-of-the-fittest gamesmanship. Within minutes he'd run off twenty-one straight points, leaving no doubt who was the better man. Then, putting his paternalistic forearm around my neck, he led me back to the house, where I was forced to listen to Michael Moriarity describe in exquisite detail the night he won his Tony. I'd been nominated for a Tony myself that year, but didn't have the heart to butt in after losing twenty-one straight points to a man who might be offering me my next job.

The next day I read *Semmelweis*. It was an ambitious, fluid piece of writing composed in a fever. The play concerned Philipp Ignaz Semmelweis's discovery of the sanitation theory in Budapest, midway through the nineteenth century. In an attempt to reform the health care system, the Austro-Hungarian Empire had set up free clinics in the city's hospitals, allowing the poor to have their babies delivered by midwives, while in adjacent wards, doctors delivered the babies of the middle class and the well to do. A horrifying epidemic of childbed fever led to mortality rates that were dramatically higher in the wards where doctors were delivering babies. Twenty years before Louis Pasteur's discovery, Semmelweis concluded that the reason for the disproportionate mortality had to do with doctors, himself included, dissecting cadavers in the mornings and then, without washing their hands, transferring decomposing matter into women's vaginas while delivering newborns in the afternoon.

Using the historical record, Howard Sackler had written a morality play about how Semmelweis's discovery was rejected by a European medical establishment that refused to admit that it had been responsible for the deaths of hundreds of thousands of women and their infants. Instead of embracing Semmelweis's asepsis theory they choose to ostracize him, labeling him a madman even as the epidemic rages on. Aware that he himself is responsible for the deaths of hundreds of women, Semmelweis goes mad, and in the final scene, while addressing a group of medical students, he crushes a test tube filled with decomposing matter in his hand, thus committing ritual suicide.

It was a fascinating play couched in the ferocious, tortured poetry that was unique to Sackler's large literary talent. Unpropitiously, it was unrelentingly fervent, it needed a cast of more than thirty, and it was hardly a barrel of laughs. Decomposing matter in women's vaginas did not carry the surefire ring of commercial viability.

From the actor's perspective, the play was dominated by the character of Semmelweis. It was an enormous role that seemed nearly impossible to pull off. Going progressively mad for two and a half hours could really wear out an audience, and playing Semmelweis would mean memorizing a part that made Hamlet seem small. If Ed wanted me to play Semmelweis, he was tapping the wrong guy. I was a comic actor. I'd tried my hand at melodrama at the Public Theater and had convinced no one, especially those two women in the second row. ("Who's he supposed to be? Groucho the Hungarian?")

I called up Ed Sherin and told him what I thought.

"I'm directing it at the Studio Arena in Buffalo in the fall. Would you like to be in it?"

"Sure. I've never been to Buffalo."

"What role do you see yourself as?" he asked me. I'd never found myself in this position before. He was asking me to pick a role.

"Skoda," I said. There was silence. Obviously I'd picked the wrong part.

"Oh. How come?" he asked.

"He's got a few scenes that lighten up the play a bit. You're going to need it. There's a lot of screaming."

"You don't see yourself as anyone else?"

"Well, I guess there's Semmelweis, but I don't think I could play him. That's a lot of work."

"All right," he said. "So it's Skoda. I'll have to bring you in to Howard before I can make an official offer. Howard lives in Spain. He's very particular about who acts in his plays."

I met Howard Sackler in a cramped second-rate rehearsal studio in the Broadway area that was famous for being rented to productions on a tight budget. It was understood that this was to be an interview, not an audition. Outside the door, a long line of actors, scripts in hand, milled around a narrow hallway. Howard and Ed sat behind a desk at the far end of the room, Ed dressed in Eddie Bauer duck hunting attire, a multipocketed safari vest that held his decision-making accouterments. Howard, on the other hand, was dressed as he would always be dressed, in black, except for a yellow silk bandana tied around his scrawny neck. He was of slight build, with a wisp of thinning blond hair and a perpetually crooked, ironic smile. Ed also did a lot of smiling, but his was wide open and toothy. He was the jock, a dominating physical presence, while Howard was small enough to fit on Ed's knee (which begged the question of who was the ventriloquist and who the dummy). Howard's lockjawed speech conveyed his intellectual superiority. He had to be either British or from a snobbish section of Bensonhurst. Actually he'd been raised in Brooklyn, although his penetrating gaze implied that North America was far too mundane a place for his genius.

"Did Ed tell you what the Studio Arena Theater pays its actors?" he asked.

"No, he didn't," I told him. "But I'll tell you how much I need to work there."

"They pay everyone, and that includes Ed and myself, four hundred dollars a week."

"That won't be enough," I parried. "I need eight hundred a week."

For the first time since our introduction an ugly look began to spread across Howard's handsome baby face.

"You know, of course, that Al Pacino is willing to work for four hundred."

"Al Pacino can afford to work for four hundred. I can't."

"I suppose that's it," he said, dismissively. For a playwright he was being surprisingly high profile when it came to salary matters. A few moments later, Ed jumped in with what turned out to be a fateful suggestion.

"Kathy—your wife, Kathy. She's an actress, isn't she?"

"Oh, yes," I said.

"What if we paid you four hundred and Kathy four hundred to be one of the women in the ward. We're casting mostly nonunion actresses in Buffalo, but we can make an exception in order to make this thing work."

"That sounds like a great idea," I said.

"Of course, she'll have to audition," said Howard.

"I'm sure she'll be thrilled to audition," I assured him.

"Don't you have a daughter?" asked Ed.

"Yes. Diana will be nine months old in September."

"Wonderful! Then we'll all be up in Buffalo together," said Ed.

"I hope it works out."

"Can Kathy scream?" asked Howard. "There'll be a great need for screaming and moaning in agony."

"She can moan in agony with the best of them," I assured him. I shared a conspiratorial wink with my friend the director and left the room.

So began my lifelong fascination with the city of Buffalo. There's something almost un-American about giving one's self up to a community that's perceived as second rate. America exports self-confidence, and Buffalo is the poster child for imperfection. There are beautiful parts of Buffalo, but Buffalo is not beautiful. With the exception of two and a half summer months, when the ceiling is high and asure and the weather is mild, a harsh wind blows in off the lake and the perpetual overcast threatens snow.

Those who live there like it, or least accept it, and that's another reason for its reputation as a half-assed city. Why accept the grubby conditions of a place that's lost half its population since the early 1950s, when you can travel an hour and a half north and live in a remarkable city like Toronto? The same can be said for the good people of Tacoma, who could just as easily travel a few miles up the highway and live in Seattle. Why live in Newark when you can live in Manhattan? Obviously, the availability of capital has something to do with it, but mostly it's about a personal outlook. People who live in Buffalo don't want to move to Toronto because they don't see any benefit in moving to Toronto. Their determination is to survive the storm of life. Work hard and plan for your retirement. The women wear a lot of blue eye shadow and the men a lot of polyester. (Did you hear about the movie star of Polish descent who slept with the screenwriter? She was brought up in western New York, just a stone's throw from the Peace Bridge.)

Like every other city, Buffalo has wealthy patrons who dedicate themselves to culture, but the town's got a bombed-out, blue-collar feel: professional football and chicken wings at the cozy Anchor Bar, where they were invented. They sell a tie-dyed tee-shirt there that reads "Buffalo, City of No Illusions."

Kathy, daughter Diana, and I drove the New York State Thruway one Sunday in our new crimson Volvo. Mindful that no one in this new city had any preconceived notions of who we were made the trip feel carefree.

> There is something very comforting when you are in the car in the rain at night alone, for then you aren't you, and not being you or anything, you can really lie back and get some rest. It is a vacation from being you. There is only the flow of the motor under your foot spinning that frail thread of sound out of its metal gut like a spider, that filament, that nexus, which isn't really there, between the you which you have just left in one place and the you which you will be when you get to the other place.
>
> – Robert Penn Warren, *All the King's Men*

This comfort of not being me is my weakness posing as salvation.

Late that afternoon we arrived in downtown Buffalo and parked in a large uncovered lot beside the Hotel Lafayette, a grand seedy relic that spoke eloquently of what I assumed would be seven weeks of limited responsibility. I loved the Hotel Lafayette. We were assigned a suite that appeared to have been decorated around the time of the McKinley assassination.

This was how I envisioned my commitment to the Studio Arena: I would watch a handsome TV actor named David Birney emote his guts out for seven weeks while I played my three scenes for a total of twenty minutes per performance. I would socialize with my fellow actors in a large communal dressing room, the subject of the play being so bleak that it would lend itself to much hilarity and gallows humor. Thereafter I would retire with a stiff drink and a good novel to my shabby hotel suite, where I would change the occasional diaper.

After the first reading Kathy and I agreed that Ed Sherin and Howard Sackler had hired an impressive cast. Sixteen New York actors were playing the larger speaking roles, and there were another sixteen nonunion actors from Buffalo. The non-Equity members, mostly young women, played the fever-ridden women in the ward or an occasional naked corpse waiting to be dissected, and a handful of men playing various medical bureaucrats rounded out the cast.

Ed and Howard had lured David Birney from Los Angeles to play the title role. The wonderful Kim Hunter was his sister, the estimable and still unknown Kathy Bates was his wife, Shepperd Strudwick was an understanding if somewhat dubious superior, and Jack Bittner, a pugnacious, rock-solid actor who reminded me of a middle-aged James Cagney, was to play Semmelweis's chief antagonist.

Birney, star of a successful sitcom, *Bridget Loves Bernie,* had been hired because the Studio Arena's artistic director, Neil Dubrock, felt he needed a recognizable name to overcome the bleak subject matter. Unlike today, when casting for the theater is predicated almost exclusively on celebrity cachet, the fear back then was that casting a sitcom actor in so demanding a role might be our undoing. Dubrock himself would have admitted he was taking a substantial risk, but David had been classically trained and had performed numerous leads for Lincoln Center Rep before his success in Hollywood. I had seen him as the lead in Synge's *Playboy of the Western World.*

David affected a midatlantic accent, enunciating like a man who lived somewhere between the Isle of Wight and Nova Scotia. It was a pretentious way of speaking that might have worked had it been accompanied by the depth of feeling required to play the part, but after a few days of rehearsal it was obvious that a form of vanity was distorting his interpretation. Given his seductive good looks, it should not have been a surprise to anyone that he would fall back on a quality that had been the foundation of his success. If you go to Hollywood and play the lead in a sitcom, it makes perfect sense to present yourself as a classically trained actor who is equally adept at being a tragedian. Watching Birney attempt the role of Semmelweis made me think how difficult it would be for any actor to capture the essence of a man who was never in emotional repose. Every scene seemed to start in midargument, which meant the audience was never allowed any downtime with the character. He was either flagellating himself or berating those unsympathetic to his cause.

And he never shut up! Fully 75 percent of the play's dialogue was his. Howard Sackler's thematic specialty was dissecting the fatal flaws of historic figures, as he'd done with Jack Johnson in *The Great White Hope.*

Semmelweis's flaw, as conceived by Howard, was his inability to comprehend the mediocre intellectual capacity of those who opposed him. He was the perfect martyr, a man unable to choose between his purpose for living and his desire to die.

From the outset it was clear that the play was thought provoking, ambitious, well cast, and had at its center an enormous hole. David Birney had neither the moral weight nor the temperament for the role. What was needed was an emotionally aggressive protagonist. The play took place in Central Europe, and our Semmelweis was playing it as if he were a character in *The Importance of Being Earnest.* Everyone connected with the production was aware that as long as the title role was in limbo we were pretty much wasting our time in Buffalo. A fatalism pervaded the first six days of rehearsal, and we spent our time trying to distract ourselves.

There's a certain type of actor who monopolizes the rehearsal process by either continually asking the director for his motivation or complaining to the playwright that his written lines don't suit him. A middle-aged actor of sweet but maddening temperament named Leslie Barrett seemed incapable of rehearsing a scene without questioning Howard's choice of syntax. The entire cast would stand around cringing, knowing that Howard was a Pulitzer Prize-winning author who had labored over every sentence. The encounter would go something like this:

"This line here: 'Now is the winter of our discontent.' It doesn't feel right. Would it be possible if I just said, 'I've been feeling a little depressed lately because it's cold outside?' "

All eyes would turn to our genius playwright, who, having weightier things on his mind than Leslie Barrett, would give him a patient, thin-lipped smile and say, "Why don't you try saying it as it's written?" We would collectively exhale and move on to the next fixable crisis.

In the last hour of our first week I noticed Sherin and Sackler heatedly conversing and pointing in my direction. Paranoia engulfed me. My interpretation of Skoda was coming together. He was a spot of calm in a tempest, and I was investing him with an ironic good nature. Now the director and the playwright were deciding to fire me because obviously I was acting our handsome leading player under the table. I had to admit that this made a certain amount of perverse sense: You couldn't have an actor in a secondary role showing up the lead. Canning me would be an outrageous injustice masquerading as a solution, but fortunately they still had to pay me. The play was doomed to failure anyway, and now I could spend the next six weeks babysitting my daughter while my wife was the actor.

After an abbreviated note session, we broke for the day. No sooner had we settled into the ramshackle sweetness of the Hotel Lafayette than Kathy handed me the phone and told me Ed was on the line.

"Lewis, this is Ed Sherin."

This would be the first of many phone conversations in which Ed would lower his voice, his tone suggesting that if the two of us handled the situation between us we could save the world. I could imagine him leaning back on the couch, Irish whisky in hand, furrowing his brow to further convince himself of the gravity of the situation.

"I've been talking to Howard," he said. Ed was always talking to Howard. If they weren't promoting themselves as womanizers, you'd have thought something was going on between them.

"Lewis." His voice was even lower and more controlled than before. "David Birney isn't working out as Semmelweis, and Howard and I would like you to step into the part."

This was astonishing. I'd almost been hoping I'd be fired.

"I've always known you were the man to play Semmelweis," Ed said, "but because of commercial considerations Howard and I were forced to go another way."

"Listen, Ed," I said. "I'm terribly flattered, but I couldn't even learn it. I mean, we have two weeks until we open. I could never learn it and rehearse it in just two weeks."

"Believe me, I understand. It's a massive undertaking. If you decide to do it, Howard and I will put ourselves at your disposal twenty-four hours a day." There was a long pause. "If you decide not to do it, we'll simply continue on with David—and that'll be a disaster. Give it some thought. We'll be awaiting your answer."

If Birney stayed on, it would be a waste of everyone's time. That realization was followed by a wash of ambition, the vanity engendered by the prospect of fame and glory. One side of my brain decreed that fame and I were incompatible. Was I too mentally lazy to achieve fame, or did I really believe there was something inherently absurd in the concept? Famous people had retinues who traveled around the country with them, teasing their twenty hairs. Then again, better men than I had made peace with fame (although at least one of them had been shot dead while attending the theater). If I became a respected person, everyone would be interested in all the foolish things I had to say. I would be perceived as an achiever.

But first I had to achieve something, and what they were asking me to do was get up at five o'clock every morning for the next two weeks and memorize a mountain of dialogue for the measly sum of four hundred dollars a week. Well, I thought, why not! If I couldn't handle a promotion on the banks of Lake Erie, when could I? I decided to throw myself into the fray, because if I refused to, I'd feel like an asshole. A few minutes later I called Ed back and told him I'd do the part.

Photo Section B

Playing the title role of *Semmelweiss* at the Studio Arena Theater in Buffalo, N.Y. (1977) Kim Hunter is on my right.

One of the few quiet moments during *Semmelweiss*.

As Ali Hakim in the 1979 touring production of *Oklahoma*. Choreographed by the great, Agnes DeMille.

The Female Odd Couple. The Broadhurst Theater (1985) From left to right. Sally Struthers, Tony Shaloub, me & Rita Moreno. Another case of falling in love on the road.

The cast and crew of the beleagured Mickey Rooney adaptation of Neil Simon's *The Sunshine Boys*. We're somewhere in Florida. (1990.) Donald O'Connor is to Mickey's right. I'm behind him reprising the role I originated seventeen years earlier.

Playing the role of Lupinsky in *To Be Or Not To Be*. (1982) I'm actually directing my fury at Mel Brooks.

One of the few quiet moments on the set of *To Be Or Not To Be*. Mel must have been at the dentist.

Addressing Mel Brook who is impersonating Hitler. He was extremely convincing.

Mel Brooks, minus his Hitler moustache.
He is actively in the process of *not* directing the film.

My most recent
professional photo.
I told the photographer
to try and make
me look like
Winston Churchill.

210 Acting Foolish

Max Bialystock in the National Touring Company of *The Producers*. (2005)
I fell in love with the nun looking up at me. (Jill Wolins)

Max Bialystock and "Hold Me, Touch me." (Nancy Johnston).

Chapter 28

Kathy and I were invited to lunch at Howard and Ed's lakeside cottage. We dined beneath a balmy sky on a manicured lawn facing Canada. It was in keeping with Howard's esthetic entitlement that he had secured such imposing digs in a down-and-out city. He'd inherited a significant amount of money from his family's pharmaceutical business, the one that bankrolled the Sackler Wing at the Metropolitan Museum of Art. His inheritance allowed Howard to spend part of the year on Majorca and split his time between a London flat he shared with his lover, the excellent English actress Eileen Atkins, and a home in Los Angeles where on occasion he stayed with his beautiful, much-put-upon wife and his two young daughters.

I'd always considered Ed a director of enormous energy and intellect. (He'd hired me twice, hadn't he?) His wife, Jane Alexander, had reinvented herself as a contemporary Ethel Barrymore. (She certainly could have aspired to something more pedestrian.) They lived beautifully on a tasteful country estate, hobnobbing with a few notable liberal politicians (that should have been a clue right there) while finding time to dedicate themselves to the American theater. (Well, Sherin was directing a play about women's vaginas in Buffalo, wasn't he?)

Ed reminded me that despite his strong hints that I should have played Semmelweis, I had turned him down. This was my opportunity to stop making timid career choices. He also reminded me that *The Great White Hope* had been similarly kicking around until Zelda Fichandler produced it at Arena Stage in Washington, and the rest was Broadway history. Howard's writing had turned James Earl Jones into a star. Robert Whitehead, known as the Gentleman Producer, was waiting to see whether the Buffalo production of *Semmelweis* succeeded before committing himself to mount it on Broadway. Neither he nor Howard underestimated the challenges ahead, but when you came right down to it, this was the kind of creative risk every artist dreams about.

Ed did most of the talking while Howard made certain the salad dressing contained the perfect ratio of oil to vinegar. I loved working with Ed Sherin. He spoke to actors in a vocabulary they could understand. His mission was to clarify the writing and transform it into feelings. His director's bedside manner was firm and selfless. When you nailed a moment, he didn't spend the next five minutes taking responsibility for the discovery. He made you do it again. He drilled it into your memory until he was certain you understood it well enough to repeat it. That's what a good director does. Five hundred discoveries later, you usually have a performance.

Most directors don't know or care about this. They decide they're going to direct a play that takes place in a miniature house that transforms itself into a giant chandelier. At some point in the second act the chandelier will lift itself above the stage and fly out into the audience, thereby reassuring the patrons that they haven't paid too much for their tickets. Directors who dedicate themselves to pulling chandeliers out of their hats are convinced that actors are on a par with the scenery. Both are part of the overall *concept*. Concept directors are incapable of illuminating a play beyond the superficial, because all they understand is the plot. They essentially carpet-bomb the audience out of the theater and into the barbecue restaurant across the street. I recognize that having communication skills that make actors feel worthy and essential doesn't necessarily make a great director. Greatness is in the eye of the press agent. I can only say that even when Ed Sherin made a casting mistake that compromised the story, he always gave it an honest effort, and for that reason alone, I enjoyed being in the same room with him.

Each character you play has his own distinctive voice, and my voice for Semmelweis was that of a man who thought he was losing his mind. I began memorizing the part at six in the morning and worked straight till noon. Then I'd walk a half mile up Main Street and begin our eight-hour rehearsal day. Everyone in the cast was enormously supportive and grateful that we now had the potential for success. Good, bad, or indifferent, I wasn't hiding behind a faux British accent.

But I *was* experiencing severe mental overload. I remember blanking out on my lines and being reduced to tears as I attempted to get my bearings. There were moments when nothing at all came out of my mouth but the raw emotion of my situation—not the situation in the play, but the scrambling of my mental faculties. The pressure of my two-week deadline was inducing a temporary kind of madness.

After our first preview performance, Ed visited my dressing room and demanded that I give up the fear and ride the play like a wave.

"When Kent Broadhurst's character dies, I want you to weep."

"I can't command myself to weep," I said.

"You can. You'll be amazed, but you can."

The next night I wept. Two weeks of sleepless panic had turned me into a volatile machine. I was powerless to resist any emotion. It was a once-in-a-lifetime symbiosis between an actor and director. Ed could walk into my dressing room and tell me to shit in my hat and I'd go out and do it.

The reviews were sterling. The drama critics of the *New York Times* and the *New York Post* came up to Buffalo and lauded the classical beauty of Howard's writing. Both raved over my performance. I hate to quote a critic directly, but this review from the *Times* is relevant to this story:

> Such a role demands great acting. Nothing in Mr. Stadlen's past performances—for example as the deliriously comic Dr. Pangloss in the musical *Candide*—has prepared us for the intensity and conviction of his Semmelweis. From Mr. Stadlen's first entrance, we can feel the man's burning commitment, his Freudian dedication to a scientific mission.
>
> In common with his playwright, Mr. Stadlen has a masterly sense of pace—darting from blazing outrage to Hamlet-like play-acting. Retiring to the quiet life of a general physician, he becomes a child who has been cheated of his birthright. Like James Earl Jones in *The Great White Hope*, Mr. Stadlen offers a performance with weight and tragic dimension, one in which he appears to expend his inmost energies.

I've certainly gotten worse reviews. The day after that, Robert Whitehead and his wife, Zoe Caldwell, joined the celebration. Zoe practically fell all over me with alcohol-fueled praise.

It was announced that the play would be remounted and produced by Whitehead on Broadway as soon as the financing was available. My dream of becoming a hero had come true; I'd sacrificed my sanity to save the show. That same night we had a cast party in the dressing circle lobby with a number of New York theater people in attendance, including Howard Sackler's literary agent, Bill Barnes.

"Do you have a legal agreement that stipulates you'll be playing the role on Broadway?" he asked me. I stared at him. What an absurd question.

"There hasn't been time. The only thing that's been done was to paint my name over David's on the sign."

"Don't you think you should get an agreement in writing?"

"Why?" I asked, nonplussed. "I don't want to force myself on anyone. I'd imagine they'd offer me the role based on the success my performance."

What I really wanted to say was, "Buster, you don't seem to get it. This entire situation is because of little old me. You wouldn't even be standing here if I hadn't stepped up and done the impossible. This play has been hanging around for ten years with no one willing to option it, and tonight they announced that Robert Whitehead is going to produce it on Broadway. I'd think Howard Sackler would rather cut off his own cock than have someone else in the role!"

Of course, I was feeling far too much like Jesus to appear immodest, so I simply lowered my eyes and told him that it wasn't my style to push myself on anyone.

"Lewis," Barnes said, "the first thing you have to do tomorrow morning is call up your agent and demand that they put the whole thing in writing."

We talked a few more minutes before I felt compelled to circulate among my many admirers. He seemed like a nice enough fellow, but I believed his professional concern was completely inappropriate.

One young woman in the cast portrayed a naked corpse. She'd lie beneath a sheet, barely breathing, with six or seven of us hovering over her. At a certain point I'd remove the shroud, exposing her naked torso from her head down to her pubic area. It was a moment that drew gasps from the audience and never failed to invigorate those of us pretending to be doctors. She was the prettiest of the Buffalo girls and the most eager. Rumor had it that during our first week of rehearsal she had spent hours in David Birney's hotel suite helping him to memorize his lines. Since she was married and had recently purchased a house with her husband, whom she was supporting while he attended graduate school, her behavior had become a hot topic of conversation in the women's dressing room.

Tall and big boned, with straight blond hair, she bore a certain resemblance to Laney Kubler. (One time, after I'd brought home a girl with straight blond hair who my father thought was unattractive, he observed that if Bert Lahr had straight blond hair I'd fall in love with him too.) Once again a woman who communicated restless discontent led me down the path of sexual obsession. If David Birney, who'd been fired after a week, could avail himself of her favors, why couldn't I?

Ninety percent of the time I was a model citizen. All right, I cheated on tests to get through high school, and I was certainly not going to march lemminglike into a transport plane to die in Vietnam, but those exceptions aside, I was as dedicated to social standards as the next guy. I just wanted a taste of what was lying on that cold white slab. I convinced myself that here lay the way to a more interesting and complete life.

After blowing off Bill Barnes's advice, I made my way across the room to flirt shamelessly with this lovely, unhappy girl, who must have suspected that lying naked in front of her family and friends would be the most daring thing she would ever do. The play would close in a month and she would be forced to spend the rest of her diminishing youth with her less than thrilling husband. Why not leap into the arms of the second Dr. Semmelweis?

My wife, obviously aware of this mutual infatuation, kissed me goodbye and left the party early so I could exorcise my sexual yearnings. I had triumphed on the stage, I was drunk, and I imagined myself dragging her into my caveman's lair by her straight blond hair. At three in the morning, a local actress named Michele Maulucci kissed me on the cheek and remarked, "I shall leave the two of you to sow the seeds of your mutual destruction." Too drunk to do much of anything, I grabbed my hat and coat and fled alone onto Buffalo's main street. There I was immediately surrounded by three gentlemen of color dressed in various shades of black, purple, and lime green who asked me for directions to a destination I was certain they cared little about. Drunk as I was, it occurred to me that it would be ironic indeed if I wound up dead on so magical an evening. Dismissing the possibility that I might be a closet racist, I broke into a gallop. They chased me for a time, yelling insults, and I realized that the day had been long and I had experienced more than my share of worldly sensations.

I've always flirted with the danger that comes with wanting what isn't mine, but in every instance I've been able to convince myself that the golden pussy lies before me. I'm not a compulsive betrayer, but when the right or wrong woman comes along, I lose my ability to reason. These women all share a general profile. They have never been affirmed by a significant male figure (usually their father). Their innate hostility toward men expresses itself by reveling in and exploiting a temporary power, the power to give themselves totally and then—usually—to withhold those favors. (I say usually, because I've sometimes been wise enough to look the other away.) Even my long-term relationships exhibit this dynamic. Women who genuinely like or love me smell my weakness and are willing to exploit it in order to sustain my interest.

A friend once said to me, "Let's face it. I love women."

"No," I told him, "you love to fuck women, at least those women you would like to fuck." I believe I do love women. They exhaust me, but so does everything else. What I do know is that it has always been an effort for me to embrace a woman's tenderness with the same conviction I bring to their passion (I think). I've shared different periods of my life with very different women and somehow, every one of them has been more or less an amplification of my unhappy mother.

The final three weeks of performing the role of Semmelweis was as fulfilling as anything I had ever experienced. I would leave my new hotel suite every afternoon at four. (Shortly after I assumed the role, the family had been transferred to the much posher Statler Hilton, where David Birney had been staying. I accepted the upgrade: remaining at the Lafayette would have been to short circuit my achievement.) Every performance gave me the feeling of regeneration. No actor could ask for more. Our Buffalo production had exceeded anything Howard Sackler and Ed Sherin had imagined. Within the year we would open out of town, at the very same Kennedy Center where Kathy and I had first met. (Pussy willows.) Only this time, we'd be traveling the road to Broadway together.

The Monday after we closed, we packed up the Volvo and left the city an hour ahead of what would thereafter be called the Great Buffalo Blizzard of 1977.

Chapter 29

At least once a month I invite myself to Sardi's for a midweek lunch. I do this because no matter how good or lousy I feel about myself, the aura of all those theater people who have dined there before me reminds me that I'm still part of a dream I wish were the truth. I once told the playwright Herb Gardner how shocked I was to see how small Sardi's looked during its renovation, when all the chairs, tables, and banquettes had been removed. "I suppose," Herb mused, "we see Sardi's as a very large place because of all the very large things that have happened to us there."

A month after our return from Buffalo, I stopped in for a casual lunch with myself. At the table next to me was Arthur Whitelaw, producer of *Minnie's Boys,* with a guest.

"Wonderful to see you. What are you up to these days?" he said as we hugged each other warmly. Not only was Arthur responsible for my first success, the two of us shared a birthday.

"Oh, I'm pleasantly biding my time," I told him. "I did a play up in Buffalo a few months ago called *Semmelweis*, and I'm just waiting to hear when we go back into rehearsal."

"September thirteenth," said the smartly dressed gentleman sitting next to Arthur. "I work at the Robert Lantz Talent Agency, and we handle Colin Blakely."

"Colin Blakely?" I asked. "I hadn't heard anything about him."

It was one of those moments you play over for the rest of your life. I began to imagine what role the British actor could conceivably be playing in *Semmelweis*. A momentary confusion befuddled me before I allowed myself to imagine the unthinkable. I don't remember how many seconds I stood there before sliding into my adjoining banquette. I was like a prizefighter who had taken a kidney punch and was too stunned to fall.

Next thing I remember I was lifting a glass of Jack Daniel's and recalculating the possibilities that either this asshole agent had gotten the name of the play wrong or that Blakely, an actor I very much admired, had decided to step into the role of Skoda, the part I had vacated after week one of rehearsal. I stared across the room at the caricatures of several famous producers, realizing through the haze of my midafternoon intoxication that Robert Whitehead was among them. Was it really possible that those motherfuckers had given my role away to an actor no one in the States had ever heard of?

I must have inhaled three more drinks before tears began to burn my cheeks and I realized I was mumbling out loud. Feigning sobriety as best I could, I bid Arthur and the messenger boy/agent good-bye and cabbed it home.

The first person I called was Ed Sherin. Jane Alexander answered the phone.

"A very humiliating thing happened to me at Sardi's today," I began with the solemnity that comes only with plenty of booze and an audacious story to tell.

"Well, that's horrible," said Jane, when I'd explained. "I know that Ed certainly doesn't know anything about it."

"Why would he know?" I said. "He's only the director. I want to speak with him."

"You can't. He's not here. He's skiing in Idaho with his children."

"What's his phone number?"

"He never gave it to me. I'll have to wait until he calls back." Jane was giving about as convincing a performance as she did as Eleanor Roosevelt, only this time you couldn't see the fake buck teeth.

"I very much want to speak with him," I said, and hung up. Within ten minutes Ed called.

"How the hell do you think *I* feel?" he yelled. "Do you really, in your right mind, believe that I want to go through the same torturous process with another actor?" He appeared to believe that a good offense was better than a simpering defense.

"I was great in that part!" I sniveled.

"Of course you were great! Do you think I haven't spent every goddamned waking hour trying to address this subject with Howard? He's like a broken record: 'I wrote the part for Colin Blakely.' And—" he paused, "that phony bitch, Zoe Caldwell. Remember when she fell all over you in Buffalo? The moment you turned your back she made a bee line for me and Howard and said, 'Get rid of him!' "

"I don't give a shit about Zoe Caldwell," I said, although this revelation clearly stung. We had spent a very pleasant weekend together up at Hume Cronyn and Jessica Tandy's house a few years earlier. "I give a shit about you!" I yelled.

"Me? What do I have to do with it?"

"Aren't you the director?"

"Have you been listening to one word I've said? Howard wrote the part for Colin Blakely. What on earth do you want *me* to do?"

"I want you to quit," I said, stating what I believed to be the obvious.

"Quit? I can't do that."

"Why not? Listen, mister—" All I could think was that this was the schmuck who hadn't allowed me to return one in twenty-one straight badminton serves. "We had words, mister. You and I had words, and now it is your moral responsibility to quit."

"You mean quit the show? Listen." I had clearly struck a nerve. "You have to speak with Howard. Nobody in this world has fought harder for you than myself and Jane."

"I didn't realize you'd have to fight for me. After all, I did save your fucking ass!"

"Can't you get it through that aggrieved head of yours that all that is water under the bridge? You have no idea what kind of a man Howard Sackler is once he sets his mind to something." I could hear him pouring a drink on the other end of the line. "He says he wrote the part for Colin Blakely. I can't move him off the dime."

"I want to speak to Howard."

"I *want* you to speak to Howard. I'm sure he'll be relieved to speak to you. Trust me, Lewis, you're accusing the wrong guy. I'm your biggest booster."

Five minutes later Howard called. He sounded in an ebullient frame of mind. Being exposed as the scumbag he was seemed to appeal to his sense of dramatic irony.

"I was waiting for the proper time to tell you," he said. "Obviously the fates intervened."

"How the hell can you do this to me?" I screamed at him. "I saved your ass. You wouldn't have another production if it weren't for me."

"I won't argue with you there." His speech was growing more clipped with every word. "You were very much the hero of the moment, and if I hadn't written the role with Colin in mind, or if by some chance he was suddenly to become unavailable, you would certainly jump to the head of the line."

"You sonofabitch! If you told me you were giving the part to Richard Burton, I could at least wrap my brain around that. He's a big fucking star! But Colin Blakely? Do you know who knows who Colin Blakely is? I do! That's who knows!"

"I couldn't disagree with you more. If I offered the role to Richard Burton solely on his ability to sell tickets, I'd be doing something immoral." At that moment I could see Howard staring out at the high Sierra, puffing away on one of his French cigarettes. "I consider Colin to be the fifth greatest actor in the English-speaking world," he said. "I remember my good friend Stanley Kubrick telling me—"

"You have no friends."

"I understand you're angry with me. Nevertheless, Stanley Kubrick impressed upon me a long time ago that one must bridge no compromise when consummating art. You're a nice young actor, and I appreciate what you did for us in Buffalo, but Colin is a great actor, and I feel no need to apologize for writing the part of Semmelweis with him in mind. In this regard I treat you no differently than I would my own family."

"You know what you are?" I yelled. "You're an artistic fascist. A black-shirted little fascist!"

"Well, that's another discussion, and hopefully we can have it around the time Colin's contract expires."

"You are so certain he's going to be better in that part than I was?"

"Let's say I'm more than willing to take that risk. To turn my back on Colin now would be to betray everything I believe in."

"You are an incredible bastard!"

"I forgive you your rage. I understand that it hasn't worked out as you had wished."

I had hardly had time to digest Howard's betrayal when a phone call came from the Gentleman Producer Robert Whitehead.

"I can only say how mortified I am at the manner in which you found out. I sincerely offer you my apology."

"Thanks." By this time I was in no mood to be placated by Whitehead's reputation for gentility. "Let me ask you a question. Don't you think what you're doing is really dumb? I mean, you've already got a rave review in the *New York Times*."

"Well—" I heard his uneasy chuckle on the other end of the line. He recognized that in order for his sincerity to be perceived as genuine he would have to endure my questions for a few minutes longer.

"You know I've been interested in producing this play for over ten years."

"But you never did," I said.

"No, I never did. As for being dumb, I'll admit I've made any number of mistakes during my years in the theater. It is possible this may turn out to be another."

He was very smooth and I believe sincerely mortified, but there was little doubt that after he hung up, my outrage would run a distant second to his self-importance. After all, he had had nothing to do with what had transpired in Buffalo. He had merely jumped on a plane with his boozy theatrical wife and, seeing something that pleased him, decided to thrill the cast by announcing he would be moving us all into the big time.

"Well, I have no complaint with you," I told him. "But what, exactly, is your apology worth? You'll be moving to Broadway in a few months and I can take my four hundred dollars a week and shove it."

I suppose I wasn't behaving like the Gentleman Actor.

It didn't take long for Ed Sherin to call back. Unaware that I had just gotten off the phone with his new boss, he was in an expansive mood. "Get hold of your congressman! Go out and get yourself a labor lawyer! They can't do this to you."

"I thought they already did," I said. "I've spoken to Howard."

"Fuck him! Listen to me. There are rules about bringing English actors into this country. You have to be an internationally recognized star or something, and Colin's no star. Secondly, they have to prove there isn't another American actor who can play the part. We all know what a pile of horseshit that is. Jesus! We have three rave reviews from the New York papers. What I'm saying is, you've got to fight this thing. It is imperative that you fight this thing! I'm the goddamned director. I'll stand up and testify for you in any court in this country. Jane is a member of the Actor's Alien Committee at the union. There's no way you can lose this fight, and now is the time to stand up for yourself and show some balls!"

"I'll look into it."

"Don't look into it, do something about it!" he said.

I called up my father and explained the situation.

"Jesus." He sounded more worried than surprised. "Don't do it. Don't make your life about this. They screwed you, now put an end to it. They're only going to fuck themselves."

"Don't do it? You want me to let them drive a tank over me? Ed Sherin said he'd testify for me in any court in the country."

"What court? What country?"

"Whatever court it takes, how the hell do I know? That's why I've got to get a lawyer and find out how these things work."

"Lewis, darling, don't do it," my father said. "Don't make yourself a martyr. Semmelweis was the martyr. Who knows what you're up against? As your father, I'm advising you, get pissed off and drop it."

"But Ed Sherin said—"

"I know what Ed Sherin said. I'm advising you not to do it."

"I'm sorry, I can't let them roll over me," I told him.

"All right. Do what you have to," he said wearily before hanging up.

Confronting people you admire who are blatantly screwing you can be confusing. Your purest reaction would be to take a machine gun and riddle them all with bullets, but a gremlin on your shoulder is telling you that perhaps you are merely suffering from a lifelong persecution complex. Maybe Colin Blakely *is* the fifth most talented actor in the English-speaking world. Perhaps there's something irrational in your inability to appeciate the refined instincts of a Gentleman Producer. Perhaps your bullying director is offering you a way out of your habitual propensity to play the victim. Perhaps all this isn't really happening.

A few days later I hired a lawyer friend by the name of Richard Brodsky. Brodsky wasn't really a practicing attorney as much as he was an aspiring politician. Another brilliant move. I found Brodsky's annoying personality perversely entertaining because he made me feel like a descendant of Prince Charming. His defining characteristic was an absolute certainty about everything. The archetype of the man who was dying to be elected to something, he was very bright, alarmingly self-confident, and actually quite charming, as long as your interaction lasted no longer than a greeting and a handshake. I had never needed an attorney before, and since he was fond of boasting that he had never lost in court ("Undefeated, Lewie!") and since his expertise lay in politics (I saw my quest in political terms: the American acting community warding off the invasion of the British, complete with visions of the Capitol dome being torched during the War of 1812), and finally, since he promised not to charge me an arm and a leg as long as I did all the scutwork (the research about Colin Blakely's career), Richard Brodsky was the lawyer/congressman that Ed Sherin had recommended I get in touch with.

For the next month I combed the archives of the Lincoln Center Theater Library to dig up whatever biographical material existed on Colin Blakely. Researching another actor's career was interesting. I'd seen Blakely perform in London, in Harold Pinter's *Old Times,* as well as in the film *Charley Bubbles,* which starred my idol Albert Finney (who really *was* one of the greatest actors in the English-speaking world). I'd enjoyed both performances very much. Blakely was a stocky, broad-shouldered Irishman with a mischievous face, a good-natured, unexceptional fellow you might have spent an evening getting drunk with at a local pub. He had an infectious everyman brand of charm, but his strong suit did not appear to be playing men who were intellectually arrogant or exceptionally intelligent.

A successful actor is usually associated with a particular essence that they draw on, with minor variations, over the course of their career. No one ever confused Claude Rains with a construction worker on the Empire State Building. George Sanders was brilliant as the well-heeled cosmopolitan snob; no one would cast him as a dolt. Nick Nolte is most effective playing a volatile underdog; but he wasn't convincing as Thomas Jefferson, who was a genius and an aristocrat.

What I was discovering about Colin Blakely was that his career was remarkably like my own. He was well respected because he was a fine actor. He was not a star in the sense of projecting an intangible sexual appeal and radiance. He reminded me of myself, only older. He was fortunate to be part of a British theater system that allowed him greater opportunity to move from role to role. What I was up against was the snobbery of those who preferred all things British, which was certainly not his fault. Yet more often than not, the roles Colin Blakely performed were of individuals who were more earthy than smart.

By the time the matter was referred to the Actor's Alien Committee, I was certain that Blakely would not be allowed to perform the role on

Broadway. To qualify, he had to meet several criteria that had been negotiated between the League of Broadway Producers and Actor's Equity.

1. He had to prove he was an internationally recognized star, which he was not.
2. He had to be the recipient of internationally recognized prizes or awards, which he was not.
3. He had to prove that he had received star billing in a commercial production of a play. This was the one area in which he qualified. He was currently playing the lead in a play in the West End entitled *Filumena*. Unfortunately for me, he was receiving star billing for the first time in his career, but *Filumena* had already been produced unsuccessfully on Broadway, and the American producer had chosen not to bring him over, believing he needed a star. The role had instead been cast with the great *Italian* actor Eli Wallach. The play closed within a week.
4. Most damaging to the other side was the producer's need to prove that no actor residing in the United States was qualified to perform the role of Semmelweis. This seemed a pretty open and shut case. How were they going to prove that no American actor could play the role, after I'd received rave reviews from the *New York Times, New York Post,* the *Newark Star-Ledger,* and several Buffalo papers? And, of course, there would be the testimony of the play's director, Ed Sherin, who would stand up and tell the world just how remarkable a performance I had given.

A couple of days before the hearing I called Ed to give him the particulars.

"What is it you'd like me to do?" he asked.

"Stand up and tell Jane and the committee that it's absurd to bring Colin Blakely over, because I was great in the part."

"Jane won't be there," he said.

"Why not?"

"She's in L.A., rehearsing a movie."

"I'm sorry to hear that."

"What are you worried about?" he said. "Everybody knows what side of the fence *she's* on. This is your own union. You're swinging through an open door. How can you possibly lose?"

"We could lose."

"I'd say it's pretty remote, wouldn't you?" His tone implied disgust with someone so openly suspicious.

"I certainly hope so."

"That's what I wanted to discuss with you." For a second time Ed lowered his voice confidentially. "You're going to win. Trust me! I have it on authority that you're going to win. This is the first of a three-step process. Why blow our wads now, when I can testify when the going gets tough and you need an ace in the hole?"

"Because the reason I went out and got a lawyer was because you promised you would testify for me in any court in the country."

"And I will. I'm just saying, why ruffle their feathers in a format Howard and Bob fully expect to lose? Save your star witness for when you need him most. Ask your lawyer, for God's sake. Does he really think you're going to lose?"

"I'd like you to testify."

"It's not the smart move. Ask your lawyer. It makes no sense to bring me out so early in the game."

"All right," I said. I'd done all the research. No one knew better than I that Colin Blakely did not meet three of the four provisions in the contract. It seemed inconceivable that my own union would rule against me. I called up Brodsky, who hesitated for a moment after hearing the news.

"Yeah, this one's pretty much a lock. I mean, there's validity to his argument. You trust the guy, right?"

"Sure."

"Hey! That's the bottom line," said Brodsky.

The next day he went in and argued my case. I was not allowed attend—at least that's what I was told by Brodsky. By late afternoon the committee had decided that Blakely failed to qualify under the terms of the alien clause in the production contract. The producers of *Semmelweis* could either accept the verdict or appeal to the elected council of Actor's Equity. As soon as the verdict was read, Robert Whitehead informed the union that he would appeal.

Two days before the case was to be argued before the council, I called Ed Sherin.

"You should meet Brodsky on the fourteenth floor of the Equity Building. I'm not allowed to be there."

"There's going to be a problem," said Ed.

"What's the problem?"

"Howard's the problem. You didn't think he was going to roll over, did you?"

"What does Howard have to do with your testifying on my behalf?"

"Everything! You spoke to him. You know what kind of a man he is. If he thinks I've in any way been responsible for keeping Colin out of the country, he'll remove me as the director, and then where will you be?"

"He's not going to remove you as the director."

"Listen to me, will you? If you win this thing on the merits, he'll have no choice but to rehire you. But if he believes there's been some collusion between the two of us, he won't allow you to play the part as a matter of principle."

"What the hell are you saying? That you aren't going to testify?"

"Have you listened to one word I've said? If I testify for you and you win, I will have completely fucked your chances."

"So if I win this round without you, what happens in the next round?"

"There may not be a next round. A next round will cost Bob Whitehead ten thousand dollars. This is about taking one baby step at a time. Do you realize that every day, Ann Roth [the costume designer] and John Wulp [the scenic designer] are telling Howard and Bob that they're insane to be fighting this thing? We've been jumping through hoops for you behind the scenes."

"Ed, this thing is costing me about four thousand dollars."

"I understand, but it's imperative that Howard sees you win the thing on the merits. That's what it's always been about. If they're dumb enough take this thing to arbitration, I say fuck them! That's the time we pull out all the stops. But if I testify for you tomorrow—you're dead."

Mel Brooks, a man with whom I've spent a fair amount of time, has built a comic philosophy around man's responsibility to be smart. Why be dumb if the alternative is to be smart? Why weigh yourself down with moral conundrums when a man's life is measured by winning? Winning silences your enemies and makes converts of your doubters. Just believe in yourself and be smart!

If I'd listened to Howard Sackler's agent, Bill Barnes, and insisted that I receive a guarantee to play Semmelweis in any subsequent commercial production, they would have stalled while I played the role in Buffalo or eventually confronted me with Howard's obsession with Colin Blakely, and how would that have changed anything? I suppose I wouldn't have confronted Ed Sherin and expressed my moral outrage, thereby relieving him of any responsibility for being my advocate and protector. I could have accepted my father's advice and allowed the matter to drop. But being smart in this case meant recognizing that just because people are talented doesn't mean they're planning to do right by you. That's a form of smart that has to be experienced before it becomes part of a person's lexicon. I may seem like a cynic, but in my heart I've always been a closet optimist.

We won the second round before council, whereupon Robert Whitehead's attorney appealed the verdict to an impartial arbitrator. Brodsky explained that the arbitrator we got depended on the luck of the draw. Some were recommended by Actor's Equity and some by the League of Broadway Producers. In the month that followed, Whitehead went to the mat and collected a bunch of letters from celebrities insisting that Colin Blakely was the finest actor of his time, and that to deprive the American public of his greatness would be an act of cultural philistinism. Katharine Hepburn and Arthur Miller were two of the letter writers. In response, I asked the three New York drama critics who had reviewed my performance to write letters on my behalf. The *Times* refused, saying such a letter would compromise the integrity of the drama desk. The *Post* reviewer refused because he was a close friend of Howard's, and he insisted he would never have taken the shlep up to Buffalo if their friendship hadn't been an issue. Emory Lewis, the critic for the *Newark Star-Ledger,* wrote a heartening letter of support. The kindest gesture came from Hume Cronyn and Jessica Tandy. Cronyn and Whitehead were first cousins. They owned adjacent homes overlooking their private lake in Pound Ridge, and the two couldn't have been closer. They took fishing trips to the Arctic together. When Whitehead asked Hume and Jessica to write letters supporting Colin Blakely, Hume said, "But I hear Lewis Stadlen was wonderful in that part." They both refused. This wasn't anything I could show to an arbitrator, but it will forever remain in my heart.

The day before the case was to be presented, I called Ed Sherin, and this time he agreed to see Richard Brodsky and me, as long as our meeting took place outside the city. Brodsky lived in Hartsdale, New York, so he suggested a restaurant off the Saw Mill River Parkway.

This phase was more complicated than the last, and Ed and Brodsky had to be on the same page when it came to his testimony. Brodsky told us he believed we stood a 70 percent chance of winning. You could never tell whether the arbitrator was in someone's pocket, but it was too late to worry about that now.

"What exactly are you going to say regarding Lewis's performance in Buffalo?" Brodsky asked Ed.

"Well, that's what I wanted to talk to you about." Ed was clearly uneasy. "You say you're almost certain Lewis is going to win?"

"I would say the odds are in our favor," Brodsky replied. "Especially after the director testifies that no one can play the part as well as Lewis."

"But that's the problem," said Ed. "How could I answer that with any certainty?" Brodsky gave me a sidelong glance.

"That's why we're here tonight. I'll phrase the question in a way you can answer with certainty."

"What if I can't?"

"What if you can't what?" asked Brodsky.

"Testify to anything with absolute certainty. Whitehead's lawyer is no fool. They've got a carload of celebrities willing to testify that Colin is the greatest thing since sliced bread. I know for a fact that the arbitrator saw Colin's performance in London. How he got there is anybody's guess."

"Are you suggesting that Robert Whitehead flew the arbitrator to London?" asked Brodsky. Ed gave a knowing shrug.

"What exactly are you suggesting?" I asked him.

"I'm suggesting—" he gulped some water and stared directly above my head, "—that since it's all but certain that you're going to win this thing, I wondered if you would mind—terribly—if I testified on behalf of Colin Blakely."

The amazing thing about the world of the theater is that just when you think you've experienced every kind of shameful chicanery, some new twist comes along. It's like good comedy writing. The audience believes it's following the joke to its logical conclusion, only to have the writer turn the screw and elicit laughter from our surprise. This I remember: I could not bear to look Ed Sherin in the face when I said, *"Yes, Ed. I would mind very much if you testified on behalf of Colin Blakely."*

Here was the man I could forgive almost anything because he was talented and because he had cast me in *The Time of Your Life*, the man who had whacked twenty-one straight badminton shuttlecocks at my face, and he turns out to be not amoral, like his symbiotic partner Francisco Franco the Playwright, he turns out to be a pathetic pussy! This was a deep personal loss for me.

The next day Ed honored me by testifying for neither Colin Blakely nor me. I suppose that was his strategy from the beginning. I wasn't at the hearing, so I never knew what transpired. Word filtered back that Brodsky was a tad abrasive for the arbitrator's taste, the arbitrator who had been flown to London to see Blakely's performance in *Filamena*. For all it mattered, that day Richard Brodsky couldn't have gotten a Du Pont off on a murder charge.

Continuing on with the farce, the arbitrator took a month to hand down his decision. His reasoning was that even though Blakely failed to qualify if one focused on the most rigid definition of the contract language, the recommendations of some of the most respected members of the artistic community, who vouched that Blakely's artistry was of the first rank, had to be acknowledged. If he was not an international star at the moment, it was only because he had never been allowed access to the American stage, and this was the opportunity that would afford him international status. Buffalo was Buffalo, and any asshole willing to work for four hundred dollars a week could not be considered a serious alternative to someone starring on the London stage. Actually, I was mentioned very little in the judgment. This was about a playwright and a theatrical producer being denied their God-given right to choose their own star. Richard Brodsky was no longer undefeated.

For some reason, when the judgment came down I was still surprised.

Chapter 30

In the throes of despair I drove the red Volvo up the Taconic to Gray Gables and walked around the grounds asking myself why this had happened. It had been fifteen years since I'd been there, and the place had ceased to be a camp a couple of years after I'd departed. Now the property belonged to a religious order of women who dressed in starched white collars and blue gingham smocks. As I made my way toward the theater, I could hear the sound of barnyard animals. The dressing rooms and waiters' quarters now housed cows. The barn converted to a theater had reverted to a barn. The earth under my feet, once the site of my sexual awakening, had been transmuted into a dairy farm for vestal virgins.

Sometime during the spring, I got a call from my favorite playwright, Howard Sackler.

"I was wondering," he said without a hint of discomfort, let alone contrition, "I seem to have misplaced my original working copy of *Semmelweis*. It's filled with notes from our Buffalo experience, and I faintly recollect that I might have given it to you. If you have it, I would love to get it back."

"I can assure you that if I do have it, I'd rather roast it over a spit and pee on it than give it back to you," I told him. Then, in the heat of the moment, and not being able to punch him through the receiver, I did something that surely deserves a place in the Self-Destructive Hall of Fame.

"Well, now that you've managed to rid yourself of me, does this mean you intend to fire my wife as well?"

"Of course not," said Howard, delighted with the opportunity to right a perceived wrong. "We'd welcome Kathy back with open arms.

We're all very fond of her, as we're extremely fond of you."

"That's damn generous of you," I said, seething, and hung up. A few minutes later I recounted the conversation to my wife. "And he said, 'Of course we won't fire Kathy. We'd welcome her back with open arms.' That miserable sonofabitch."

Kathy continued washing dishes for a few minutes before returning to the subject. "So what do you think about my moving on with the show?"

"What do I think about it?" I said, flabbergasted. "I'd like to plant a bomb in the theater. I'd like everyone connected with that show to die, and if you were in the show I'd want *you* to die."

"Even if this is my only opportunity to act in a Broadway show?"

"This isn't your only opportunity. This is just the opportunity they're offering you at the moment." What I really wanted to tell her was that if I hadn't needed the extra four hundred dollars to go to Buffalo, she wouldn't even have had that opportunity. But being the great guy I was, I decided to shield her from the truth and appeal to her sense of loyalty.

"I've decided to do it," she said. "You're always lecturing me on how I never make decisions concerning my own life, and now I'm going to make one. I did good work in that show, and just because they screwed you doesn't mean I have to be sacrificed. Besides, we could use the money. I've decided to do it."

"And the baby?"

"You can take care of Diana for the month I'll be away. For five hours a day she'll be in day care. Listen, you did a show in Princeton the week Diana was born. Why shouldn't I bring home the money for once?"

"You're collaborating with my betrayers."

"Please. Are you suggesting you'd have given up your part if they'd fired me?"

"That's different. I was the fucking lead."

"It's not different. I'm going to do the show. I know it's a sensitive issue, but I'm not going to betray myself."

A few months later Kathy began rehearsing the new and improved version of *Semmelweis* starring the fifth greatest actor in the English-speaking world. I had no one to blame but myself.

People who make their living in the theater are consumed by envy. You sit down in a theater and if you're not involved in it, you hope the enterprise fails. Yet somehow the theater's regenerative power mutes your mean-spirited impulses and allows you to open your heart to what's transpiring on the stage. The negative impulses arise from the misconception that another actor's or director's success is diminishing your own career. This is a ridiculous notion, but one that's difficult to shed.

The problem I was facing as *Semmelweis* reentered rehearsals was that in this situation another actor's potential success *was* subtracting from my career. My dream life was haunted by people telling me Colin Blakely was the most brilliant actor in the world and would utterly eclipse my Buffalo interpretation of Semmelweis. During this period my sense of reality was completely dominated by a play that had cast me aside, and I imagined the entire world was equally obsessed with the first public performance of *Semmelweis*. Howard Sackler's play was an affliction. On one occasion I walked past a framed picture of myself in the role of Semmelweis and with no regard for my physical safety, ripped it off the wall and smashed it to pieces. Miraculously, the shards of glass missed my eyes.

Every evening I waited for the sound of Kathy's key in the lock so I could maniacally cross-examine her about the day's events.

"How's he doing?"

"He's doing all right. He's different," she would say, heading toward the kitchen for a drink. "His conception of the part is different."

"Is his conception better or worse?"

"I'd say he's still finding his way."

Not long thereafter she came home in an expansive mood and poured herself a glass of wine. "Today he really got it! For the first time you could see it's all coming together!" I went completely insane.

When she finally packed her things and sped off to Washington, it seemed merciful. Left alone, however, my mood darkened further. Each morning after I'd packed my eighteen-month-old daughter off to day care, I found myself entertaining sexual obsessions about my wife, the whore who had sold herself for Broadway minimum. I began searching out tangled thickets on the Palisades Parkway where I planned to drive her when she returned on her day off. I'd rip her clothes off and fuck her on the ground. None of this boded well for the future of our marriage.

Semmelweis opened at the Kennedy Center on a Monday. Kathy called that evening to tell me that the audience's reaction was respectful but reserved. I waited in a state of near panic for the *Variety* review due out Wednesday. That morning, after I'd dropped Diana off (my poor little girl had to know that something very weird was going on between

Mommy and Daddy), I hit the nearest newsstand and with trembling fingers opened the paper. It was as strange a notice as I had ever read. I suppose you'd call it a modified approval. Most of the commentary concerned Howard's track record as a Pulitzer Prize winner and the fact that the play took on a difficult subject. (The bulk of the review was an explanation of historical circumstances that affected the plot.) It mentioned that the play's dialogue was somewhat fevered, but said the effect was more episodic than dramatic. It also said the play was too long but in the critic's estimation was fixable with time and work. Not until the third to last paragraph was Colin Blakely's name mentioned: "And Colin Blakely makes a subtly persuasive American debut in the title role."

I beg your pardon? The role of Semmelweis was the entire reason for the play. This was like ignoring the actor playing Hamlet until the conclusion of the review. I was in such a state of traumatized confusion that I didn't know whether to laugh or cry. What I concluded was that I had dodged a bullet. My worst nightmares had not come to pass. They hadn't said that here was a performance that made the theater the religious experience it was meant to be. Was it possible that the whole thing would be recorded as a nonevent and go out with a whimper?

"It's going all right," Kathy said over the phone after her Friday night performance. "I think Ed's a little frustrated. He keeps telling Colin to do the scenes the way you did them."

"Good."

"We're getting some walkouts. But most of the reviews were positive."

"Yeah. I read *Variety*."

"I'm looking forward to coming home on Sunday," she said sweetly.

"Yeah. So am I." I didn't tell her about my big plans to splendor her in the grass.

Next morning I was sitting in my den with a cup of coffee, foraging through the major league box scores, when the telephone rang.

"Lewis?" I recognized the intonation in Ed Sherin's voice. "This is Ed Sherin. Listen, Colin Blakely isn't working out, and Howard and I were wondering if you would consider coming back to replace him."

Now, I'd entertained any number of fantasies since that afternoon at Sardi's, but most of them had to do with burning down Ed and Jane's house. Somewhere along the line I had accepted that Sir Colin Blakely was the genius he was purported to be, so most of my fantasies were either defensive or revenge oriented.

"You know I always felt that casting Colin was an enormous mistake," Ed continued. "The only thing that's changed around here is that Howard has finally seen the light. The situation is complicated, and there isn't a great deal of time. Would you still be interested in replacing Colin?"

I had to hand it to Ed. This could not have been an easy phone call to make. But figuring out Ed's motives was sort of like entering the greased pig contest at a county fair.

"I'd be interested if the money was right," I told him coolly. In reality I was feeling like Fred Astaire dancing on the ceiling in *Royal Wedding*. I couldn't believe this was happening.

"I'll tell you what. I'm going to hang up now and let you speak to Howard." Of course! You had to be a complete idiot not to know that Howard was sitting right beside him in their shared suite at the Watergate Hotel.

Ten seconds later my phone rang.

"Lewis?" said Howard in those clipped tones I had grown to despise. "Would you like me to eat humble pie?" That was the thing about Howard. He was such a miserable bastard that nothing he said or did made you want to do anything but cry.

"I've made a terrible mistake. An amateurish mistake," he said, assuring me that his objectivity would forever remain intact. "If you agree to come back we'll have plenty of time over drinks for postmortems. Colin's just hideously wrong in the part. He's been resistant to everything Ed has been trying to unlock, and it's obvious that we've reached the point of no return."

What a guy! For the same reasons he had advanced as he handed me my hat, he was now dumping his good friend Colin Blakely for the sake of the Artistic Ideal.

"I'm willing to come back if the money's right," I told him, my righteous passion now reduced to numbers on a paycheck. I certainly couldn't deceive myself that it was about anything else.

"Here's the problem," said Howard. "Ed and I have been leaning on Bob Whitehead since the middle of the week to make the change, but he has thus far resisted. I believe he's angry with you. As a matter of fact he thinks Ed and I are both crazy. I told him I'd rather be crazy than an amateur. It's obvious that Colin has failed in the role. Anyone can see that." Poor Howard. He'd gambled on Whitehead being his esthetic peer, and now he felt betrayed.

"At the moment he owns the license rights to the play, but if Ed and I walk away and refuse to work on it, he'll have no course but to accept you back or close the show. So don't be faint of heart! We already have another producer waiting in the wings who's willing to remount it as soon as Bob drops out."

Once again the weight had shifted back onto my shoulders. His memory of my brilliant performance meant that Howard was now willing to screw Colin Blakely, Robert Whitehead, and all the financial backers. Howard had seen the light. In his kaleidoscopic view of artistic perfection, I had just elevated myself past the fifth greatest actor in the English-speaking world.

I called Kathy.

"I knew this would happen," she told me. "I fantasized about this the moment I took the job." (Yeah, and I've got a couple of fantasies in store for you too, baby!)

I was told not to waste a moment. I should drive down to Washington, Diana strapped into the backseat, so I could watch the Saturday evening performance. All this would be clandestine. They would sneak me into the Eisenhower Theater's presidential box. (I wound up sitting next to Roger Stevens, head of the Kennedy Center and also one of the producers of *Semmelweis*. He was quite drunk and hadn't the faintest idea who I was. Why should he?)

The play stank! For two and a half hours I tried not to scream. It was only a play, not my life! I kept asking myself who was the bigger fool—me, for a year's worth of suffering over this leaden entertainment, or everyone else for allowing themselves to be hornswoggled by Howard Sackler's monumental self-importance. Poor Colin Blakely. He was a victim all right, but victimization and tragedy are different dynamics. He had made the worst possible miscalculation. His anxiety about pulling off the role had led him to decide that because the medical establishment was crazy for not accepting Semmelweis's sanitation theory, Semmelweis could be portrayed as reasonable and rational at all times, and the audience could decide for itself who was sane and who was not (a very British decision). But this let all the air out of the play. Just like David Birney, he was playing the role as if he were in a play by Oscar Wilde. You'd think nothing had been learned since the first day of rehearsal in Buffalo. A disclaimer: It was the circumstances I was forced to endure—the lack of rehearsal time and sleep deprivation—that led me into the madness that was in large part responsible for the success of my performance in *Semmelweis*.

But there's a lesson in this. There's a qualitative difference between the talents of Maggie Smith and Zoe Caldwell, Paul Scofield and Tom Conti, Albert Finney and Colin Blakely. English actors, (Zoe Caldwell is Australian) who come to the States and repeat a role they've done successfully on the London stage are feted by the American critics as if they were geniuses. When we were performing *The Sunshine Boys* on Broadway, Alan Bates was across the street doing his two thousandth performance in a minor British comedy called *Butley*. They were selling the text of the play in the lobby as if *Butley* were *Uncle Vanya*. That year the Tony went to Alan Bates, a wonderful actor, rather than to Jack Albertson, who was giving a better performance. It's time for American drama critics to recognize that when their publications send them over to England to review a week's worth of plays, they're in a far more receptive mood than when they're at home, dashing to get to the theater on time after forgetting to pick up their dry cleaning.

Watching *Semmelweis* that evening left me seriously underwhelmed. I was thrilled to be vindicated, but now, robbed of my outrage, I felt unmoored. I drove back to New York the following night with my daughter asleep in the backseat. Somewhere around Elizabeth, New Jersey, I looked up and saw a gargantuan disc hovering at an indeterminate distance above me, its shape defined by what appeared to be a million particles of light. "My goodness," I said, in a hypnotic state of calm. "It's a flying saucer." Within seconds it dematerialized. Two days later, Walter Cronkite announced on the evening news, "And for those of you in northern New Jersey who thought you saw a flying saucer, the National Aeronautics and Space Administration reports that you were witnessing a flight of millions of migrating bugs trapped in a light pattern."

Robert Whitehead was soon to learn what Herman Levin had experienced after producing Howard's other play, *The Great White Hope*. Levin had optioned *Great White* after seeing it performed at Arena Stage in Washington. (Ed Sherin had directed that play as well.) Levin had been a successful theatrical accountant until the mid-1950s, when he decided to produce a musical that more experienced Broadway producers had refused to touch. The musical was *My Fair Lady*, and Levin made a fortune. After its initial success at Arena Stage, *The Great White Hope* opened at the Alvin Theater in New York.

In its first week of previews the play was running well over three hours, and Levin demanded that Howard make some cuts and restructure the play to eliminate a second intermission. (One can only wonder where Ed Sherin came down in all of this.) Howard adamantly refused to change anything, and to hammer home his point he began legal proceedings challenging Levin's right to produce the play even as it continued its run at the Alvin. Levin promptly countersued and was quickly exonerated, since he'd paid Howard for the option rights and therefore owned the license to the play for the duration of its Broadway run. Howard was forced to make the cuts, and Herman Levin refused to ever speak to him again.

The day after my visit to Washington, Howard and Ed demanded that Robert Whitehead fire Colin Blakely and replace him with me. I can just imagine the look on Whitehead's face. This time it was the producer's turn to refuse Howard's demand, and because no consensus seemed possible, Howard and Ed told Whitehead they were stepping aside and would have nothing to do with *Semmelweis* unless I took over the part. Since the play was doing horrible business at the Kennedy Center and since Colin Blakely's name had inspired not even a hint of a Broadway advance, Whitehead put up the closing notice the next day, and *Semmelweis* shut down three weeks into its out-of-town run. Under the aegis of artistic principle, Howard Sackler (with Ed Sherin lapping at his heels) put a cast of more than thirty actors out of work on the vague promise that another producer, Terry Allen Kramer, was going to come to their rescue and remount the production the way Howard and Ed wanted to present it.

Even before the dust settled I was asked to see Howard's agent, Billy Barnes—the same Billy Barnes who had warned me to get my name on a contract. We were to powwow over plans to remount the play with me starring in it. Patricia Routledge, the excellent English actress who had replaced Kim Hunter (Kim had refused to continue with the play after they sacked me), scampered back to England immediately after the show folded. Plans were to have Kim return to the cast as soon we went back into rehearsal. Are you following me so far?

At Barnes's spacious ICM office I was greeted by Ed Sherin, whom I hadn't seen since our dinner near the Saw Mill River Parkway. From that day on the sight of Sherin filled me with sadness as well as nausea. It's distressing to mourn a friendship when you're completely alert to a former friend's bullshit. But even the skepticism I brought to this meeting couldn't prepare me for the *chutzpah* I'd encounter. Ed, in his accustomed physical manner, greeted me with a huge bear hug and invited me to take a seat in the most unprepossessing chair in the room. Billy Barnes sat behind his desk. Surprisingly, Howard was absent.

"I can only imagine the incalculable pain you have experienced these past few months," Ed began, "because I know the pain I've experienced myself." He was stalking around the room in confident-director mode. Because the two of us had once been close, they must have decided that Ed should be the one to welcome me back.

"There's been quite a stink since the closing of the play," he said sorrowfully. "We plan to begin rehearsals seven weeks from the official closing of the Washington run. I'm terribly excited, because we're finally going to produce the play the way it should have been produced in the first place." Ed put his large hands together and sat on the edge of Billy Barnes's cluttered desk.

"We're going to structure this thing so that everyone in the cast receives a small share of the profits. It's a truly, truly revolutionary concept, and in exchange for all of us being partners, everyone is going to work for minimum."

"You want me to work for minimum?" I asked him. "Do you remember when you called me up last week and asked me if I was interested in coming back to the show? Do you remember what I told you? I said I would consider it if the money was right. Do you remember my saying that?"

"My friend," he said, leaning toward me with the patience of a kindly guardian. "You have no idea what professional jeopardy Howard and I have put ourselves in by walking away from that Washington run. The situation today is completely different than what it was two weeks ago."

I glanced over at Billy Barnes. My onetime defender stood arms folded and poker-faced. (It couldn't have been easy being Howard Sackler's agent.)

"Ed," I said, trying not to appear too emotional. It occurred to me that these boys most have spent their formative years burning flies to death with a magnifying glass. "I'm embarrassed to say that because I did so much research on Colin Blakely to keep my legal fees down, I probably know more about Colin Blakely than he knows about himself. I am also fully aware of what he was paid. Colin Blakely's salary for failing in the part was two thousand, five hundred dollars a week. If you want me to play Semmelweis, you will pay me two thousand, five hundred and one dollars a week. That's it! That's the end of the negotiation."

A pained expression spread across Ed's face. I could see that some part of him actually believed I was going to embrace his revolutionary Buffalo to Broadway/Favored Nations pay scale.

"Howard will never agree to that," he said. Whereupon I burst into hysterical laughter.

"Can I ask you a personal question?" he said as I struggled into my coat. "Do you actually hunger to play the role of Semmelweis?"

"That's a good question," I said, halfway out the door. "Because if I did agree to do the play, I'd have to dedicate myself to making it a success, and between you and me, I'm not certain I want this play to be a success. Does that answer your question?"

That night I got a call from Jane Alexander, who I hadn't spoken to since that fateful afternoon at Sardi's.

"Lewis!" she said. Her voice bristled with impatience, as if this was a continuation of a long conversation. "Do you want to play the part of Semmelweis?"

"As I told your husband, Jane, I'm not at all certain that I do. But not to worry! The discussion this afternoon was strictly about money."

"Do you know where I'm calling from?" she whispered. "I'm on the set of *Kramer vs. Kramer*. I snuck away because I just heard that if you don't accept their offer, Howard is ready to move on and offer the part to Dustin Hoffman."

Of all the cheap, underhanded betrayals, this was the most revolting.

"Jane, I'm begging you. Please convey to the boys that they should definitely hire Dustin Hoffman. If I played the part it might possibly win a Pulitzer Prize and run a maximum of six months—after all, it's a story about decomposing matter in women's vaginas. But if Dustin Hoffman plays the part, it would run for as long as he chooses to be associated with it. And Jane, I want you to know how deeply touched I am by your personal concern."

I found no reason to speak to her for another twenty-five years.

Chapter 31

The Terry Allen Kramer production of *Semmelweis* never came to be. The stink was indeed huge, and for a while the principals dispersed and the offstage drama became as dead as the play itself. The relief of being released from so ghastly an obsession was undermined by a sense of defeat. Defeat also compromised my marriage. I no longer felt compelled to honor my wife, and although I pretty much stuck close to home a pervasive anger soured the air, and I began to fixate on women who made their way through life by earning a living.

Soon it would be time to pick out a school for Diana, and Kathy was having none of the public kind. Diana would be attending one of those expensive private schools along the lines of Brearley or Dalton, and if I couldn't afford it, Kathy was content to ask her mother to pay for it. This was the first real philosophical disagreement in our marriage, one that was exacerbated by our disillusionment with each other.

I remember a Saturday afternoon at a Central Park playground when a guy came over to Kathy and introduced himself as an old classmate of hers from Beverly Hills High. "I'd like you to meet my husband, Lewis Stadlen," she said to him. "Lewis is a relatively successful actor." A relatively successful actor, am I? The bloom was definitely off the pussy willows.

If I had gained anything from the *Semmelweis* experience, it should have been a healthy respect for the dispensation of ghosts. Colin Blakely's job was made impossible because he was being crowded out of the picture by another performer's interpretation. Something unholy had transpired, and whether Ed or Howard would admit it to themselves, replacing me lessened their ability to communicate with my successor. In such a difficult role, you need all the confidence you can muster. What hung in the air was the fact of comparison. Nothing Blakely accomplished could stand on its own terms. My voice, my mannerisms, my finished performance—whether it was good, bad, or indifferent—denied Blakely a clean start. Everything about his performance differed from my own, and in the end he had chosen the opposite of a performance he had never seen but almost everyone else associated with the production had.

You can fuck a guy over because it makes you feel powerful, but in this instance an innocent paid the price just trying to figure out how to do the work. It's amazing how often this misstep is repeated in the theater. Those willing to lend their artistry to a project that pays little or nothing are more often than not cast aside and denied the opportunity to share in the emotional rewards of the finished product.

With private school tuition looming and my fiscal integrity about to be tested, I was approached by a director named Bud who wanted to cast me as Ali Hakim, the Persian peddler in a road company of *Oklahoma!* The plan was to tour it for a year before opening on Broadway the next season.

"Here's the potential problem," Bud said. "That cantankerous old bitch Agnes de Mille is restaging her original choreography and has final casting approval. I've got to get you past her." Cantankerous old bitch? The opportunity to work with Agnes de Mille was reason enough to suffer the usual show business humiliations. I would crawl a country mile for an Agnes de Mille.

"Before the audition," Bud told me on the phone, "I want to rehearse you and Will Parker and Ado Annie so we can figure out how to play the scenes in front of Agnes."

Terrific! The role of Ali Hakim, the old Jewish bullshit artist from the Lower East Side, was just what I needed to cleanse my palate after *Semmelweis*. Playing Ali Hakim was not brain surgery. *Oklahoma!* was the granddaddy of all modern musicals. Every show that followed it borrowed something from its formula. De Mille's Dream Ballet had been an evolution in the musical comedy form. The show was basically foolproof. All you had to do was open your eyes and breathe, and Rodgers and Hammerstein's magnificent score would carry you away.

I awoke the day of my audition confident and in good cheer. I believed I had the characterization down. The role had been played a thousand times before, and the laughs were as predictable as rain. An hour before the audition Bud had me read three scenes with David Eric and Maureen Moore.

"What you just did was very amusing," Bud said to me after we'd finished, "but completely wrong."

"Completely wrong?" I thought I had a perfect handle on the role.

"Yes, completely wrong. You're playing Ali Hakim as if he were Jewish."

In the past year I may have left a quarter of my brain on the altar of High Art, but I still had faith in the three-quarters that was left.

"He *is* Jewish," I said resolutely.

"No, he's Persian. It says so in the script at least ten times. It says he's a Persian peddler."

"I understand, but that's the funny part. He calls himself a Persian peddler because he's in the middle of Oklahoma. If they believed he was a Jew from Delancey Street they might tar and feather him."

"No, he's Persian," Bud insisted.

This reminded me of my conversation with Victor French as he described his theory of stage territory. "But what if the director doesn't want you to go where you want to go?" I remember asking him. "You go there anyway," he'd said. "In a few days he'll realize you're doing him a big favor."

"Bud," I said plaintively, "the role was originated by Joseph Buloff. I believe *Oklahoma!* was his English-speaking debut. He and his wife were big stars in the Yiddish theater."

"Lewis, you can't play a Persian peddler with a Jewish accent."

"What would you like me to do?" I asked him, gazing at my watch. "You want me to play him with an Iranian accent? I don't know how to do an Iranian accent. Trust me, Bud. The guy has always been played Jewish."

"No, he's supposed to be Persian."

Bud was presenting me with a real dilemma, insisting that I contradict my basic instinct. In five minutes I'd be facing Agnes de Mille, and whether or not it was in the cards for me to play the role, an actor can't contradict his instincts. Many a performance has been destroyed by a director who insists you play the part his way instead of the way you know is right. What happens is that after you attempt to meet him halfway you wind up playing the role no way. I don't mean to suggest that I'm immune to a director's input; in fact the opposite is true. It's a privilege to work with someone gifted. (See Sidney Lumet or Jerry Zaks.) Actors are grateful for all the help they can get. But when you're told you should be interpreting a character one hundred and eighty degrees from the way your gut is telling you he should be played, in most cases you're dealing with an insecure director. That's why whenever my agent calls to tell me about a project, my first question is Who's the director?

Agnes de Mille had recently suffered a stroke, and half her body was paralyzed. I entered the rehearsal room at the end of a line of actors waiting to audition. Agnes was one of many people in the room. Several people ahead of me had already met with her silent disapproval. It's amazing how many actors cannot comprehend the style of a piece. Several people that day had chosen to audition for *Oklahoma!* singing what amounted to rock and roll. Agnes was not amused. This was 1970s, and today the problem has increased tenfold. As the sense of history recedes, society seems to be evolving at the expense of every achievement that has preceded it. When it comes to live theater, there couldn't be a more misguided assumption.

When it was my turn, I took my place in the center of the room and looked the old girl over. Agnes was so haughty, with a glorious beak of an old woman's nose. She was obviously opinionated and so scarred from a lifetime of fighting the good fight that a glow of redemption surrounded her. Occupying a different level from the rest of us, she had done more in her life than oversee hits: she had *innovated*, and no matter how abrasive she could be, she always communicated honestly, affected less by her ego than by an obsession to get things right.

I knew immediately that I had no choice but to give my Ali Hakim a thick Yiddish accent. Halfway through my audition, Agnes bellowed, "Who the hell is he? He's good!"

I got the job.

During rehearsals, whenever I didn't have to be with the actors, I'd race into the studio where Agnes was directing the dancers. Most of them had extensive backgrounds in ballet. Agnes sat in a wheelchair while her choreography was taught and demonstrated by her longtime assistant, Gemzie DeLapp, who had been a lead dancer in many of her shows and ballets. For hours at a time I sat behind Agnes listening to her descriptions of how her work should be danced. She was brilliant at communicating the psychology behind each movement. Having invented her own vocabulary for dance, her economy of language was impeccable. In one room the actors were being led by a well-meaning fellow whose obligation was to put the show on its feet. What Agnes did was make it fly.

The first act of *Oklahoma!* ends with her historic Dream Ballet. In one segment four postcard girls, who are actually prostitutes, take center stage, their left hands provocatively placed on their hips. The movement connotes pure sexual enticement, but the girls dancing the roles were innocently pristine. Agnes stopped them.

"Just remember, girls," she said, slightly slurring her words, "this is the dream of a very good girl. And no one has a dirtier mind than a very good girl." Instantly the girls were transformed, their centers of gravity descending to their groins. Agnes, darling, I love you!

Shortly after the original *Oklahoma!* opened on Broadway in 1943, Agnes was walking down the street when she met a friend who asked how it felt to have choreographed the greatest sensation in Broadway history. Agnes replied that she hadn't realized it was the greatest sensation, but after leaving her friend she headed straight for the offices of the Theatre Guild, where she had a chat with the head man, Lawrence Langner. Agnes was making fifty dollars a week, and she told Langner that since she believed her contribution to *Oklahoma!*'s success was substantial and since it was selling out every week, she thought she deserved a raise.

"What kind of a raise are we talking about?" Langner inquired.

"I think seventy-five dollars a week would be fair," she said. Langner shook his head a few times before casting his eyes to the heavens.

"No," he said, "I could never justify that large a raise to my investors."

Within months Agnes de Mille had organized the Society of Stage Directors and Choreographers. Never again would a choreographer have to beg a producer for a handout, and all because Langner assumed he was sitting across the desk from just another cowed minion. I'm not casting aspersions on Lawrence Langner. The only way progress is made in this world is when the unexpected happens and someone like Agnes fights back. There is little doubt in my mind that without theatrical unions, producers would demand that performers pay for the privilege of being in show business. I can see both sides of the argument. Everyone has the right to fight for what they believe is in their own best interest. What has always amazed me is that if theatrical producers simply offered actors more than they expected (like Manny Azenberg) but less than they actually needed, most negotiations would conclude quickly and satisfactorily for both sides. Or maybe not. A lot of people suspect generosity to be a ploy. This goes back to Stella Adler's metaphor about those who recognize the glass for what it cost, while others recognize the glass for its esthetic value. Each day is another battle, and I've always greatly admired those artists willing to fight for the money. If we don't take some part of it for ourselves, the other side will make a religion out of it and pray to it.

Our production of *Oklahoma!* opened at the Jackie Gleason Theater in Miami Beach. What I discovered playing Ali Hakim was that I could take the curse off playing asshole roles by imbuing characters with sexual energy. As television has swallowed up the industry, the relationship between the leading and supporting player has become more linear, compared, say, to the way a Frank Morgan related to a Jimmy Stewart or a Walter Brennan to a John Wayne. Too often these days the character actor's job is to be insulted by the lead. He's the jerk you love to hate. There are few nuances, few opportunities to play, for example, a warm-hearted, slightly tyrannical man who is hurting and confused because the wife he adores is cheating on him. Television comedy rarely allows itself the time to explore the complexity of the human condition; it's too busy putting on simpleminded little shows to sell the products that subsidize it. So from a contemporary actor's point of view, the choice often comes down to whether you're going to take the money and run with a cardboard creation or hold out for a real human being who isn't going to wind up with the girl.

Ali Hakim was the first time I decided to impose an element of sexual voraciousness on a character who doesn't have to be played that way. It was my attempt to dignify the cosmetically unprepossessing people of this world, of whom I am definitely one. Outside the States, not everybody looks like Brad Pitt. They have large noses and receding chins, but what they have in common with the rest of mankind is that they all want to get laid. A libidinous person is interesting to an audience and fun to play.

Here's an example of how great a musical comedy *Oklahoma!* is if you don't screw it up. This happened at our first performance in Miami in front of a paying audience. At the very end of the show, Ali Hakim, who's been flirting shamelessly with Ado Annie throughout the play, returns to town with his new wife, a local girl named Giggling Gertie. (It was a shotgun wedding.) While Ali is talking to Will Parker, who has hooked up with Ado Annie, a fight breaks out between Gertie and a few of the other girls. As soon as the girls begin to shriek and holler, Will starts toward them to break up the fight.

"What are you doing?" asks Ali.

"I'm gonna make sure those girls don't kill your wife," says Will.

Heading into the home stretch of my first performance, for a nanosecond my mind went completely blank. At the very last moment the line came back to me, and I said it without the slightest intonation: "Mind your own damn business!" I said.

I've gotten many big laughs during my career, but none as thunderous as that one. The irony is that I was simply saying the line in self-defense. The audience screamed because it was a laugh built for the ages. Just don't try to deconstruct *Oklahoma!*'s meaning and Oscar Hammerstein's brilliance will brighten your world.

Chapter 32

When I was young I visualized myself primarily as a man of the theater, although I thought I'd make a handful of movies—of course memorable ones—and an occasional foray into television, where I'd appear as a recurring guest on *The Dean Martin Show*. I chose to fantasize about singing medleys with Dean, both of us in tuxedos, because he was the one person of his breed who appealed to my mother. She appreciated his public image as a womanizing drunk because she believed he was being honest. This reinforced her conviction that all male entertainers were irresponsible, and Martin's comic lewdness allowed her to let down her guard just enough to be charmed. My mother and I watched *The Dean Martin Show* religiously, so I decided if I were ever to lower my standards and appear on television, singing love songs with Dean Martin in black tie would meet with her approval. (My mother's distaste for actors mirrored the attitudes of producers. Producers feel comfortable with the occasional nut job who specializes in making impossible demands because it confirms their belief that all actors are overgrown, egocentric children. If every actor is a potential pain in the ass, then to exploit them and refuse to take them seriously is actually an altruistic act.)

My fantasy appearances on *The Dean Martin Show* notwithstanding, television had never been a major influence on my imagination. When I was a kid I would sit with my mother and watch *Father Knows Best*, *The Adventures of Dobie Gillis*, *Ben Casey* and *Stoney Burke*. I also adored *Amos 'n' Andy*, which I watched alone. Twenty-five years later I would make it a point to spend Saturdays watching *The Bob Newhart* and *Mary Tyler Moore Shows,* and I was also a fan of *Buffalo Bill,* a mean-spirited, short-lived sitcom. Most of what I watched on television was news and sports. Perhaps because my father had made his initial success in it, I never aspired to be on television.

Before I began touring in *Oklahoma!,* I had arranged to take my family to Jamaica for a vacation. A few days before we were to leave I got a call from my newest agent, Susan Smith, who spent most of her time in Los Angeles and was high powered and well connected.

"You have to cancel your vacation," she said. "The creators of *The Mary Tyler Moore Show* are coming to New York and I've set up an audition for you for their new series, *Taxi.* It's the finest pilot script I've ever read. This show is going to make everyone connected with it a star."

Against my better judgment I canceled my trip and met with a fellow who began my interview by telling me he had been born and raised in New York but was now thoroughly revolted by the state of decrepitude the city had fallen into. "Every time I look out the window of my hotel and see the ugliness of this city I cannot believe that I lived here as long as I did," he said moments before my audition. I don't remember exactly what I said in response, but I'm pretty sure I didn't take his denigration of my hometown lying down, especially after swallowing the price of three round-trip tickets to Jamaica. What I do remember was that I gave an excellent audition.

When I hadn't heard anything after a week, I called Susan Smith.

"*Leeew-isss,*" she said, drawing out my name as if it was an unwelcome smell wafting in from the next apartment. I seem to have a first name that speaks volumes when someone wants to impress on me that I've behaved irresponsibly. The name *Lewis* comes off the tongue like Don't step in that sinkhole! or, Don't trip over that thing lying in the street! or, Do you really want to buy that before I wrap it up?

"*Lewis,*" she said. "Those of us who know you—really know you—understand that you're a sensitive, talented, and passionate human being. But certain people who meet you for the first time—" this was obviously painful for her to say, "certain people find you shockingly abrasive!"

"Susan, darling, what did they think of my audition?"

"They liked your talent," she continued. "They just didn't like you."

Now, this business is difficult enough without your agent telling you you've flunked the *Entertainment Tonight* likability contest. Hadn't anybody heard of Wallace Beery or Frank Faye? This is a criticism that stings, especially when the messenger is implying that this is not a one-time occurrence. (I tell you this unpleasant truth to prevent you from being unlikable in the future!)

What I really wanted to do was fire Susan Smith on the spot, but since nobody wants to hear that they're sickening to others, what it did was make me wish for another opportunity to impress on some television sitcom executive that I was really a nice, shockingly unabrasive New York kind of guy. All of a sudden being an actor on a television sitcom had a certain allure.

Before I left to do *Oklahoma!* (where I should have stayed), I put myself on tape for another television pilot entitled *Benson,* a spinoff of the sitcom *Soap.* In that show Benson was a manservant in the household of a wildly dysfunctional family. Its TV creators now wanted to spin off the character, setting their show in the governor's mansion of some fictitious state and making the manservant the show's anchor. When I did a taped audition in New York I was wearing a mustache, and I was told I hadn't gotten the job because I was too much like Groucho Marx.

A couple of months later, while vacationing in Hawaii, a harried Susan Smith called to say they'd shot the pilot but had fired the actor who'd gotten the role I'd auditioned for. Could I fly back to Los Angeles and re-audition for the same role? I agreed, only this time I was savvy enough to shave off my mustache.

"It's the finest pilot script I've ever read," said Susan. "You must get this part. Besides, being an annuity, it'll allow you to come back to Broadway and be cast in any part you want." Anton Chekhov, here I come!

The next day I was whisked into the offices of Witt-Thomas Productions, and this time they loved my audition. (Groucho who?) What I was beginning to figure out was that I had walked into a situation where Tony Thomas (son of my least favorite comedian, Danny Thomas) and Paul Younger Witt (Wittstein, to those who knew him at Forest Hills High) were fighting a political battle with an ABC executive. They were furious that a certain network suit had the power to veto their casting choices. After my audition I was immediately dragged over to Studio City, where they used me as a pretext to challenge the authority of some young woman (an embryo in a suit) who was either going to approve or reject me. I'd become the chum in their battle for casting supremacy. Later that afternoon Susan called with the news that I'd been approved by the network. Like it or not, I was now a member of the cast of *Benson.*

I stayed on tour in *Oklahoma!* for a mere five weeks and then left the Dream Ballet to become a weekly guest in the homes of Mr. and Mrs. America. Who needed the theater anyway, after the way they'd treated me with *Semmelweis*? Of course, I couldn't admit to myself that I was signing a seven-year contract to appear on a TV sitcom. Certainly not! I convinced myself that I was appearing in a half-hour modern dress version of *Volpone*, and I was playing the role of Mosca.

Having driven the Volvo cross-country with my good friend Michael Scott, I was led into a screening room at the Witt-Thomas offices and shown the pilot episode of *Benson*. When the lights came up I was asked my opinion.

"I think it's the funniest TV pilot I've ever seen," I said.

Nothing in my life had prepared me for what I was about to experience. Many years later I spent a couple of weeks in Czechoslovakia, and as much as I adored the place, I couldn't believe the mindset of people who were forced to live under Communism. Their so-called rule of law was imposed on them by the Russians, who actually walked around in long black leather coats (KGB) to advertise their presence. The majority of Czechs found them terrifying and at the same time patently absurd. The nightly news showed the politicians of this one-party system raising their hands in zombielike approval or disapproval of some measure handed down by those who had sold their souls for luxuries provided by the state. The politics of Hollywood weren't that different. As disappointing as it can be, at least the theater isn't predicated on our drinking the Kool Aid of bureaucratic conformity. (That was still a few decades away.)

I don't excuse myself for toeing the party line after seeing the *Benson* pilot. If I screened it for a lifetime, I wouldn't laugh once. Something in the air that day made me lie. Or, to quote a disgruntled actress who got tired of listening to me complain, "You know, for a guy with a lot of integrity, you sell out a lot."

When an actor signs on to do a sitcom, he's reacting to the voice inside his head that's begging him to do the sensible thing. If some star-crossed Dallas multimillionaire invites the entire cast of a musical comedy out for a midnight supper in hopes of enticing a long-legged chorus girl to sleep with him, you're not going to refuse the invitation out of moral pique. You're going to eat and drink his free booze and have a good time and hope he gets lucky. Signing a seven-year contract is a more serious proposition, not all that different from being confronted in an alley by a masked stranger who asks you to accept more money than you've ever dreamed of making in exchange for shutting your mouth for the next seven years. It's a totalitarian ethic.

The lead in *Benson* was Robert Guillaume, a longtime theater veteran who had distinguished himself mostly in musicals. He had a marvelous singing voice of near operatic quality, and as a middle-aged black man in 1979, he had been pushed around plenty. I had seen him perform as Nathan Detroit in a rather ridiculous all-black version of *Guys and Dolls*. Bob's style of comedy was to spin his sardonic dialogue in a falling register. He'd scored in *Soap* by delivering wisecracks sotto voce, the joke being that the white family he worked for couldn't hear him. This premise was now moved into the political arena, where he was the only intelligent member of a white household that included an addled governor, played by another theater veteran, James Noble; his eight-year-old daughter, played by Missy Gold; a German cook, played by the marvelous Inga Swenson, who for two seasons had become a legitimate musical comedy star on Broadway (a lyric soprano, her career was derailed by the ascendance of the rock musical, specifically *Hair*); the governor's secretary, played by Carolyn MacWilliams, a sexy, offbeat comedian; and, as Taylor, the anal-retentive assistant to the governor who is always wrong, yours truly.

The theater is an actor's medium. Once that curtain goes up you're on your own. The director shows up at intervals during the run, but the responsibility for maintaining a performance belongs to the actor. The motion picture industry is a director's medium. Along with an editor, the director translates the actor's performance onto the screen. The film director sets the style and pace of the storytelling.

A television situation comedy is a producer's medium. The director is merely a glorified stage manager who decides, in a six-camera setup like the one we had on *Benson,* which camera photographs which action. He rarely discusses motivation with the actors, who after the first few episodes are playing fairly standard types. It's the producer who has daily story conferences with the writers and then returns to the set to watch run-throughs, direct the actors, and structure the action. In the case of *Benson,* Tony Thomas and Paul Younger Witt, having spent much time and energy convincing the networks that they were infallible sitcom geniuses, brought to the set a narcotic-induced arrogance not unlike that of

James Cagney's character Cody Jarrett in the film *White Heat*. (Top of the world, Ma!) With wagonloads of money rolling in, they had reinvented themselves as professors of comedy.

The day I arrived in Los Angeles I was invited to the home of an actor I'd directed five years before in a failed Off Broadway play. He'd become rich writing situation comedies, and all his guests that evening were transplanted New Yorkers who were also making tons of money in the sitcom field after years of struggling in the New York theater. Having convinced myself that I wasn't really in Los Angeles, I listened in horror as one married couple after another recited the same litany about how New York was a bastion of cultural elitists and how now, as loyal Angelenos, they were willing ("Hey, those Lakers aren't too shabby. Ask Jack") to root for the local teams. There were also torturous discussions of what automobiles they were driving and how they were desperately looking to purchase more expensive models. Every once in a while one of the transplanted moms would drop her infant into a baby swing before inhaling a couple of lines of nose powder. It took me quite a while to realize that no one was actually pulling my leg. It seemed like a comedy sketch on materialism. I remember leaving the party dispirited.

As my day-to-day commitment to *Benson* stretched into weeks, I became overwhelmed by what seemed the dishonest atmosphere surrounding the show. The more experienced actors, like Jimmy Noble and Inga Swenson, tried to impress on me how fortunate we all were to have landed the gig. Both had struggled mightily, and they were not going to make a federal case over the lies bandied around the table in order to placate the egos of our sociopathic producers. "We're thrilled that we're twenty-seventh in the ratings instead of being in the top ten," was Paul's refrain in the show's opening weeks. "If you're in the top ten there's no place to go but down. We're building slowly, just the way we planned it from the beginning."

Jimmy and Inga let most of it roll off their backs—they had kids to put through college—while I let it drive me crazy. As a matter of fact, everything about Los Angeles was driving me crazy. I couldn't bear being invited to some transplanted actor's apartment to celebrate a television performance that consisted of him running down an alley and being shot.

"What did you think?" I was asked by this perfectly sweet fellow over a beer and salsa chips.

"You were wonderful. Totally believable," I told him.

"I think it'll make an excellent addition to my reel. Put a fire under my agent."

"Absolutely."

"It's the first acting I've done in the nine months since I've been out here."

"No kidding?"

"Yeah. But this is the beginning of something special. I could feel the positive endorphins on the set."

Then there was the dinner party at a neighbor's newly acquired cheesebox house at the top of Bel Air. They'd bought what looked to be a mobile home for more than four hundred thousand dollars.

"What we really love about the place is that we're above the smog line."

"You don't get any smog up here?" I said.

"No. We look down on the smog."

That evening, as we returned to our hideous hacienda of unpainted cinder blocks (sale price a million two), Kathy asked me why I felt compelled to challenge the illusions of people who believed their new home was worth four hundred thousand dollars.

"Why not spend two hundred thousand dollars on a spoon?" I said.

"If that's what the market will bear, why not? People spend hundreds of thousands of dollars on a painted egg. Why must you point out the absurdity of everything people believe around here?"

"Because when you're being told a pack of lies about everything from the smog line to the price of rice in China, it's the responsible thing to set the record straight."

"No it's not. It's the responsible thing to leave well enough alone. I don't see you giving back any money. You made a decision to be on *Benson*, now live with it."

A couple of weeks later Kathy told me she was pregnant with our second child.

My greatest fear was that the show would run for seven years and I'd be forever typecast as Taylor the imbecile. It never occurred to me that being typecast was the whole point of being on a television series. Why worry about defining yourself as one thing when you're in an industry that only feels comfortable with everything defined? It's the actor who has the ability to transform himself who's going to have a difficult time. Create the illusion that you're a pilot for Iberian Airlines and people are going to believe you're a pilot for Iberian Airlines. Paul Muni went from *Scarface* to *Louis Pasteur* to *The Good Earth* to *Juarez*, but that kind of acting career is extremely rare. Most American actors build solid careers on a single personality trait. Frank Morgan, one of my idols, played a subtle variation of himself for his entire career, and I wanted to be just like him. If I had to play an archetype, I didn't want it to be the one I played on *Benson*.

Around Thanksgiving, the eight-year-old Missy Gold began to show signs of a nervous breakdown. Her parents were pressuring her because they were being pressured by the producers, who didn't feel she was adorable enough to meet their demanding standards. Apparently, being twenty-seventh in the ratings wasn't the bonanza it was initially thought to be. Every Friday morning, when we sat down to read the new episode, the poor kid would be so anxious she couldn't read her lines. The simplest words confused her, and we'd all sit by helplessly as she reacted to her parents' scorn. It's no easy trick having your eight-year-old daughter earn your living for you. If there'd been a show trial, Missy Gold would have been the first member of the cast to confess.

Two weeks before Christmas, Paul Younger Witt showed up before our Friday table reading to make an important announcement. *Benson*'s weekly competition was a new incarnation of the old outer space classic *Flash Gordon* and, more threateningly, the final season of the fabulously successful *Waltons* series. Though we were a bit of a disappointment to our advertisers and the network, *Benson* was regularly winning its time slot, with the exception of certain holiday episodes of *The Waltons*.

You can't really appreciate the emphasis put on the Nielsen ratings unless you're in the midst of shooting a television series. The Nielsens are a scam created by the networks to enhance advertising revenues. In the early days of television, individual shows had individual sponsors: Milton Berle's show was *The Texaco Star Theater;* Bulova was the sole advertiser for the evening news. Then some marketing genius came up with the idea of having advertisers pay sponsorship fees based on the popularity of the program they bought time on, and the Nielsen rating system was invented to measure viewership. These ratings were highly unscientific, but after a while the system became so entrenched that the networks became the victims of their own idea. Suddenly the little monster let loose in the cellar had more influence than the network's CEO.

Everyone connected with a television series is advised to pay close attention to the Nielsen ratings in order to gauge how long they'll be employed.

"This week," said Paul Younger Witt, "we'll be up against a ratings juggernaut on NBC. I'm talking about *Rudolph the fucking Rednosed Reindeer!* Every Christmas they swoop down and destroy everything in their path. But this year—we're going to beat their fucking asses!" And with that he left the studio.

"No, we're not," I said as soon as he was out of earshot.

"What do you mean we're not?" said Bob Guillaume.

"I say we're not going to beat *Rudolph the fucking Rednosed Reindeer* in the ratings," I said.

"Why are you are so damned negative?" Bob responded. "Why would you contemplate saying a thing like that?"

"Because he's a big liar," I said. "The idea that he took the time to announce that we were going to beat *Rudolph the Rednosed Reindeer* means that we aren't."

Bob was very angry with me because a couple of weeks before I had implored him to use his influence to alter a scene in which they had him eating a piece of watermelon.

"You're the star of the show, Bob. Tell them you don't want to eat a piece of watermelon."

"What's wrong with eating watermelon?"

"What's wrong with it? It's the worst kind of racist stereotype."

"Don't talk to me about racism. You don't know shit about racism," he told me. "It's a joke. It's satire."

"Well, if it's satire it sure is *unclever* satire. You mean to tell me they can't come up with anything better than a black man eating a piece of watermelon?"

"It's satire, goddamn it!" And that was the end of that.

Now Bob was really exercised about this *Rudolph the Rednosed Reindeer* thing, and I *was* being a wiseass, but I couldn't quite forgive myself for falling into a rabbit hole.

"I'll make you a twenty-dollar bet that we beat the fuck out of *Rudolph the Rednosed Reindeer*," Bob said in front of everyone associated with *Benson*.

"You got it," I told him.

There are two separate Nielsen ratings. The first are the overnights, which are the demographics that come in from major cities like New York, Los Angeles, Chicago, San Francisco, and so on, and then there are the full Nielsen ratings, released a few days later, which report the viewership of the entire country. *Benson* was considered an urban comedy with a large black following, so we had to defeat our competition in the overnights by at least 15 points in order to emerge the winner when the ratings from Nebraska came in. It's like the Democrats having to win big in the cities in order to overcome a large Republican rural vote.

The day after our Thursday night airing, I walked over to the table with the coffee and doughnuts and picked up the printed overnight results. *Benson* had beat *Rudolph* by only 13 points. I figured my wager was safe, but when I got to the studio after the weekend Bob was waiting for me with a huge grin on his face.

"Can we all gather around, please?" he said to the entire cast. "Did you or did you not say that we wouldn't beat *Rudolph the fucking Rednosed Reindeer* in the ratings?"

"I said we wouldn't."

"Well, hand over your twenty bucks, because we beat their asses!"

"Really?" I said.

"Absolutely!" Then we began to rehearse.

If this had been anyplace in the country other than Los Angeles, there would have been no doubt in my mind that when a person says he won a bet, he won a bet. But for a full half hour it nagged at me that all I had to do was walk over to the table with the coffee and doughnuts and check the Nielsens for myself. I only waited as long as I did because I was ashamed to be entertaining such cynical thoughts, but finally my hatred for my job got the best of me, and I made my way over to the table to check out the results for myself.

We had lost to *Rudolph* by close to two rating points. It was almost the final straw. When I felt it was appropriate, I took Bob aside and, masking my outrage as best I could, inquired why he had assembled the entire cast to announce something that was patently false.

"You really don't get it," he said, looking me over with utter contempt. "*Rudolph the Rednosed Reindeer* is a ratings monster. Year after year it's mowed down everything in its path. The fact that we came so close to beating them means we actually won!"

I'd heard a few beauts since my Volvo with the broken fan belt had huffed its way over the Colorado Rockies, but aside from the conventional L.A. wisdom that houses built on stilts above the Hollywood Hills were the safest place to be during an earthquake, this one was making my head spasm.

"Bob," I said, trying to control myself, "nobody's going to tell me that coming in second is coming in first and coming in first is coming in second. Now give me my forty dollars!"

And that's the way it was, moving west!

"Get me the hell out of here," I said to Susan Smith.

"What are you talking about? The show's a hit."

"I hate it. I hate going to work in the morning, and I'm telling you it'll take an elephant dragging me across the Rocky Mountains in chains before I come back for another season. How do I get out?"

"The way you get out is to take a meeting with Paul and Tony and explain to them how unhappy you are. Nobody wants an unhappy actor around."

"You're telling me that all I have to do is say I'm unhappy and they'll let me out of a seven-year contract?"

"That's usually the way it works."

I knew it would never happen that way. It wouldn't happen because it was beyond their comprehension that I would want to. Why would I want out, when there were a thousand actors in Hollywood salivating to take my place? They would see it as a ploy to extort money from them. It couldn't be that I didn't want to be on television: everybody in America wanted to be on television (and this was 1979). How could they believe I didn't want to be part of a show that more often than not ended with Bob Guillaume sitting little, nearly psychotic Missy Gold down beside him—at a safe distance, I might add; he was still a black man and she a little blond girl—to tell her that the reason she was feeling depressed was because she hadn't told her father the absolute truth. We must always tell the truth, because deception is the devil's tool.

A lawyer friend advised me that if I refused to go back to *Benson*, the producers could legally prohibit me from working anyplace else, which meant I wouldn't be able to do theater in New York. I considered starting a fictitious letter-writing campaign implying that my character was an insult to the Jewish people, but I realized that wouldn't work because these two guys would rise to my defense and fight all the harder to keep me on the show. (There's nothing more nauseating than a liberal Hollywood producer exploiting a social issue.) I would just have to bide my time.

Within the week, while we were doing one of our twenty-minute run-throughs, Paul, the director, Tony Thomas, and whoever had written the show that week were sitting in their canvas director's chairs taking voluminous notes, a long row of spit-polished Gucci loafers. At the end of every scene, Paul and Tony would critique our performances.

"That line we wrote for you, Lew," said Tony. "There are really only two ways of doing it. You could either play it like a complete asshole, or I suppose you could do it with some semblance of dignity."

"Aha," I said, nodding thoughtfully. "I understand, yes."

"Well, what way *are* you going to do it?" said Paul.

"I think I'll do it with some semblance of dignity," I told him.

Tony and Paul conferred. "We'd prefer you do it like a complete asshole."

"This is good," I said. "I'm glad we're delving into this area, because I have a pretty clear concept of what you would like my character to be. You want me to be the man you love to hate, like Ted Knight on the *Mary Tyler Moore Show*. The difference is, when Ted Knight comes on he does something actively insensitive, and everyone sees what a fool he is. But my character never does anything active. I walk into the governor's mansion and you have Benson say something like, 'The idiot has arrived!' I think that's a lot less clever than allowing me to do something idiotic myself."

I knew exactly what I was doing. I knew these guys would not look kindly on my venting an opinion in a public forum. I was certain they would conspire to show me up at the first possible opportunity, so I began a disingenuous form of playacting—which, considering the venue, seemed entirely appropriate.

At the next table reading, Tony Thomas turned up to see how I'd react to having Benson insult my character at every opportunity. ("How are you, pizza face?" was one of their more clever bons mots.) I was elated that they'd so heedlessly fallen into my trap. The rest of the cast sincerely sympathized with my situation, which made me feel I was betraying their confidence by pretending to grow more enraged with every clumsy insult. This was the moment to make my escape. All I had to do was embarrass Danny Thomas's son in front of everyone he employed, and that included the little blond girl and her parents. Just go for his throat, I told myself. Pretend you're having a brawl with someone you really care about.

"I thought I expressed myself rather cogently at the last note session," I began, feigning a kind of seething outrage. "But obviously, because you pay my salary, you think you can embarrass me in front of thirty million fucking people each week!"—some nonsense like that. It was all playacting, although I was legitimately close to having a nervous breakdown.

"I won't allow you to embarrass yourself any further," said Tony Thomas as he made his way off the soundstage.

"Fire me!" I told him. "I'm begging you! Fire my ass!"

I was instantly surrounded by well-meaning colleagues who wanted to know if I was all right. I hadn't the heart to tell them I'd never felt better.

About half an hour later Tony returned, and we took a walk around the grounds of the ABC studios. "We're going to give you what you want," he said, engaging in a bit of playacting himself. "At the end of the year we're going to let you out of your contract. But you're not going to get any money." This remark reminded me of the polite soldier at my draft physical telling me to accept the subway tokens. Here was my opportunity to express how morally aggrieved I actually was.

"I don't want your money," I snapped. Which was true. What I wanted was to go back to New York and stop pretending I was doing the smart thing when I knew in my heart I was doing the dumb thing.

There was to be one final episode in my serpentine journey through prime-time television. When I'd first arrived in Los Angeles, Susan Smith told me that the cast of *Benson* was scheduled to appear on the popular quiz show *Celebrity Family Feud.* East Coast sophisticate that I was, I immediately refused, until it was explained to me that for a day's work, I would receive a check for five grand. I allowed myself to be persuaded.

On the Sunday afternoon the show was taped, actors performing on various ABC shows were picked up and driven to the studio in individual stretch limos. Everything was stage-managed so the performers had to expend minimum effort. At the studio we would be treated to a large catered buffet, where one could gaze admiringly at actors who were pulling down huge salaries on shows like *Dallas, Knot's Landing,* and various situation comedies. The concept was that each cast was a family, competing against the others. Whoever won would receive a check for twenty thousand dollars made out to the charity of their choice. It was a harmless way to publicize your product on a lazy Sunday afternoon.

When we appeared on the show in early autumn, we were quickly defeated by the cast of *Dallas*, and I collected my paycheck and went home. Several weeks before the final episode of *Benson* was to be taped, the cast was asked to appear on *Family Feud* again. Conscious that my days of television affluence were coming to an end, this time I had few reservations about saying yes. The only rub was a mild case of self-contempt. The freshly made-up streetwalkers I drove past each day on Sunset Boulevard were at least working hard, looking sexy, and performing an invaluable service. What was I but a prime-time polluter? I felt complicit in the dumbing-down of America.

Two days before we were to reappear on *Family Feud*, Bob Guillaume called the cast together and derided us for not taking the competition on the show seriously enough.

"We just didn't concentrate the last time," he lectured. "We allowed those people from *Dallas* to whip our ass!"

"Are you fucking serious?" I asked him.

"You're damn right I'm serious. This time we'll be playing for sickle cell anemia, and I want everyone to hunker down and kick their butts!"

Bob's pep rally inspired me to head straight to our kindly hair stylist, who made a substantial living on the side supplying hallucinogens to the West Coast acting community. Angel dust, mescaline, airplane glue, whatever you wanted, he had it.

"I'd like to buy some marijuana," I said as he greased my hair.

"I've got just the thing. Have you ever smoked Maui Wowie? Awesome, man, but expensive."

"How much?"

"Eight hundred an ounce."

"Bring the mother on." I knew he was ripping me off, but what did it matter? It was dirty money anyhow.

That Sunday afternoon I settled into the leather seat in the *Family Feud* limo and removed a neatly wrapped reefer from my breast pocket. I rolled down the window and took a few discreet blasts off my eight-hundred-dollar purchase. By the time we idled past the Bel Air gate I was completely wasted. I was hallucinating, although somewhere inside my addled brain lurked the recognition that in an hour and a half I would be appearing as a celebrity contestant.

Donald O'Connor once told me that during ten years of sustained alcoholism, he had spent every waking moment faking sobriety. As my mental capacities faded into a hallucinogenic L.A. sunset, the possibility of winning the grand prize for sickle cell anemia appeared as remote as remembering my first name. I would do everything in my power to sublimate my desire to make love to a chicken, but first I had to figure out how to get out of the car. In the studio, Bob was exhorting the cast to win this one for all the black people who were leading desperate lives in the projects of South Chicago. I couldn't even see.

By some miracle I managed to fake my way through the first twenty minutes of the taping without drooling on my colleagues. Fortunately for me, every question asked by the show's host, Richard Dawson, could be answered after a group conference. It was easy to pretend I was huddling with the others before Bob volunteered the answers. My problem was that my brain was rapidly deteriorating into rice pudding, and the words being spoken were coming at me like a foreign language.

At some point in my stoned dementia I became faintly aware that *Benson* had been declared the winner and that a single member of our winning team was being asked to stand in the center of the garish quiz-show set and answer several questions.

"You do it," said Bob, shoving me toward Richard Dawson. "You're smart."

"No! Please, no!" I begged him, fighting my way back behind the podium. "I can't do it."

"What are you, nuts? Go out there and answer the questions," said Bob. And with one final shove I found myself standing in a circle of light beside Richard Dawson.

"Answer these questions within sixty seconds and *Benson* will win twenty thousand dollars for sickle cell anemia!" he announced, looking fairly medicated himself.

"Name a city famous for its restaurants," he said. This was a tough one but I did my best.

"Spinach," I answered.

"I said a city," he repeated.

"South America!"

"All right, we'll move on to the next question. What's the coldest season of the year?"

"Snow," I answered.

"Season?"

"January." By this time the audience had to believe I was doing one of the most original comedy acts in history.

"Next question. In what country do the citizens swim in subfreezing temperatures?"

"Coney Island" was my considered answer as the sixty seconds ran out. By this time the audience was in hysterics. I didn't have the courage to look over at Bob.

"Listen," said Dawson, grateful that something had happened to arouse him from his quiz-show torpor. "People were laughing so hard at his ridiculous answers that he couldn't hear the questions. For twenty thousand dollars—who's buried in Grant's Tomb?"

"Mister Grant?" I ventured.

"Grant is the correct answer!" crowed Dawson. Within seconds, my remaining viable brain cells evaporated beneath the glare of the overhead lights.

Three years later I got a check in the mail for five thousand dollars. My appearance on *Celebrity Family Feud* had been chosen for *Television's Most Famous Bloopers*.

Chapter 33

Burt Lancaster used to say that when he chose to do a movie, he did one for himself and one for the pope, meaning he chose one he believed in artistically and one commercial enough to allow him to do the next good one. If you're not a star, your best hope is to be cast in a project that can reasonably be defined as acting. Most of the time you're lending your presence to a story in need of nothing more than a body. In which case the body is yours.

In 1973 I had done the film *Serpico* for Sidney Lumet. Sidney is one of the truly gifted directors, always associated with projects of merit. He directs with the understanding that his work is to be both artistic and money-making. In 1981 he cast me in *The Verdict,* starring Paul Newman, who played a down-on-his-luck, alcoholic attorney hired to bring a medical negligence suit against a hospital run by the Catholic archdiocese. This was the first time in a while that my talents needed to be worthy of the material and not the other way around.

Sidney liked to cast me in roles in which I portrayed white-collar types who were morally vacuous. He liked the way I took the edge off the characters' corruption. In *Serpico* I played the deputy mayor of New York, who appears to put himself on the line for the title character (Al Pacino), but who later reveals himself to be more talk than action and eventually puts Frank Serpico in harm's way. In *The Verdict* I was cast as a prominent surgeon, Dr. Gruber, who alerts Paul Newman's character that his client has been turned into a vegetable by medical malfeasance and that if Newman decides to do the right thing and litigate, Gruber will serve as his chief witness. (Are you listening Ed Sherin?) Gruber turns out to be as corrupt as the next guy, and instead of testifying is bought off by the archdiocese and is never seen again. The role consisted of one terrific scene with Paul Newman that begins in the locker room of a hospital and continues down a flight of stairs and through a winding corridor. Gruber delivers his information to the attorney, Frank Galvin, before stepping into a Jaguar and peeling off into the night. He has 90 percent of the dialogue.

When we shot *Serpico*, Sidney filmed the scenes like segments on the evening news. There was a relentless this-is-happening-right-now-on-the-streets-of-New-York feeling. The two major scenes I had with Pacino were shot almost in real time, as if the camera were recording a critical,clandestine meeting. After a couple of takes we were done. *The Verdict* was rehearsed like a play, in a large studio on Broadway and Nineteenth Street. Every day the cast, which included James Mason, Charlotte Rampling, Jack Warden, Milo O'Shea, and many others, would run through the screenplay in sequence, a luxury unheard of for a movie.

Because my scene with Newman was to be an extended tracking shot, Sidney had the two of us rehearse it by walking at a furious pace around the perimeter of the studio. I was very excited to be working with Newman, whom I greatly admired as an actor but also related to as a fan. Sidney kept imploring me to treat him with disdain. "Don't wait for him to catch up to you. He's a drunk. You're an important man in a hurry." This was easier said than done, because I wanted to spend as much time making eye contact with Paul Newman as possible.

Then Sidney gave me an inspired piece of direction. A bad director speaks metaphorically: You're like a meteorite hurtling through space!— which, of course, is unplayable. Sidney said, "You're having an affair with a twenty-five-year-old intern who lives across the Charles River in Cambridge. You've got two and a half hours to get to her apartment, spend time with her, and get back to the hospital." Suddenly, I wasn't waiting around for Paul Newman. I was conveying my information with the utmost urgency, because Gruber had a hidden agenda. Add to the scenario that he's a married man and you have the element of corruption that makes Gruber an intriguing character. That is great direction.

I've for the most part been blessed in my professional opportunities. I've played the great Groucho Marx. After listening innumerable times as a child to the cast recording of *Candide*, I played the starring role in the successful revival. I was allowed to re-create David Burns's role of Senex in the Broadway revival of *A Funny Thing Happened on the Way to the Forum*. In these endeavors I've been lucky to be able to translate fond childhood memories into professional accomplishments.

When I was in my early teens my father brought home a 16-millimeter print of Ernst Lubitsch's wonderful World War Two comedy, *To Be or Not to Be*, starring Jack Benny and Carole Lombard. Everything about the film struck me as comic perfection. The story involves a Polish acting troupe's attempt to survive the Nazi occupation of Warsaw. Benny and Lombard played the Toras, the most famous acting couple in Poland. As in all of Lubitsch's films, a delicate undercurrent of hostility illuminates the battle of the sexes, with each character's foolishness demonstrating human folly. Even a Nazi SS captain, played brilliantly by Sig Rumon, possesses some ludicrous comic charm that allows us to settle back as an audience and forgive.

There was only one Ernst Lubitsch, the undisputed genius of the seriocomic, European-influenced American cinema. When he died, in his late fifties, two of his most successful protégés, Billy Wilder and William Wyler, were carrying his coffin to its final resting place. Wilder whispered to Wyler, "No more Lubitsch."

"Worse!" said Wyler. "No more Lubitsch pictures!"

For the only sustained period in my career I was making movies. *The Verdict* was followed by a ten-week shoot in Chicago for a film entitled *All the Sad Young Men*, later released as *Windy City*. In this one the story was completely restructured in the editing room and turned out to be dreadful. A few months later I was asked to audition in New York for a remake of *To Be or Not to Be*, to be produced and directed by another of my idols, Mel Brooks.

Perhaps idol is too strong a word. Let's just say I was enormously grateful to a person who, like Agnes de Mille, had invented his own unique vocabulary. Mel's comic argot had infiltrated the speech patterns of every Jewish actor of my generation. I could repeat from memory most of his dialogue from his first film, *The Producers*, as well as his *Two Thousand* and *Two Thousand and One Year Old Man* albums. Mel evoked the same chauvinistic response in Jewish men as did our few Jewish athletes. He was the Hank Greenberg and Sid Luckman of comedy because his style was aggressive and unapologetic. He pushed his point of view in people's faces, reminding the world that the Jews had been around for a very long time.

In the Lubitsch *To Be or Not to Be,* the role of a Jewish spear-carrier who wanted to play Shylock was given a dignified, lighthearted touch by the European actor Felix Bressart. A Lubitsch favorite, he had given a memorable performance as the gentle clerk and friend of Jimmy Stewart in *The Shop Around the Corner,* one of the deftest comic films of all time. It was the Bressart role that I auditioned for, and whatever I lacked in skill I made up for by reprising the style of the original.

Bressart, besides being a better actor than I was at the time, had the perspective of middle age as well as the directorial help of a genius. At thirty-five I was too young for the part. The actor playing Lupinsky (the name given the character in the Mel Brooks version) should have been twenty years my senior. I misinterpreted Bressart's nuanced resignation for a weepiness that wasn't anywhere near as affecting. What was pivotal to playing the role was the character's ability to perform Shylock's famous speech "Hath not a Jew eyes?" twice. The first time, the speech is delivered off the cuff for the edification of his spear-carrying colleague; the second time it's performed in front of the Nazi high command in an effort to save the troupe from extermination. Once again I was well served by my talent for mimicry. There's something to be said for appreciating those who have come before you.

A week or so after my taped audition, I was flown to Hollywood to audition for Brooks. I arrived on a Sunday afternoon and was taken by limo to a fancy hotel on Pico Boulevard. There I sat for two days before I picked up the phone and called 20th Century Fox to inquire if anyone was planning to set up a time for me to meet with Mel. Later that afternoon, very much an afterthought, I was driven onto the Fox lot and led to a large room, where I was given a chair facing Brooks and a hundred other people who had crowded in behind him. Sitting at Mel's feet was the majestic Anne Bancroft.

Something about Mel has always reminded me of a street tough trying to escape the body of an elderly Jewish woman. It's like he's holding a knife to your throat and demanding that you eat chicken soup. After I'd auditioned every scene the character had in the film, Mel looked as if he'd eaten a bad clam. "I can't make up my mind!" he barked. My interpretation had troubled him. "Listen, go back to where you came from, and I'll have to think about this, because I can't make up my mind."

It was apparent that in addition to Mel's comedic talents he harbored a Meyer Lansky-like need to exercise control. By sending me back across the continent without a hint of whether the part was mine, he had instantly elevated himself into the most important person in my life. My world would grind to a halt as I awaited his Solomonic decision.

"Listen, Mel," I said, "I think I'm uniquely qualified to play this part because even when I eat my eggs in the morning, I do it with a Holocaust sensibility."

Everybody laughed but Mel. He glared back at me as if my very presence in the room was undermining his confidence in the Jewish people. "I'm sorry. I just can't make up my mind," he said over the restless din of his entourage. "Maybe in a week or two, you never know. It could come to me in my sleep."

"Mel," I said, "if you want me to play this part—" I decided to hit him with one of his own lines from *The Producers*, "—if you want me to play this part, all you have to do is ask me!" Again a hundred people laughed, but not Brooks. Silence ensued. Getting a big laugh was definitely not the way to his heart.

"Wait a minute, that's my line!" he yelled back at me. "You just stole my line!"

"Yes!" said Anne Bancroft, begging him to see the humor in the situation.

"I can't make up my mind," he repeated, sounding even more like a big-breasted Jewish woman hanging out a Brooklyn window. "When I make up my mind, I'll have someone contact your agent."

A few days later he made up his mind, but it was obvious that his decision had come during a tortured sleep. Jewish people have this thing about other Jewish people. This is difficult to admit, but it's not unusual to be especially hard on your own. An example: When I was doing *Benson*, the eight-year-old Missy Gold had a Jewish father and a Christian mother. The mother I forgave: after all, she had a couple of beautiful kids, and what the hell else was she going to do with her life? The father I wanted to slap around. I hadn't realized it yet, but something about me rubbed Mel Brooks the wrong way. He didn't trust my adoration because the possibility existed that I might fall out of love with him the moment I got to know him better. He saw me as simultaneously fawning and hypercritical.

The conceit of the Mel Brooks version of *To Be or Not to Be* was that Brooks was not the film's director. The talented choreographer Alan Johnson, who had staged the musical numbers in *The Producers*, was to be the director, but anyone who ever listened to *The Two Thousand Year Old Man* knew that Mel wasn't going to walk quietly into the Southern California surf. Mel was the producer, the coauthor of the screenplay, and the film's costar alongside his wife, Anne Bancroft, Mel and Anne playing the Benny and Lombard roles.

I'm certain there wasn't anyone who respected the original version of *To Be or Not to Be* more than Brooks. For this reason he didn't want the critics to compare his own in-your-face directorial style with the deft genius of Ernst Lubitsch. But Mel *was* directing the film, and while we all had to pretend he wasn't, he absolutely demanded that we recognize that he was. A few years later I suggested that Israel should declare him the modern-day king of the Jews. He pondered my suggestion seriously before replying, "You're right! I *should* be the king of the Jews!" That's a good healthy ego.

A few days before we began shooting, the cast, which included Jose Ferrer, Charles Durning, George Gaines, Ronnie Graham, Tim Mathison, and Mel and Anne, assembled in a conference room at 20th Century Fox to read through the screenplay. When we got to the section where Lupinsky delivers the first casual reading of "Hath not a Jew eyes?," I was interrupted midsentence by Brooks, who yelled at me in front of the entire cast, "Now that is the *very opposite* way I want you to do that speech!" It was an embarrassing and totally disproportionate emotional outburst. I would come to understand that whenever Mel lacked confidence in a situation, he believed he was totally within his rights to punish the source of his doubt. When we took a break, Ronnie Graham came running over to me and put one of his long arms around my shoulders.

"I thought you did that speech wonderfully," he said, leading me down a hallway away from the room.

"I wasn't aware that we were expected to deliver a finished product."

"You have to understand Mel," said Ronnie. "He's a wonderful, warmhearted human being. He's just in the habit of saying whatever comes into his mind."

"Why are you apologizing for me!" screamed Mel, who, unbeknownst to us had followed us down the hall.

"I was just telling Lewis—"

"Don't tell Lewis anything! Stop being the best boy! He doesn't understand how to do the speech!" He pushed his way past us and went into the bathroom.

The first time I stepped before the camera was to deliver a monologue in front of the troupe's theater curtain informing the audience of a sudden change of program. Because the Polish authorities had forbidden a play lampooning the Nazis, Mel's character, a noted Polish ham, would instead be performing his infamous *Highlights from Hamlet*. After the audience groaned, I registered my own disapproval by deadpanning the word "Yes."

It was vintage Mel Brooks, the implication being Yes, I agree he's a terrible actor, but what can I do, he's Mel Brooks!

Because Mel was not the director, he wasn't there. The scene was directed by Alan Johnson and Mel's associate producer, Irene Waltzer. Irene handled Mel with fastidious care. She loved working as a producer at Brooks Films, and when she appeared on the set she brought with her a much-needed aura of calm. The first time they filmed the speech was as a long shot. On the second take the camera closed in and shot me from the waist up. My third take was a close-up. After I'd finished, Irene yelled from the back of the soundstage, "That was wonderful, Lewis. But then you're always wonderful!"

In the afternoon Mel walked onto the set for the first time that day, dressed in his Elizabethan Hamlet costume and wearing a blond wig that made him look like Harpo Marx. He was agitated, because he was about to re-create one of the most memorable moments from the original film: As Mel's character begins to recite "To Be or Not to Be," a handsome young air force pilot, played by Tim Mathison, stands up and walks out of the theater. Humiliated by what he believes to be the rejection of his talent, he is unaware that his speech is the pilot's signal to go backstage and rendezvous with his glamorous wife in her dressing room. In the original version Jack Benny played the scene to perfection, a reality that hung over Mel Brooks like the disapproval of a judgmental aunt.

Stalling for time, Mel gathered the entire cast and crew around a television monitor that contained video footage of everything that had been shot that morning. Sitting in his director's chair in his blond wig and blue Shakespearean tights, he seemed to be gathering strength from the absurdity of his appearance, the class clown having merged with the school principal. The first thing that flashed on the screen was the long shot of my curtain speech. It wasn't very good. My performance was self-conscious and overgesticulated, and I cringed watching myself.

"What is that idiot *doing?*" Mel screamed, like the fishwife he had in him. I was standing two feet away. "The man is an absolute moron!" Moments later my second take appeared on the screen. It wasn't very good either—although it was considerably more economical. I could see I was beginning to work things out.

"The man is a complete *imbecile*!" he ranted. Suddenly everyone standing on my side of the monitor began to shift over to Mel's side. Within seconds I was alone. (That's Hollywood for ya!)

"I hate actors! I hate Lewis Stadlen!" he yelled in apoplectic fury. Seconds later my close-up came up. Mercifully, I'd given a funny performance.

"O.K. That's good!" said Mel, instantaneously composed.

It was an ugly moment, and as soon as Mel walked away, several colleagues came over to see if I was still breathing.

"I'll be all right," I told them, "as soon as I take a nap."

But I wasn't all right. No one had ever bullied or embarrassed me that way. I was not a confident enough film actor to be berated at the beginning of what was certain to be a challenging eight-week process. Nothing Mel had said could be construed as constructive criticism. Instead of telling me what he wanted, he just kept insisting I stank.

The next day I could see Mel looking for a pretext to come over and have a little chat. It was my romantic notion that the night before, just before she dozed off, Anne Bancroft had she'd whispered in her beloved's ear, "You know, Mel, for a great man you sure can be a terrible prick. You have to apologize to Lewis Stadlen. Either that or you're going to have a basket case on your hands."

During a break Mel walked over and gave me an impersonal poke. "So you were in a Broadway show? *Minnie Boy*?"

"*Minnie's Boys*, Mel. It was about the Marx Brothers."

Then, in a voice dripping with condescension, "This is your first movie?"

"No, it's my seventh."

"Your seventh!" he said, regaining his composure. "I've only done five. How come I never heard of you?" It was a great line, and I'm sure I'd have laughed hysterically had it been directed at someone else.

The next day I did my first important scene, the one in which Lupinsky recites the "Hath not a Jew eyes?" speech for his spear-carrying buddy, the two of us standing in a stairwell. This time Mel was there to direct. He gave me two takes. After the second one he said, "Well, the first part's a piece of shit and the second part's all right. All right, print it!" I never got to see how I did. He cut it from the film.

It had been a horrible first few days. I was hurt and disillusioned, but I was also really pissed at Mel Brooks. I wasn't the only person he was treating badly. Later that week he showed up on the set after root canal surgery, and he was a Jewish man in pain. Anne Bancroft and Charley Durning were doing terrific work on a scene, but Mel wasn't satisfied and began berating their performances.

"Let me get this straight," Anne said. "Mel Brooks is telling Anne Bancroft and Charles Durning how to act? Ha ha ha ha!" she snorted and haughtily departed the soundstage with Mel in hot pursuit.

"I'm going to send you to an acting teacher," he told me a few days later. "Have you ever heard of Bobby Lewis?"

"Yes, I've heard of Bobby Lewis," I said. Mel figured New York had lost most of its intellectual wattage the day he decided to move to Los Angeles.

"I'm going to send you to Bobby Lewis because you don't understand the speech. I want to let you in on a little story," he told me. "I was working with a young actress doing one of my films, and I told her 'You have to study with Bobby Lewis,' and she says, 'Excuse me, Mister Brooks, but I know what I'm doing and I don't need an acting teacher.' Five minutes later, my wife says, 'Where's Bobby Lewis? I have to study with Bobby Lewis!' The little *pisher* says no, but the greatest actress in America wants to study with Bobby Lewis!"

The idea of Mel sending me to an acting teacher was truly insulting. They were paying me a substantial weekly salary, and as much as I admired Mel as a comic innovator (I was beyond referring to him as a genius), I thought he was a terrible actor. What was probably bugging him about my performance was that early on I was playing Lupinsky like a victim. That quip about my having a Holocaust sensibility was getting in the way of my work. Felix Bressart had played the part like a man with little power who chooses to be watchful as circumstances close in around him. He remains hopeful throughout the twists and turns of the plot. I was playing the role knowing what would happen to Europe's six million Jews instead of taking a page out of Luther Adler's book and playing the guy as hopeful. (If you want to impress your buddy with how well you can do the Shylock speech, just do it well. Don't try to show the public you're representing the Jewish race.) I had fallen into the trap of playing Lupinsky as a victim, which isn't really interesting. To play a victim is to play a quality. To be watchful is active and positive.

Unfortunately, Mel didn't have the acting vocabulary to say "Stop playing a victim. Play him like a winner, and events will take care of themselves." His approach was to tell me I didn't understand a great piece of literature because I wasn't a good enough actor.

A few mornings later I was sitting next to Anne Bancroft in the makeup trailer when an assistant director told another actor that Mel was so displeased with his performance he expected him to come over to his house in Beverly Hills that Saturday to rehearse. This was strictly against union rules. The working week for a movie shoot on a Hollywood lot is Monday through Friday. All weekend rehearsals are voluntary, with the provision that if you comply, you must be paid an additional fifth of your weekly salary. There but for the grace of God go I, I thought.

"Oh, Lewie," said Bancroft, in that devilish way she had of tempting you into trouble. "It isn't official yet, but I was there when the decision was made. Mel wants you to come over to the house on Saturday too." O brother, where art thou?

Later that day I was talking with fellow cast member George Wyner when Mel materialized in full Nazi regalia as Adolf Hitler. (Part of the movie's plot involved Mel impersonating the Nazi madman.) There he stood with his hair combed over his forehead and the infamous Hitler mustache pasted beneath his prominent Eastern European nose.

"So you'll come over to the house on Saturday morning," he barked, "because you don't understand the speech!" Then, as an afterthought, "But you'll call up the union first so you don't get into any trouble!"

The moment he walked away, George, who was a genius at getting along with people, said, "I like that phrase 'You'll call up the union first so *you* don't get into any trouble.' "

"I know," I said. "What am I going to do about that?"

"What are you going to do?" said George. "You're going to do nothing, that's what you're going to do!"

"Oh, I don't know about that," I told him. "I mean, it's one thing to be patronized, and quite another not to be paid. You know, I was quite a hell-raiser in my time. I was an Equity deputy and everything."

George Wyner was a model Hollywood citizen. What I admired most about him was how satisfied he seemed to be with his life. He loved his wife and children and the house they lived in. He'd been raised in the penthouse suite of the Boston Ritz-Carlton. His father had invented the hotel. Perhaps for this reason his temperament remained mild and his emotional grounding imperturbable. Talk about a room outside the womb.

"The thing I don't understand about you," George said, "is that you're the only one here who refuses to play Mel's game. Why is that?"

"What are you talking about?" I said. "I came into this experience revering the bastard. I worshipped at his shrine. I wanted him to love me."

"No you don't," George replied. "If Mel Brooks comes over and asks you to do something, what do you do?"

"I listen to what he has to say and I think about it."

"Exactly!" said George. "When Mel Brooks asks you to do something, he wants you to shake your head yes and then go out and do it. He doesn't appreciate your weighing whether it's a good or bad idea. Just shake your head yes! Try it my way," he added. "It works."

A few hours later I was driving out the gate of 20th Century Fox when I was stopped by a breathless Jack Riley, who played my sidekick. Because of his sincere loyalty, Mel had found parts for him in most of his recent films. "Mel needs to speak with you," he told me. He had run all the way. With great annoyance I turned around and drove back to Mel's trailer. He was waiting for me in a satin robe, still made up as Hitler.

"Did you call the union about Saturday?" he said. "Because I don't want you to get into any trouble."

I won't pretend that I wasn't a little afraid of Brooks. He exuded authority, and he had a very loud voice. But I had taken quite enough. I've always believed that no individual is that strong, nor am I that weak.

"There'll be no trouble with the union," I told him, then paused. "But you're going to have to pay."

A much longer pause ensued. Mel looked at me with the insolence of someone who had never been told he wasn't everybody's favorite. He searched my face as if trying to determine what manner of man I was, to tell him an unpleasant truth.

"So what are you doing on *Friday?*" he said.

"I'm not doing anything on Friday."

"Good. So you'll come on Friday during the lunch break—because you don't understand the speech!" With that he retired into his trailer.

On Friday I met him at the same spot. He was in his robe again, made up as Hitler. "Do you like it here in Los Angeles?" he asked me.

"No, I don't."

"You don't like it here? Why not? You don't like the smell of azaleas?"

"I guess nothing good has ever happened to me here."

"That's too bad, because it's a very beautiful place." If Mel Brooks could be submissive, this was as close as he was ever going to get. "I'm going to show you how to do the speech," he said, "because from the very beginning you have never understood the meaning of that speech. Listen to the way I do it: *Hath* not a Jew eyes?" he intoned in a singsong cadence. "*Hath* not a Jew hands? Did you see what I did there? The operative word of the first two sentences is *hath*. You have to stress the *hath*." Then his eyes grew searching. "Wait a minute. I'm wrong. The operative word is *not*, not hath! Hath *not* a Jew eyes? Hath *not* a Jew hands?" He was reciting it just like his two-thousand-year-old man, but in classical style. "Wait a minute. Goddamn it! I'm wrong again. The operative word is *Jew*. Hath not a *Jew* eyes? Hath not a *Jew* hands?" Then, remembering that a warm pastrami sandwich was waiting for him across the room, he ended our clinic by saying, "Do you see the way the poetry rolls off my lips?"

I had gained Mel's respect by facing him down on the money. Now I just wanted to figure out how to do that speech. This is the speech: "Hath not a Jew eyes? hath not a Jew hands? organs, dimensions, senses, affections, passions? fed with the same food, hurt with the same weapons, subject to the same diseases…If you prick us, do we not bleed? if you tickle us, do we not laugh? if you poison, us do we not die? and if you wrong us, shall we not revenge?…"

Mel and I were two Jewish boys who hadn't gone to college. How could two men who revered intelligence possibly admit that they couldn't figure out Shakespeare? Worse, Mel had pointed me in the wrong direction. What was it, exactly, I had to figure out? Was I so dense that I couldn't grasp the meaning of the words? This was a huge dramatic moment in the film. If I couldn't deliver that speech convincingly, my performance would be a complete failure, and I would also have failed the film.

What I wasn't taking into consideration was the circumstance Lupinsky finds himself in when he's compelled to give the speech. It's delivered after he's been caught by a group of Nazi storm troopers. They think he's saying it to Hitler, but it's really Mel's character dressed up as Hitler. The action takes place in a dressing circle lobby while the real Hitler is addressing the SS inside the theater. The night before we were to shoot it, in desperation I figured out how to do the speech. I would pretend I was talking to the real Hitler and not Mel Brooks. The speech would be my way of kicking ass for the Jews. It was definitely the right choice. Stick it in Hitler's face. Be brave. Be courageous. Don't be sad. (Thank you, Luther Adler.)

The next day Mel was very nervous, and fortunately for me, he set up the camera on himself while I delivered the speech out of the frame. But I wasn't doing it the way I'd envisioned it. Kicking ass wasn't enough; it had to be moving. After lunch Ronnie Graham came over to me and said, "Mel's not letting you do it the way you want, is he?" At this point I would have loved to blame it on Mel, but in truth I couldn't quite figure out what I had done so magnificently the night before in my living room.

In the sequence just before I was to deliver the speech, I exited a theater lavatory and ran straight at Mel's Hitler. Before I could reach him, three huge blond boys from Orange County dressed in black SS uniforms grabbed me by the arms, which caused me some pain. *That was it!* That was the one element I hadn't taken into consideration. These Nazi bastards were going to kill me if I didn't deliver a hot rendition of that speech. In the end, it was a combination of fury mixed with fear. Only part of it had to do with Shakespeare's prose. I wasn't playing Shylock, I was a spear-carrier acting for my life.

Mel announced that I was such a brilliant actor that I had to be referred to by three names. "That's why we're forced to call him Lewis J. Stadlen." In the end, I wasn't as good as Felix Bressart—with one exception. I did the Shylock speech better.

Chapter 34

Playing a sixty-year-old man at thirty-five is no way to advance your career. Our *To Be or Not to Be,* like the Lubitisch version, was a flop at the box office. In show business you're rewarded only when the show makes money.

The problems in my marriage were exacerbated by the birth of a second child. Peter Julius Stadlen, named after Groucho, was a sweet, Buddha-like child, very calm and wise beyond his years. His parents were not. Kathy kept telling me to go out and get a new suit so I could present myself to the world as a winner. "You're just frustrated because I'm doing something for myself and you're sitting home getting stoned," she told me one afternoon while I lay on the couch getting stoned. She was going to a psychiatrist whose practice catered to so many show business people that her waiting room looked like an opening night party at Tavern on the Green.

Walking along Madison Avenue one day with a four-day growth of beard, looking extremely unprosperous, I passed Brooks Brothers and, with Kathy's criticism ringing in my ears, decided to step inside and look for a suit. It was symptomatic of my confusion that I would choose Brooks Brothers. I'd reached a stage in my life where I'd completely run out of fuel. I could barely decide whether I needed to go to the toilet, let alone what style of clothing I should consider.

As I walked around the store I noticed a man being fitted for a suit in a mirrored enclosure. His back was to me, but something about his posture was extremely familiar. The woman facing him also looked familiar, but for the life of me I couldn't figure out who they were. Then I got it. I was staring at Richard and Pat Nixon. Standing in proximity to a man I had hated from afar but who now looked so human compelled me to belabor the nearest salesman.

"I think it's an outrage that you're selling clothes to that man," I said, totally forgetting that I looked like a panhandler.

"What do you want us to do?" said the salesman. "He's an American citizen just like anybody else."

"That may be the case," I told him, "but I'll never shop in this store again."

I was tired. The past few years had been one battle after another, and I was feeling my age. At thirty-seven all I could hear was Peggy Lee's haunting rendition of "Is That All There Is?" I was also beset by fear. An astrologer friend had convinced me that the world was going to end in 1984. I wanted to lose myself in something that felt good, but I was at a loss as to where to find it.

I was having a difficult time getting up in the morning, partly because Ronald Reagan's popularity had really thrown me for a loop. I know it's never talked about, but one of the real selling points of the Reagan presidency was that he didn't seem to like black people any more than the average white citizen did. He was affable but certainly not convinced that black people were having a beneficial effect on things most Americans cared about, like real estate and crime. I understand that a large part of a president's job is being a cheerleader for the country, but the president also has the duty to set the moral and cultural tone for the nation. Reagan surrounded himself with a lot of rich white guys who preferred suspicion to tolerance. I mean, the guy was a joke, and he was one of the most popular presidents in the nation's history.

I did a lot of hiding out in a one-room office I'd rented on Broadway and Forty-seventh Street. I needed to get out of the house. The scripts that crossed my desk didn't interest me. Depression was blinding me. It was not a terribly different mindset than the one I found myself in before I crashed the opening night party for *Fiddler on the Roof.* I was susceptible to a big jolt, and I found it because of a baseball game.

I'd been called at the last possible moment by a casting director to audition for the role of Tartuffe, at the Yale Rep. They had obviously lost an actor hours before, and were scrambling to find a replacement. My prized possession at the time was a pair of season tickets for the Mets, situated in what was arguably the finest location at ugly old Shea Stadium. Aware that the casting director was a huge Mets fan, I entered my audition by disingenuously asking her, "When are the two of us finally going to go to a Mets game together?"

"How about tonight?" she said, calling my bluff.

"What a terrific idea," I said, although I wanted to stab myself gently with a kitchen knife. "What time should I pick you up? Where do you live?"

"The West Village."

"Great! I'll pick you up at six."

When I started out in show business in 1967, there was really no such thing as an independent casting director. Prolific producers like David Merrick, Alexander H. Cohen, and Harold Prince had in-house casting directors. It was the film industry, drawing on the talent pools on both coasts, that revolutionized the way actors gained access to the audition process. Soon casting directors themselves were represented by theatrical agents. By the 1980s the casting director, like the sound man who orchestrates microphone levels on a console in the back of every theater, had achieved a position of importance when essentially he hadn't existed a decade before.

The casting director now has a powerful but ultimately unfulfilling role in the theater. Like the gatekeeper in *The Wizard of Oz*, he is initially all-powerful, controlling everyone's access to the formidable wizard. But as soon as the final creative decisions are made he fades from the scene, locked out of the process until an original cast member has to be replaced. His dilemma is not unlike that of a stage director who realizes (if he's wise) that he must eventually hand over maintenance of his creative vision to the actors.

An uneasy relationship exists between casting directors and actors. Casting directors have favorites as well as those they consider untouchable. Actors concede the casting director's power by either currying favor or throwing up their hands and saying the hell with it. In the case of this individual, our relationship ran hot and cold. She recognized my talent, but I had turned down one of her projects a couple of years before, and because of this she had mostly frozen me out. I generally resist hustling those in a position to help me, but there have been times when my reluctance to kiss someone's ass has deferred to the voice that whispers in my ear that to survive I must play the game. This was such a time.

The moment I picked her up I realized I was in for a punishing evening. Cognizant that I'd fought Robert Whitehead over the Actor's Alien Clause, the first thing she confided to me was her outrage at not being able to cast Namita Braithwaite (not her real name) in some Off Broadway play she was working on.

"Who's Namita Braithwaite?" I inquired.

"Who's Namita Braithwaite? She's only the finest actress in South Africa."

"I never heard of her," I said.

"I find that hard to believe. All I can say is, if Actor's Equity blocks her from appearing in this country, I will seriously think of leaving the business." Oy. The conversation shifted to the recent Democratic convention, where Walter Mondale had been chosen to run against Ronald Reagan. On this subject we agreed perfectly, although I was finding it increasingly difficult to stomach some of her more liberal stances—which, incidentally, were completely at odds with the way she behaved as a casting director. But soon Shea Stadium's lights beckoned in the distance, and who needed to argue about anything when we were minutes away from immersing ourselves in the world's most beautiful game?

For seven innings I kept up my end of the bargain, before I decided that she had eaten enough hot dogs and drunk enough beer on my dime. By the eighth inning I was hoping one of us would be knocked unconscious by a foul ball. The Mets were losing to Cincinnati 4-1 entering the bottom of the ninth. The Cincinnati pitcher, John Franco, needed only three more outs before I could drive her home. Maybe she'd take pity on me and throw me a few auditions as summer drew to a close.

As fanatical a Mets fan as I am, I was praying they'd lose. I had run short of cash and conversation. Boom, boom, boom—a single, a double, and a two-out, two-strike home run, and we were going to extra innings. The Mets won an hour and a half later, in fourteen innings. The moral of the story: Never take a female casting director to the single place on earth where you feel at one with yourself.

On the ride back to the West Village she once again brought up Namita Braithwaite, and this time she managed to get a rise out of me. I implied that perhaps she should consider voting for Reagan if she couldn't connect the dots between the interests of American workers and those who pay their taxes in South Africa. I had given her exactly what she had demanded. I had kissed her ass, but she had forced me to savor the experience.

This is the way show business really works. Young actors straight out of college are desperate to have an agent, but what an agent does is serve as a conduit between the casting director and the actor.

"I have an audition for you for a new play, *Ma Rainey's Black Bottom*," my agent said proudly the next morning, "and later in the day I have another one for you, a female version of Neil Simon's *Odd Couple*." These auditions had come about not because my agent had lifted a finger, but because I had sat through fourteen innings with that casting director the night before.

As grateful as I was for the opportunities, each of these auditions came with a hitch. It's difficult to put Stella Adler's theater of the imagination theory into practice when you haven't been given time to read the play, but that's the way the world works, and part of being a professional is your ability to adapt to a less than ideal scenario. This can even work to your advantage: lack of time and information sometimes forces you to make a bold, intuitive guess.

The downside of my baseball companion's largess was that all the good roles in *Ma Rainey's Black Bottom* were black, and the one white role seemed insignificant. As for *The Odd Couple,* they were looking for a bald, middle-aged Hispanic man, and I was none of those things.

It took only one reading of August Wilson's prose for me to be captivated by the playwright's vision. His writing was the real deal; nothing about this play was insignificant. I auditioned for it at noon and gave a good enough reading to merit a callback for the following day. Whereupon I retired to a Central Park bench to figure out how to play a bald, middle-aged Hispanic man for *The Odd Couple*. My first instinct was to bag that audition. What Neil Simon had done was reverse the genders of all the characters in the original play. Felix and Oscar were now Florence and Olive. The British Pigeon sisters who come down to Oscar and Felix's apartment for a hot date were now two Spanish brothers who worked for Iberian Airlines. The big question was, why?

The scene I was to read was moderately funny, packed with jokes that played off the men's mispronunciation and misunderstanding of the English language. There was a running gag about the men's baldness and their lack of physical appeal. I had spent my entire career warding off such parts. You can make a pretty decent living if you reconcile yourself to playing fat and unattractive, but I wasn't about to give in to the temptation of playing a joke. What made the scene inferior to the original was that the Pigeon sisters were knockouts. When Felix subverts the possibility of sex by telling them how much he loves his wife, Oscar wants to kill him for screwing up a sure thing. The two women who enter the apartment hot to trot end up crying on the couch. In the female Version, the Costazuela brothers were courtly but unattractive. The possibility of a sexual outcome had no audience appeal because the men were not written as sexually viable. When everyone starts weeping on the couch you're thankful nothing has transpired. There's no comic payoff.

I decided I was in no position to blow off the audition. I'd try to come up with something good enough not to embarrass myself, then put it behind me and concentrate on *Ma Rainey's Black Bottom.* Deciding it would be a good idea to work on the scene in the air-conditioned rehearsal studio, I arrived to find only a bald, slightly rotund Hispanic man sitting beside the sign-up sheet.

"Are you the stage manager?" I asked.

"No, I'm playing one of the Costazuela brothers. I'm here to read with the actors auditioning for the part of my brother."

"Where's this production going?" I asked him. "Is this going to be a Broadway show?"

"Perhaps eventually," he responded in an authentic Spanish accent. "We open in Dallas and play the road for six months. Rita Moreno and Sally Struthers are our two stars. I'm very grateful to be in it." He seemed a kind, sweet-tempered man. I was happy for him, and I realized that my first clue to the character was to match his kindly manner.

Over the next forty minutes the hallway filled up with bald, middle-aged Hispanic actors. Then the casting director walked in. She was having a wicked belly laugh at my expense.

Actors spend a good deal of time evaluating each other's work: What is it about that fellow that allows him to slide so effortlessly from one job to the next? Why is he the critics' favorite? Some sniping is based on envy, and some is based on a genuine lack of regard. At age thirty-seven I was mystified by the success of quite a few performers. Near the top of my list was Raul Julia. I found him an enormously charming and likable fellow offstage, but I couldn't for the life of me understand why he had such a stellar reputation. Although I felt he played every role the same way, his opportunities seemed limitless. (A few years later I would change my mind.) He had a laconic, easygoing manner, but whether he played Shakespeare, Pinter, or Chekhov, he did them all with a pronounced Puerto Rican accent. It drove me crazy watching him perform in Noel Coward's *Design for Living.* Why did everyone give him a pass? If I played

Shakespeare with a Brooklyn accent I'd be laughed off the stage. And then came a thunderbolt: If Raul Julia could play Noel Coward, I could play Raul Julia!

The distaff *Odd Couple* was the brainchild of Danny Simon, Neil's older brother. The original *Odd Couple* had been based on an incident in Danny's life when he separated from his wife and moved in with a male friend. Danny wrote a short treatment but never took it any further. Neil approached him as the idea languished and asked if he could take a shot at turning it into a full-length play. Danny gave him permission in exchange for a percentage, and that's how *The Odd Couple* was born.

The two brothers had a complicated relationship that was fictionalized in any number of Neil Simon's plays. Danny was aggressive, pugnacious, and an accomplished ladies' man while Neil was more intellectual and painfully shy. The two started out together with Danny making the contacts and having some initial success, but as their careers matured it was Neil who gained the acclaim while Danny's talent lay in his role as a punch-up man, a writer who could contribute a punch line for a sketch but who lacked the confidence and sensitivity to write a full-length narrative.

Since the female version of *The Odd Couple* had been Danny's idea, and since he'd directed any number of his brother's plays in stock, Danny was being thrown a bone by his successful younger brother by being allowed to direct the play. I auditioned for him that afternoon, reading alongside the kindly actor who had already been cast as the older brother. I had done many Raul Julia imitations for my friends, playing an Englishman with a thick Puerto Rican accent in the musical *Where's Charley?* The moment I began to speak, placing my (Raul's) voice in the back of my throat, Danny Simon and the casting director broke up. The actor already cast was initially appreciative, but soon a look of alarm spread across his face. The two of us looked nothing alike. Whatever I was doing was redefining the scene. I could see him beginning to worry. He was thinking, This fellow is very funny, but is that a good thing for me?

When I'd finished, Danny Simon asked if I would consider shaving my head for the role. I replied that I'd jump off that bridge when I came to it. "Could you be this man's brother?" he asked me.

"I don't think so," I said, thinking only of making a graceful exit from the room. I'd been set up by the casting director to fail, and I'd dodged the bullet.

"Would you come back tomorrow and read for Neil?" Danny asked.

"I'll think about it," I said as I was led out the door by the casting director. "Let me ask you something," I said to her. "I've got that callback for *Ma Rainey's Black Bottom* tomorrow. I'd rather concentrate on that. Do you think there's any chance I could be cast in this part?"

She paused thoughtfully. "Not a chance," she said.

"All right. Tell them I'm not interested." And I went home and concentrated on the other play.

I'd bought a suit (at Barney's, of course, not Brooks Brothers) because I agreed with my wife that I needed to look and feel like a winner. The prospect of sending two children to private school was looming very large and I didn't want to break my vow and take the money from my mother-in-law. You'd have thought this financial pressure would make me a little less picky, but for whatever reason (and it turned out to be a very good one), I decided that the female version of *The Odd Couple* was not for me.

The next morning, as I prepared for *Ma Rainey's Black Bottom*, I got a conference call from Danny Simon and Manny Azenberg, with whom I hadn't spoken since *The Sunshine Boys*. In the eleven years that had intervened, Manny's partnership with Gene Wolsk had dissolved and he had gone on to produce all Neil Simon's plays.

"Why aren't you coming in to read for Neil?" he wanted to know. "Danny tells me your audition was flat-out hilarious."

"I'm wrong for the part."

"Let us be the judge of that. Come down to the Alvin and read for Neil."

When you're in a state of mind that tells you you'd rather do anything than be trapped in an actor's life, you tell yourself you're too good for a stunt like a female version of a play that's perfectly fine the way it is. What's next, an all-black production of *Oklahoma!*? (I wasn't far off.) The problem is that the backstage in a Broadway theater has an irresistible allure. It reminds you of what you've always wanted, no matter how hardscrabble the road you've traveled. The moment I caught sight of the poor devil who had been cast as the brother, I began to boil over in anticipation, and within minutes I was hooked on the opium of laughter emanating from the rear of the orchestra.

"What are you, fucking nuts?" said Neil Simon as we met at the lip of the stage after my audition. "You weren't going to come down to audition for this?"

"I'm not bald. I'm not middle-aged. I'm not Hispanic."

"I'll change it. One scratch of my pencil and you're no longer bald."

"We want you to play the older brother," said Manny.

"You've already cast the older brother."

"Don't worry about it," said Manny. Then he said something in Yiddish that I couldn't make out but completely understood, something along the lines of "Life's unfair. You're the guy we want now."

When I walked into the wings I was confronted by the casting director who'd set the whole thing up as a joke. "You realize there's no negotiation," she said. "Everybody works for twelve hundred dollars a week. If you don't agree right now, we'll look for someone else."

I knew I could probably negotiate for more money, but something was telling me to say yes to everything. This was my ticket out of a disintegrating marriage. I'd have the money to put my kids through private school. Five months on the road. Don't worry about what other people think, take the job! said the voice in my head. Don't complicate the situation. For once in your life, go out there and be a contented whore.

"That's fine," I said. Before I left the theater I was met by the actor they were going to fire even before he had begun.

"Congratulations," he said to me enthusiastically. "I'm really looking forward to working with you."

Show business! I'd gotten the job, but I'd gotten it off another actor's back.

The moment I walked out of the Alvin, a pigeon shat all over my new gray suit.

"That's supposed to be good luck," offered a slightly bemused passerby.

Chapter 35

The difference between a stock director and a serious director is that a stock director has to stage a show in a limited amount of time. He can't promote himself as an original mind; the play has to be staged as written. The serious director can indulge in the novelty of creative thinking. He can search for hidden meaning in something as obvious as a burlesque sketch. For this reason the revival of a classic American play in a suburban theater in Chicago or in the basement of a Staten Island synagogue is usually closer to the original intent of the playwright than some manically conceived revival scheduled for Broadway.

The stock director's instinct is to keep *Fiddler on the Roof* in Russia. The serious director conceives of moving the play to some idyllic village that looks a lot like Scandinavia, with no Jews.

The stock director will begin *Annie Get Your Gun* the way Irving Berlin wrote it. The serious director will add several songs cut from other Irving Berlin shows and will have the libretto rewritten by an American Indian.

The stock director will present *Damn Yankees* the way he remembered it from the movie. The serious director will make the point that people in the 1950s had terrible taste and that the devil spent a lot of time in gay bars.

The stock director will direct *Design for Living* with the two male leads dressed in tuxedos. The serious director will give the play a homoerotic subtext and have the two male characters blowing each other in silhouette. (I doubt that *Design for Living* is ever done in stock.)

The stock director stages the show knowing he will soon move on to the next project. His major concern is getting a cheap flight home. The serious director is thinking up a flashy new concept that might translate into a movie deal.

Danny Simon was a stock director of limited invention who had us all giggling under our breath because he was kind, enthusiastic, and a little dense. He was a lot easier to be around than his successful younger brother, because life had exhausted him and he was grateful for the gig. The female version of *The Odd Couple* was strictly a back-burner project for Neil Simon and Manny Azenberg. They had booked it for a five-month road tour while they concentrated on one of Neil's best plays, *Biloxi Blues*.

I never liked her work. I always thought she performed with too much muscle and promoted herself as a Beloved Entertainer. I could always see the work. After the first reading she took me aside and asked me if that was the way I was planning to do my part. I was furious enough to run to a female friend and predict we were destined to not get along.

"You two are going to get along just fine," said my friend.

The cast was excellent: Mary Louise Wilson, Jenny O'Hara, Marilyn Cooper, Kathleen Doyle, Rita Moreno, Sally Struthers, and Tony Shalhoub as my brother, Jesus.

On the third day of rehearsal she walked into the studio with an eye infection, her face cleansed of all makeup. Her skin was so soft and smooth she looked like an ancient infant. I couldn't help staring. She was the most beautiful thing I had ever seen.

Danny Simon was cute. He loved rehearsing the scene Tony and I did with Sally and Rita. He just kept laughing and repeating the same phrase over and over: "The two of you are like Alphonse amd Gaston." That's all he ever said.

There were two obvious weaknesses with the gender alteration. The poker game didn't have the believability of the original men's game. Poker is a masculine ritual. Men behave differently when they win and when they lose. Men play cards to dominate; women schmooze. The poker sequences lost their edge.

The second problem was the contrast between Oscar as the world's biggest slob and Felix as an anal compulsive. Sally's character remained obsessively neat, but Neil thought an audience wouldn't accept a slovenly woman, so Rita's character was written as ultra-rational while Sally remained an infuriating nudnick. The Olive character was left without a dynamic comic flaw, a structural weakness even Neil Simon couldn't fix.

All the people associated with the production—with the exception of Tony, our understudy David Ardao, and the stage manager, Martin Gold—were women, and that included another stage manager, Bonnie Panson, and our company manager, Noel Gilmore. I was going out on the road for half a year with ten women and three men. The road is a luxurious incandescent fog. Besides the play there is nothing else to do but feel and observe. Everyone lives down the hall. You choose your friends and dine and drink and tell each other the very worst thing you've ever done within hours of arriving at your first temporary destination. The road allows you to save your apologies for later.

Drunk, I would stand across the street and stare up at her window in the Dallas Hotel. She wouldn't stay with the rest of us because her husband made sure to keep her on a short leash. He was the perennial outsider who would never understand her life. She would search my eyes and gently cuddle my wrist and tell me in the strictest confidence, My husband is my jailer. Who was this shallow fellow who dominated her waking life? Thin-lipped, not so nice, hiding behind a facade of affability, telling anecdotes without a point. That's what I told myself as I pursued another guy's wife.

The cast understood that direction of *The Odd Couple* was essentially on loan to Danny Simon. This was how the relationship between these two middle-aged brothers was to play out: If we opened to sterling reviews in Dallas, it was assumed that Danny might survive, but everyone knew there was little chance of that. Neil turned up for technical rehearsals and the official opening but was soon flushed out of Texas by his second wife, Marsha Mason, who was making a film in Oklahoma and was trying to track Neil down to finalize their multimillion-dollar divorce agreement.

I've done four Neil Simon plays from scratch, and every one of them has been a personal drama that could compete with a work of semi-autobiographical fiction. His addiction to prominence dictates a life spent mostly in front of a typewriter. His professional life screams out for control: If I hadn't invented your laughter-filled world, all of you actors wouldn't be here. I have earned the right not to feel guilty about anything I do. I'm the gifted child, while my not so gifted brother accepts what I offer him. There must be a certain agony involved in growing past an older sibling and realizing he's now your dependent, but there was something brutal about the Simons' unspoken resentment of each other. Danny was hired to be fired, and several days after the Dallas reviews came out (Dallas reviews?), with Neil out of town, Danny Simon disappeared. It was announced that he had returned to Southern California for reasons of declining health. That's show business!

The notices said the play was a stunt. Sally Struthers's role was better defined and therefore more entertaining; Rita Moreno seemed lost. The scene with the two brothers was the best moment in a who-cares evening. Actually, Struthers was great. I had admired her work in *All in the Family* and the film *Five Easy Pieces*, but I was unprepared for what an inspired comedian she was. As anyone who has seen her in one of those commercials for the Christian Children's Fund knows, she could cry over a bent fork.

The two women were complete opposites. No one could feel sorrier for herself than Sally Struthers. Rita Moreno had the comportment of a lifeboat occupant watching her husband go down on the *Titanic*. It didn't take long for the cast to divide into Rita and Sally factions. A needier and more inclusive person, Sally was the more popular.

Traveling with ten women and only a couple of guys was fun and instructive. Anyone holding on to the romantic notion that the world's problems would dissolve in a society controlled by women should have stepped on the bus I was riding on. There was a lot of crying and bucking each other up and complaining and drinking and swearing and competing, just like the men who preyed on them. As a minority, we males were given the benefit of the doubt, since there were far fewer of us to run to or feel oppressed by. I could also afford to reveal my feminine side while knocking off the other two guys, who seemed oblivious to the secret garden we had fallen into. It's all part of the enchanting lack of reality that envelops a person continually on the move. What I wasn't aware of was that my ardor was getting the best of me. I was falling for a woman who could eat me for lunch and spit out the seeds.

Our critical reception in Chicago was slightly less chilly than in Dallas. Sally received the better mentions, but Rita was treated respectfully. They blamed her lack of impact on the part. Unique to our situation was the fact that we had no director to reshape the play and provide guidance to the cast. We were told that Neil Simon had decided to rewrite the poker sequences by replacing them with a game of Trivial Pursuit. *Trivial Pursuit?* Much outrage was directed toward our psychologically impaired middle-aged Jewish playwright, who was addicted to blond shiksas. Only he could come up with an idea as patronizing to women as a weekly game of Trivial Pursuit.

As the women went into feminist mourning, I made my move, or was led to believe I was making my move.

"And what would you hope to accomplish in your life?" she asked me the day her husband flew back to L.A.

"I want to be happy," I told her.

"You tell funny stories," she observed as we sipped our margaritas. "If I may make an observation, you start a lot of them by telling me you were humiliated by this situation or that. Humiliation is a state of mind." She took a long sensuous swill of her drink. "I suggest you never feel humiliated again." Like the advice of Luther Adler, Victor French, and Sam Levene, this was a keeper. I was more than grateful, however; I was madly in love with her strength and resolute character. She did more than work for a living. She carried her entire family around on her sturdy, tapping feet. She smelled of places I had never been. She was ten times more worldly and a thousand times more beautiful. I wanted to caress her while she saved me from my past.

It had been a long time since a woman had meant this much to me, if one ever had. I pursued her with unapologetic zeal while she stared at me in disbelief, a look I would see at important intervals over the following two years. For someone who delighted in lying, she could speak a mean truth. Nothing she said or did could deter me. I had never feasted in so primitive a jungle. Everything I was before I met her seemed pampered and safe, and if I needed an excuse to deceive myself further, all I had to do was run my hands through her great mane of hair or slip down beneath her stomach to the smooth parchment between her legs. Nothing I could possibly hate her for could diminish what she allowed me to feel. Within a month I was the most pussy-whipped man in America. It's not a state of being I would recommend for a lifetime, but it certainly had its temporary benefits.

Manny Azenberg flew to Chicago to tell us we would continue to tour through Washington, D.C., and then take a three-week break before rehearsing Neil's new Trivial Pursuit rewrite. Gene Saks, one of Broadway's best, would be our new director. The improved version of the female *Odd Couple* would play a six-week engagement at the Ahmanson Theater in Los Angeles before opening at the Broadhurst in New York.

"Although your contracts will officially terminate after the Washington run," said our general manager, Bob Kamlot, "there'll be no renegotiation." That made me laugh. I've always felt comfortable around horse thieves. The horse thief recognizes that negotiating a salary is all a game, and 95 percent of the time he'll win. Actors are easily cowed. A commercial general manager like Bob Kamlot is usually more honest—and certainly more engaging—than the not-for-profit or corporate general manager, who is so wed to his company he can't see the difference between Albert Finney and Joe Schmo. The commercial horse thief wants to keep the money for himself. That's the fun of the job. The corporate general manager demands that everyone make the same money. At least when it comes to paying the talent, he ardently believes in socialism.

In Chicago on election eve 1984, I was sitting in a bar on State Street with one of our stagehands, Robert Curry. Big Bob was a six-foot-six, bearded, redheaded Irishman who suffered from a debilitating disease: integrity. A superb stage manager for years, he had pretty much blackballed himself for speaking honestly to those in power. Several years before, he'd taken out a tour of *Fiddler on the Roof* starring Herschel Bernardi. *Fiddler* had been touring on and off since 1966, but this time it was tanking at the box office. One Saturday, Bernardi called in sick for the matinee. Curry was standing in the back of the orchestra taking notes when he saw Bernardi chatting with the tour's producer, Gene Wolsk. At intermission he walked over to Bernardi, who was seated in a box.

"What are you doing here?" Curry asked him. "I thought you were sick."

"Let's just say I'm exercising my prerogative as the star," said Bernardi.

"I don't give a damn about your prerogative. Either get up on the stage or go back to your hotel." Curry was fired the next day.

This night on State Street, Curry, a passionate Democrat, raised his glass of Irish whisky and announced to the bar, "Tomorrow morning I have the fullest confidence that the American people will have elected Walter Mondale as the next president of the United States."

Curry and the stagehands were furious because they'd just been told by Manny Azenberg and Bob Kamlot that they would be replaced by a Los Angeles crew when the show moved to the Ahmanson. They could rejoin us after we opened on Broadway, but that meant an unpaid ten-week layoff. The money the producers were saving couldn't possibly have amounted to the price of their loyalty.

"To Manny Azenberg!" said Bob, lifting his glass. "The best of the worst!"

A few days before we opened on Broadway I was walking along Ninth Avenue when I ran into Martin Gottfried, who had been the drama critic for *Women's Wear Daily* and the *New York Post*. Martin was so highly regarded in theatrical literary circles that he had been a finalist to take over the job at the *Times*.

"How's this version of *The Odd Couple*?" he asked.

"I think it's mostly terrific. Gene Saks has done a great job."

"Has Neil finally addressed the gay issue in this version?" he wanted to know.

"The gay issue? What gay issue?"

"I've always believed *The Odd Couple* was about a homosexual relationship written in code. I've done several articles about it."

"You kidding me? You mean, like George and Martha in *Who's Afraid of Virginia Woolf?*"

"Precisely."

"Marty," I said to the man who had nearly become the drama critic for the *New York Times*, "*The Odd Couple* is based on Neil Simon's brother Danny, who was kicked out of his apartment by his wife. What makes you think it's about gay men?"

"Let me ask you this. How come when the Pigeon sisters come down to dinner, Felix fucks up the date?"

"Marty," I said, resisting the urge to whack him over the head with a stone, "that's what we call the funny part!"

The Odd Couple opened on July 11, 1986, to mostly negative reviews that ignored the excellence of Neil's rewrite and the overall quality of the production. The Trivial Pursuit game was hilariously written, and Marilyn Cooper's performance alone was worth the price of admission. Sally was inspired, and Rita's performance was classy and understated. The scene with the Costazuela brothers was as hilarious as anything seen on Broadway in years. Instead of lauding these assets, the critics chose to bemoan the decline of the contemporary commercial theater as exemplified by us. (They should have waited a few years.) Anyone reading the play today would see that it contains some superb comic writing. We closed eight months later.

One Saturday before a matinee, I led my eight-year-old daughter and five-year-old son onto the naturalistic set that had been designed by David Mitchell. Upstage center was a door that led to an imaginary offstage bathroom that was nothing more than a small canvas and wood enclosure. When Diana and Peter expressed amazement that a set that seemed so genuine could veer into this zone of unreality, I explained that the artificial bathroom was an illusion, while the rest of the set was grounded in reality. For the next twenty minutes they raced around the stage touching lamps, plates, wall sconces, picture frames, and the dining room set, asking "Is this illusion or reality?"

Defining props on the set of *The Odd Couple* was much simpler than untangling the romantic mess I'd made of my life. My marriage was in ruins. I had fallen in love with a woman I knew would never leave the comfort of her current situation, but I didn't really care. I'd found the bridge that would let me walk away from a dissolving relationship. Nothing mattered more than wallowing in the illusion of romance with a woman I probably wouldn't have had twenty things to say to if we'd been able to share a life together. She was beautiful and she made me feel beautiful, and I was willing to sacrifice everything for a double life that ultimately renders all passion profane.

PART THREE

what the hell happened to you?

Chapter 36

What the hell happened to you? was what I asked myself as I stared into the full-length mirror above my neighborhood bar one warm summer afternoon. I was well beyond the feeling-good stage after the fourth swallow of my second drink. I'd been driven out of my apartment by the epic argumentativeness of my longtime girlfriend, Vicki Lewis, and into the bosom of an establishment that served booze in tankard-sized glasses.

Actually, a lot had happened. I had forsaken the illusion of an orderly life, and although I was now quite poor, I'd been playing classical roles for paltry salaries all over the country. And I was nearing the end of a six-year relationship with a powerful, talented little redhead, the latter stages of the liaison a form of penance I'd inflicted on myself for betraying Kathy, who had remained loyal to me and the family unit and deserved better, I suppose.

After six years with Vicki I felt that in terms of karma, I was either even or slightly ahead of the game. Not that I didn't love her madly. Who wouldn't love a girl who had inquired over cocktails whether the Jews bore some responsibility for what had befallen them during the Second World War.

"What exactly are you driving at?" I asked, mesmerized by her long nose.

"Don't you think they may have brought the whole thing on themselves by being slightly..." she paused to find the right words "obnoxious?"

"Let's accept your supposition that every Jew in Europe was incredibly obnoxious. What exactly is your point?"

A relatively stable Jewish man would have taken the hint and skipped the coffee, but not I. I was intoxicated by her pluck. I suddenly found her beautiful. She was tremendously bright and talented, and for a few years we managed to save each other from our own ignorance. Each was strong in the areas where the other was weak, but now, petrified though we were about moving on, we were desperate to get out of each other's lives.

I had to admit, teary-eyed and drunk that afternoon at Miss Ellie's Homesick Bar, that I might just be what Vicki had accused me of the day before. "Let's face it," she'd said after we'd spent the morning deluding ourselves that what was missing from our relationship was a larger apartment. "You and I have turned into the loser couple."

Vicki Lewis was a career maniac. Thirteen years my junior, she spent a disproportionate amount of time torturing herself with the idea that she would forever teeter on the cusp of success. Her views on show business were strident and embarrassingly direct. She approached the acting profession with no illusion that she was upholding some honored principle passed down through the ages. She wanted money and fame, and she was tired of waiting around for it.

"What I really want to be is a rock star," she said to me one day. At the time she was doubled over in pain from a stomach ailment that interrupted our dinner and sent us racing to the nearest emergency room.

There was a magnificent morbidity to her quest for personal recognition. She had no real interests except an intoxication with the putative benefits of fame. I spent hours positing the superficiality of her beliefs, knowing she was destined to break free from the pack and leave me behind. All the while I was advancing some romantic argument I knew had no merit in the marketplace. I was running out of room to maneuver. If I was so hell-bent on dedicating myself to my ideals, why was I sitting in a bar at four o'clock in the afternoon with no prospects?

The 1992 revival of *Guys and Dolls* was such a sensation that *New York Times* drama critic Frank Rich's rave appeared on the front page. The show's success was doubly painful to Vicki and me because the actors playing Miss Adelaide and Nathan Detroit were our friends, Faith Prince and Nathan Lane. We included in our joint resentment the play's director, Jerry Zaks.

"Why does he hate me?" Vicki would ask me, as if I were somehow to blame.

"He doesn't hate you. He doesn't even know you're alive. I'm the one he hates. What the hell did I ever do to him?"

"Because we're not on the A team," she would sing out with pain.

"We're not even on the D team! We're not even on the who-do-I-have-to-blow-to-get-an-audition team?"

The good thing about these creative discussions was that they got me out of the house.

One afternoon I was sitting in my friend Ron Raine's apartment when he mentioned that a road company of *Guys and Dolls* was in the works. I immediately put in a call to my agent of the moment.

"*Guys and Dolls*," I said. "I want an audition." There was a long silence. I could tell that my representative was racking his brain to figure out what role I might possibly be right for. "Nathan Detroit!" I said, putting him out of his misery. "I may not have changed my name from Joe Lane to Nathan Lane, but Sam Levene, who originated the role, happened to be a very good friend of mine."

"I'm warning you, there's no money in it, and they're insisting you sign a two-year contract."

"Why don't you just get me an audition, Bob," I said. "If they want me we can negotiate for more money. I believe I'm uniquely qualified to play the part."

"Listen, I'll do anything you say," he said defensively. "I'm just giving you the scoop because we handle Lorna Luft. Lorna's set to play Miss Adelaide." Lorna Luft is Judy Garland's daughter. Now my agent could die happy, smelling Judy Garland's socks.

The night before my audition I decided to pay a visit to a prestigious acting coach who lived in my apartment building. I'd never gone to an acting coach before.

"I can't quite figure the guy out," I told her. "Can you help me?"

"Well..." she mused, "he's dumb. He's really very dumb."

"He is?"

"Absolutely. Just play him like he's dumb and the part's yours."

So the next day I went in and auditioned for Jerry Zaks, playing Nathan Detroit very, very dumb. It died. When I heard I hadn't gotten the part I was suffused with bitterness. That sonofabitch Zaks had it in for me. He was jealous because I'd been a more successful actor than he had. Now he wanted nothing to do with me because I'd known him before he was a great man. That's what I told myself.

Nathan Lane ran into him a few hours after my audition. "How did Lewis do?" he asked.

"Terrible," he said. "Totally unspontaneous."

"Give him the part," Nathan implored him.

"How can I give him the part? He gave a lousy audition."

"He's a terrific actor," said Nathan. "Listen, maybe he's not feeling so good about himself. As a matter of fact, I know he's not feeling so good about himself. Trust me. He won't play it like me. He'll be different. Give him the part."

"How can I give him the part?" said Zaks. "Not only did he not play Nathan Detroit like he was the smartest guy in Runyonland, he played him like he was the dumbest." So much for an acting coach!

The role was offered to someone else, but Lane's recommendation must have affected Jerry's thinking. The salary offered the other actor was insultingly low, which meant that Zaks still felt conflicted about his choice.

A week later Vicki returned to our West Side apartment after attending a Friday night performance of the show. "How was it?" I asked her, expecting her to say she'd hated every minute of it.

"It's great!" she bubbled. "Everyone's great: Faith, Nathan, Jerry's direction. We went out afterwards. They told me about your audition."

"What did they say?"

"They said you were terrible! Nathan told me not to tell you this, but apparently you totally blew it. They had nobody else to play the part and were praying you'd be good. The role was yours. Jerry said you lacked spontaneity."

"I wasn't that bad," I protested.

"I'm just telling you what they told me," she said, leaving me to mull it over at the kitchen table.

I awoke early the next morning, slipped into some rumpled clothes, bought a pack of cigarettes at the corner bodega, and headed toward Riverside Park. The upside of living with Vicki Lewis was that you could always expect the brutal truth to emerge from among the lies. ("Nathan told me not to tell you this, but...") I'd blown it. Several quickly inhaled cigarettes later I was stripped of my rage. Was it possible that there was no one to blame but myself? Within the hour I had exhausted the pack and every excuse that had to led to despair. I didn't know what to do with the next minute of my life.

I checked my watch. It was eleven o'clock on a Saturday morning. If I hustled back to the apartment and showered and dressed, I might be able to pick up a ticket for the matinee of *Guys and Dolls*. It was an idea unclouded by regret.

In the shower, Stella Adler's voice resonated in my head: "Only your own deep need to salvage something from the void—to act or to write or to create, not to have a 'profession'—can keep you from the commonplace and from dying out. But you must have a deep recognitioin of your solitude to live the way you should live, not the way it is agreed upon, and not to fall for this big thing around you."

At the Martin Beck Theater I was told there'd just been a cancellation on a fourth-row-center seat. Once settled, I struck up a conversation with the woman next to me and told her I was there because I might be playing the role of Nathan Detroit in the national touring company. I still don't know why I said that.

From the moment the curtain went up, I sat there and cried with joy. It had been a long time since I'd been immersed in such beauty. The production was perfection, the story profound. If I can't be a part of this, I told myself, I can't be a part of anything. This is the center of my being. When they offer me a chance to prove myself again, and I know they will, I'll know exactly how it should be done.

Television is swallowing America. Once there were movie, TV, and theater stars; now there are only the people you see on television. Even movie stars have to pay tribute to the television extravaganza to promote their film careers. We find ourselves arranging our day around the overhyped television interview that airs an hour and a half before the gigantic awards ceremony. Then there are the endless promotional guest appearances on the late night or early morning talk shows. If an actor or writer or politician hasn't entered our living room via the tube, he's been unfaithful to the public's desire to revel in fame. Being important enough to appear on television signifies success, and what better form of success is there than to be rich? We love Jerry Seinfield because he's funny, likable, and incredibly wealthy. We listen to his fellow cast members complain that although they're incredibly wealthy too, they're not wealthy enough. The system has screwed them. In their innocence they accepted an inferior deal. All of this bullshit filters down to become a shared societal conviction that only dreamers and fools would turn their backs on the lottery that's now the American way of life.

The obsession about winning the grand prize carries an unpleasant corollary in which talent loses its viability. There was a time when we purchased a theater ticket to see the likes of Julie Harris, Maureen Stapleton, Jason Robards Jr., Alfred Drake, Zero Mostel, Alfred Lunt and Lynn Fontanne, George C. Scott, Ethel Merman, and Mary Martin—not because they were rich, but because they could do something better than the rest of us. As television has shanghaied our appetite for culture, the theater producer has decided to do away with the theater star. A successful businessman has to live with the realities of a changing world. Why publicize some brilliant new talent if his or her departure from the show would sink the production? Actors who want to be theater stars are encouraged to leave the stage and make their names on television or in films.

Today, with the exception of Nathan Lane and Bernadette Peters, there is nobody you can point to as a theater star. Now celebrities have taken over as the stars, but usually they're minor celebrities or they wouldn't be doing theater in the first place. Eight performances a week is a grind. Show me a television has-been and I'll show you a name on a Broadway marquee. (But only for a month. The work may prove too taxing.) Sadly, celebrities often do enhance box office receipts for the month or two they're contracted to appear, but at the expense of quality. Some shows never recover from the soporific effects of celebrity ineptitude. When Robert Preston left the cast of *The Music Man*, he was replaced by Eddie Albert. Today it might be Chubby Checker.

What distinguished the 1992 revival of *Guys and Dolls* from previous incarnations was its glorious pace. It remained faithful to the original production while adjusting the musical's sensory delights to the contemporary urban pulse. High-energy optimism peremeated the singing, dancing, and dialogue. When the curtain rose on the Martin Beck's stage you were transported into a surrealistic world where gangsters and molls didn't murder anybody; they made outlandish bets on the size of cheesecake, loved each other with abandon, and sometimes begged to be left alone. I don't know of any piece of entertainment that dramatizes the dynamic between men and women more profoundly.

The moment Nathan Lane burst onto the stage I saw how wrongheaded my audition had been. Baboom! All the dialogue was shot from guns. Nathan Detroit was a character spinning several plates at the same time, like a juggler on the *Ed Sullivan Show*. If any character was trying to stay one step ahead of the dogcatcher it was good old reliable

Nathan. What kind of arrogance and obliviousness to nuance had possessed me to audition for *Guys and Dolls* without seeing how the piece was being performed? Plenty of actors refuse to see someone else's performance for fear it might inhibit their own, but nothing could be more self-destructive. What harm can there be in watching a comic artist like Nathan Lane performing a great and difficult role? They don't throw actors in prison for stealing from each other.

By a stroke of good fortune, the actor who'd been offered the insulting salary declined the role. The road company was now weeks away from going into rehearsal, and still they had no one to play Nathan Detroit. Nathan Lane successfully campaigned with Jerry Zaks to re-audition me, and now, desperate to make amends for my mental laziness and with a good sense of the style of the play, I went in with the material memorized.

Zaks is a diminutive Jewish man whose face is dominated by two sparkling rows of teeth. When he's pleased with you, the teeth reach out in a tender embrace. When he's displeased, the teeth stare at you like the grillework on an Edsel. No matter how well I auditioned that day—and he had me up on the stage of the Martin Beck for close to an hour—his downturned mouth suggested that I'd forever be considered a work in progress. I just didn't have the goods to replicate Nathan Lane's comic brilliance. When my audition was finished I exited into the wings, where I was given a two-thumbs-up endorsement from an actress named Pat Kennedy, who'd been waiting patiently for me to finish. "That was great," she said. She had the prettiest of smiles.

"I don't know. That guy just doesn't get me," I told her. Nevertheless, this time I felt like a winner. If Jerry Zaks still didn't want me, he could take a flying leap. I had acquitted myself to the best of my ability, and given the opportunity, I knew I could play the hell out of Nathan Detroit. The verdict had yet to be delivered, but as far as I was concerned, I'd returned to the land of the living.

A week went by, with various indications that they were about to offer me the part. On Friday night my agent called to say that an offer had gone out to another actor, a big star.

"Who's this big star?" I asked.

"I'll tell you, but you didn't hear it from me."

"Who'll I tell? The bartender at Sardi's?"

"It's John Rubinstein."

"John Rubinstein is a big star?"

"He's a bigger star than you are."

"Not to my mother, he's not."

A couple of days later John Rubinstein turned down the part, I suppose because he couldn't see the benefit of spending our second week in Hershey, Pennsylvania, during the off season. By the time they came back to me I was riproaring mad.

"Tell them I want two and a half times what they're offering, and if they won't pay it they can find themselves another big star."

I was quite aware that they were starting rehearsals in a matter of days. When it comes to negotiating, I'm blessed with the sang-froid of Groucho Marx: I wouldn't want to have anything to do with a club that would have me as a member.

In a perfect universe I'd be touring with *Guys and Dolls* to this day. I loved the world of the play, the comic argot, set designer Tony Walton's evocation of Broadway. The dolls! The guys! I'll even give a pass to Lorna Luft. The highlight of the experience, besides meeting my second wife, Mary MacLeod, was Jerry Zaks's direction. He taught me two lessons in comic acting that are applicable to plays written by men as disparate as Abe Burrows and Arthur Miller.

First, always protect the possibility of a happy ending. I learned this on the second day of rehearsal. *Guys and Dolls* begins with with a fifteen-minute scene involving Nathan Detroit and his sidekicks, Nicely-Nicely Johnson and Benny Southstreet. The scene sets up the conflict of the play, which is how to bankroll the Oldest Established, Permanent Floating Crap Game in New York. We're also introduced to Nathan's longtime lover, Miss Adelaide, who yearns to become an honest woman by finally getting Nathan to marry her.

Early in the scene, Benny Southstreet says, "Nathan, can't you do something?"

"What can I do?" says Nathan. "I'm broke. I couldn't even buy Adelaide a present today, and you know what day today is? It's mine and Adelaide's fourteenth anniversary."

"Yeah?" say Nicely and Benny.

"Yeah," says Nathan. "We've been engaged fourteen years."

This establishes one of the running gags in the play: when will circumstances trap Nathan into marrying Adelaide? Later in the scene Adelaide makes her entrance and this dialogue ensues:

"Hello, Nathan dear!"

"Hello, pigeon!"

"Nathan, happy anniversary!" (She hands him a present.)

"A present for me?"

"I hope you like it."

"A belt."

"Read the card."

"'Sugar is sweet and so is jelly. So put this belt around your belly!' That is so sweet. Look, honey, about your present. I was going to get you a diamond wristwatch with a gold band and two rubies on the side."

"Nathan, you shouldn't."

"It's all right, I didn't!"

Here lies the challenge. The joke is indestructible on paper, but the actor must find a successful way to deliver it. Being the well-trained thespian that I was, I assumed that since Nathan had admitted earlier in the scene that he was broke and didn't have the money to buy Adelaide a present, when the time comes for him to accept her gift, he feels guilty.

(Guiltily) "A present for me?"

"No, no!" said Jerry Zaks. "Deliver the line as positively as possible. You're delighted to have received the belt so when the time comes to tell her about the diamond watch when you deliver the punch line "It's all right, I didn't," you've said it like you've done her a great favor."

That's the second lesson: If you want to be funny, don't be overly contemplative. Be positive about everything, so when the pie eventually hits you in the face, the audience is taken by surprise. That's great direction. It allows you as you're working your way through the play to spin dialogue in a positive direction. If you don't believe me, think Bob Hope.

Chapter 37

My association with Jerry Zaks spanned the 1990s and continues up to the present. In 1993, on the thirtieth anniversary of John F. Kennedy's assassination, Neil Simon's *Laughter on the Twenty-third Floor*, a play about the comedy writers who wrote the *Sid Caesar Show*, opened at the Richard Rodgers Theater on West Forty-sixth Street. Nathan Lane played Sid Caesar and I played Milt Fields, a fictional version of the writer Sheldon Keller. I loved playing Milt, who was the least gifted and most insecure writer of the group but one of the funniest characters in the play.

Once again Neil Simon's ego affected the project's destiny. He had conducted a well-publicized feud with the *New York Times* drama critic Frank Rich, who was retiring the week we were to open. Neil had written an open letter to the *Times* accusing the paper of nepotism after it had hired Rich's girlfriend, Alex Witchell. As drama critic, Rich was to be succeeded within days by the former *Washington Posta* critic David Richards, who was at the time writing followup reviews in the Arts & Leisure section of the *Sunday Times*. Neil went so far as to accuse Rich of panning his plays in retaliation for the nepotism letter. Now, all he had to do was wait Rich out and open *Laughter on the Twenty-third Floor* the following week. He refused.

Rich's final reviews were of *Laughter*, which he hated (no big surprise), and Tony Kushner's terrific *Perestroika*. The latter he lauded as a masterwork, adding a few blistering comments about Neil's lame one-liners by comparing them to Kushner's gift for eliciting laughter through serious character development. It was like comparing *A Streetcar Named Desire* to *Come Blow Your Horn*. The two men continued their pissing contest right to the end.

Three days later, David Richards gave us an an excellent review in the *Sunday Times*. We ran for ten months, but the project was seen as déclassé. The major problem with *Laughter* was its porous ending. After two hours of jokes, the audience was unmoved by the play's conclusion. The story's message was that television of such uncompromising quality would never happen again. The genius of Sid Caesar was defeated on the commercial battlefield by Lawrence Welk.

Jerry Zaks had done admirable work as director, pacing the play at breakneck speed, but after its critical failure he was accorded most of the blame. The revisionist sentiment of the brass was that he had somehow robbed the play of its warm heart, which was poppycock. He had assembled a charming and talented cast that included John Slattery, J. K. Simmons, Randy Graff, Bitty Schram, Ron Orbach, Stephen Mailer, and Mark Linn Baker. For whatever it's worth, most of us remained friends long after the play's demise, an exceedingly rare occurrence in the transitory world of show business.

Chapter 38

In 1996, on the prowl for his long-awaited Tony Award, Nathan Lane set in motion a revival of *A Funny Thing Happened on the Way to the Forum*, directed by Jerry Zaks. The production had been delayed a year to allow Nathan to costar in the film *The Birdcage*. I'd been offered the role of Lycus the whoremaster, a part I had little inclination to play. Nathan suggested I approach Jerry about playing Senex, the character so memorably performed by my first inspiration, David Burns. It had been more than thirty years since I'd accompanied my father to Davy's dressing room after seeing him in the original production.

Nathan is a wunderkind, albeit the hardest working wunderkind in the business. I must reiterate here that stardom, which Nathan was just beginning to achieve, is not as much a matter of luck as of intensity of desire. Fame is no less an addiction than coffee or cigarettes. One of its negative manifestations is the inability of certain people to enjoy its benefits. Remaining a star becomes a career in itself and can swallow one's capacity to enjoy the small pleasures in life (the Four Seasons Hotel or Nothing Syndrome). If you're not careful, it can erode your entire perspective. How can you be discriminating when the cultural oligarchs, a necessary part of the journey, are telling you that *Frazier* is a work of unmatched comic invention?

What differentiates Nathan Lane from the rest of us, besides his enormous talent, is his desperation to be at the center of things. Not since Luther Adler have I encountered an actor more at war with his audience. It's Nathan's limitless hostility that makes him a thrilling performer. It's like being worked over by a brilliantly intuitive lover who is willing to sacrifice themselves for the illusion of total control, and it's how Nathan manages to remain Nathan no matter how idiosyncratic his characterization. He's not grateful in any way for the experience; the audience is his enemy, out to destroy his equilibrium. Acting with him is like cavorting in an elite, spontaneous playground, as satisfying as it is exhausting.

Two weeks into the rehearsal process I asked Jerry Zaks if my characterization was anything more than a cheap imitation of David Burns's original performance.

"The sad thing," Jerry said, flashing those incandescent teeth, "is that you and I and a hundred other people know who David Burns is. You're offering us the essence of what you remember about his performance. You're honoring him, not ripping him off."

A Funny Thing Happened was a solid hit that earned a rave review from Vincent Canby, who was then the critic for the *New York Times*. I was shocked the next morning to discover that the rest of the reviews were decidedly mixed. This was the last time in memory that an esteemed musical comedy had been given an altogether respectful revival. All the participants honored the creative genius of the show's predecessors. Jerry Zaks did not attempt to reinvent the wheel or delude himself that the original director, George Abbott, was his inferior. He studied the original production, put his personal touch on the opening number, "Comedy Tonight," and then worked tirelessly to figure out how best to honor the piece.

Today, revivals are entirely reinvented by directors and producers who seem to think that those who created them were sadly deficient and old fashioned. If George Abbott had cut a number out of town, put the number back in. After all, what did a hundred-and-seven-year-old man like Abbott know about his own musical, anyway?

My performance as Senex garnered my second nomination for a Tony (the first in 1973 for *Candide*), but the best supporting actor in a musical that year went to a young actor who played a transvestite dying of AIDS in the musical *Rent*. When he accepted his award he thanked the universe. If I had won, I was planning to thank Sam Levene. Later that evening, drunk and envious, I began to complain to my children that it was never a good idea to win a Tony for your first Equity job.

"What do you know about it?" said my sixteen-year-old son, Peter, whose attendance at the ceremonies had set me back five hundred bucks for his and his sister's balcony seats. He had seen *Rent* twice and the show had really spoken to him. "You haven't even seen *Rent*," he said.

"No, I haven't!" I fired back. "But I was forced to listen to one of the musical numbers tonight, and it reminded me of another show called *Hair*—only those songs actually had a melody."

"That guy who won tonight was great!" my son insisted. "His performance was fabulous!"

"Well, if you thought he was so great," I told him, "if you thought he was so fabulous, why don't you ask him to put you through college?"

Chapter 39

I couldn't understand why Nathan Lane would even consider acting in a Broadway musical version of Mel Brooks's film *The Producers*. At the time we were appearing together again in the Roundabout Theater production of *The Man Who Came to Dinner*, directed by--who else?--Jerry Zaks. A few months earlier Nathan had referred to the Broadway revival of *The Music Man*, directed and choreographed by Susan Stroman, as the worst direction he had ever seen in a musical. "It's so confused you can't even tell who's talking," he'd claimed. Susan Stroman was about to direct and choreograph *The Producers*.

"Why do it?" I asked him. "It's never going to be as good as the movie. Zero Mostel was definitive."

"Wouldn't you do it if someone asked *you* to play Max Bialystock?"

"No, I don't believe I would."

"You'd do it," he said.

As the weeks went by the subject of *The Producers* became a serious matter of contention between us, because I honestly believed the project was a recipe for disaster. And there lies a major difference between Nathan Lane and Lewis J. Stadlen. Nathan had the courage and the ambition to reach out for glory while I remained neurotically respectful of Zero Mostel and the past.

There's a wonderful Fassbinder movie entitled *Lola* that involves a morally upright man who falls in love with a young prostitute in postwar Germany. His unrequited passion for Lola distorts his moral compass. At the close of the film he's confronted by an unapologetically corrupt businessman whose motives are shaped by his understanding of the real world. "I don't understand your problem," he says to the obsessed man. "She's a whore. Just throw her on the bed and fuck her!" This exemplifies my relationship with the American theater. I know what it is, yet I pretend it's something else.

A few days before *The Producers* opened in New York, my wife Mary and I attended a performance at the St. James Theater. As is my habit, I sat with my arms petulantly folded, daring the production to entertain me. By the fourth musical number I'd been completely won over. Nathan and company were mostly terrific. Mel Brooks and his coauthor, Thomas Meehan, had improved the story by turning the sexy Swedish secretary, Ulla, into Leo Bloom's love interest. The music was tuneful and unpretentious, and Susan Stroman's choreography was witty and delightful. In an era of spectacularly lousy musicals, *The Producers* was the real deal.

After the performance we made our way back to Nathan's dressing room, where I prostrated myself and admitted I had been wrong *again*.

That same year I had the leading role in Neil Simon's new comedy, *Forty-five Seconds from Broadway*. The play seemed snakebit from the beginning. Our first full day of rehearsal was September 11, 2001. The day we were reviewed in the papers, a jetliner crashed into a Far Rockaway neighborhood. Fear of terrorism led officials to prohibit anyone from entering or leaving Manhattan.

Forty-five Seconds from Broadway concerned the unremarkable comings and goings of a group of regulars at the Edison Hotel coffee shop. I played a comedian named Mickey Fox, based on Jackie Mason. Things seemed to be going well enough until Neil became seriously ill and left for his home in Los Angeles. After our first preview we never saw him again. A few cursory rewrites were faxed from the West Coast, but Neil was in declining health and in too much pain to continue revising the play. Months later it was determined that he needed a kidney transplant. Our critical reception was mostly horrible, and we closed in nine weeks.

As the New Year dawned I could not have been more depressed. This had been, after all, my middle-aged shot. Instead of public acclaim I'd been the leading player in a flop. It seemed as if luck had deserted me for the long term.

Then Nathan Lane called to ask if I was interested in replacing him when he left *The Producers* in March. I told him I wasn't, but I wouldn't mind playing Max Bialystock when they put together the road company.

"I don't want to be rehearsed in a vacuum and then parachuted into your shoes," I told him. "It's too difficult a part. Besides, if I do it on Broadway it'll only be about replacing Nathan Lane. I'd like the chance to have a full rehearsal process with my own company."

"Well, it's never going to happen unless you get your agent on it," he bellowed into the phone.

"Sure, sure," I told him, too depressed to imagine ever being hired to play a leading role again.

We do tickle each other, Nathan and I. Opposite sides of the same coin. I'm Nathan's dubious alter ego, and he's the theater the way I want to remember it.

The Producers was more than a smash hit; it was a sociological phenomenon. Not only had it won twelve Tony Awards, it also heralded Mel Brooks's comeback. For those who thought he'd become irrelevant, the success of *The Producers* was a classic showbiz feel-good story. No matter how much we revile them while they're doing well, nobody likes to see the Boston Celtics or the Dallas Cowboys wallowing in the cellar. Mel had given the world too many laughs to be relegated to oblivion. Seeing him rehabilitated made everyone feel more confident.

The Producers was a sendup of American capitalism that featured two lovable thieves, one innocent and the other too knowing. At his best, Mel is a truly subversive humorist. The musical number "Springtime for Hitler" is more subversive than Brecht, as Mel takes civilized behavior and stands it on its ear. *The Producers* is not only hilarious when performed by good actors, it's also a titillating distillation of Mel's libido. The characters behave the way people really want to behave: long-legged showgirls are given permission to be worldly and compliant; eccentric gay men parade around in sequined evening gowns; nostalgic Nazis are too dumb to live; and, at its core, a mendacious wiseguy is willing to make love to old ladies and an idiot savant fulfills our secret desire to break all the rules and still get the girl.

By the time Nathan Lane and Matthew Broderick had decided to leave *The Producers*, all those connected with the show's success believed they were geniuses. And because the show was a hilarious exploration of larceny, those handling its financial end began to see themselves in the same lovable light as the two main characters. (Such is the narcotic that results from cashing enormous residual checks on a weekly basis.) Management began to think that *The Producers* was as indestructible an entity as *Guys and Dolls* and *My Fair Lady*, and that duplicating its initial success would be a piece of cake. Nearly forgotten was the titanic contribution of Nathan Lane, who had had the good sense to recognize the brilliance of Zero Mostel's original creation. After a year of endless hype and self-congratulation, exactly who had been responsible for what, and who had been just plain lucky, began to blur in the corporate imagination.

The day I auditioned to play Max Bialystock in the first national company, those who'd considered themselves omnipotent only a few weeks before were now panicking over what would happen once Henry Goodman, the British actor who was replacing Nathan Lane, and Steven Weber, who was replacing Matthew Broderick, took over the roles on Broadway. Neither man wanted to replicate—or was able to replicate—the performances of the originals. Nor were they being helped by rehearsing in an empty studio with a stage manager and several of Susan Stroman's acolytes, who were force-feeding them bits of comic business as if they were two Big Whoppers coming off an assembly-line grill.

Henry Goodman had made the enormous mistake of not watching Nathan's performance for fear it would inhibit his own. He had played Shylock in *The Merchant of Venice* in the West End to considerable acclaim, and of course both characters being Jewish and crooked made him an obvious choice to replace Nathan Lane—who was Irish. Weber, as charming and good looking as Matthew Broderick, had been the comic romantic lead on a successful television situation comedy, *Wings*. Susan Stroman had won a Tony for her direction, but it was unclear how much she had shaped the performances of the actors and how much the actors had shaped themselves. Broadway reputations being what they are, nobody wants to relinquish the illusion that they are in large part responsible for a show's success. Now that the two stars were leaving, the bill was coming due.

When I arrived for my audition on a Saturday afternoon, the word was that Mel had watched a midweek run-through with his two new leads and had offered a two-word critique: They Stink! (Where had I heard that one before?) I hadn't seen Mel in twenty years and was prepared to have it out with him if he so much as looked at me sideways. Much to my surprise, when I saw him outside the rehearsal studio, he embraced me and told me that if it were up to him, he'd give me the part, but Susan Stroman wasn't certain I had what it took to play Bialystock. My hostility defused, and basking in

Mel's approval (he spoke admiringly of my performances in *Laughter on the Twenty-third Floor* and *The Man Who Came to Dinner*), I entered the audition room in a confident and self-possessed state of mind.

I mention my mindset because the dynamic involved in a successful audition has everything to do with externalities. It was one thing for me to believe they'd be lucky to have me, and quite another for them to agree with me. I auditioned very well that day, but much of their approval was related not to my performance but to the desperation they'd been feeling. I'd solved their problem; now they could feel like geniuses again.

When I arrived several months later to begin rehearsals, Susan Stroman hugged me warmly. After several seconds I began to disengage, but her arms remained clasped around me, and she refused to let me go. What exactly was she doing? Was this a trust exercise? Was she inordinately attracted to me, or was she making a statement about who was in control? As much as I love the warmth of a woman's embrace, there is definitely a time to let go.

My two-and-a-half-year stint in *The Producers* generated enough material for a book of its own. Besides falling in love again, (My next book) I performed the role of Max Bialystock 761 times, in Pittsburgh, Cleveland, Cincinnati, Minneapolis, St. Louis, San Diego, Phoenix, Seattle, Portland, San Francisco, the St. James Theater in New York, Denver, Houston, San Antonio, New Orleans, Nashville, Atlanta, Tampa, Fort Lauderdale, Palm Beach, Orlando, Washington, D,C., Hartford, Wallingford, Providence, Richmond, Charlotte, Raleigh, Toledo, Grand Rapids, Kalamazoo, Rochester, Buffalo, Syracuse, and again in Cleveland and Pittsburgh. I was lucky enough to work opposite the best actors who ever played Leo Bloom, Don Stephenson and Alan Ruck. Neither received his due, particularly Stephenson.

I'm proud of earning the concomitants of stardom without having to dedicate my life to the pursuit of them. Performing in the national company of *The Producers* was the happiest and most fulfilling experience of a career that has been mostly blessed.

Chapter 40

I see the dream clearly, in all its specifics. While I push my pencils around and rustle my looseleaf paper to create the illusion that I'm doing what I've been commanded to do, I drift off into a distant future that will someday be my present. Above the marquee is the theater's name, the Diana Lew. It's not a large theater, a shade under a thousand seats. It's named after me, but obliquely, because I've become, almost, a leader of men. It would be too egotistical to call it the Lewis J. Stadlen Theater, so I tip my hat modestly to the throngs of people who pass through its lobby doors. Perhaps one in a hundred realizes it owes its name to its not so famous, but certainly famous enough, theatrical entrepreneur and his devilishly attractive lady friend, Diana, who sits at his side at Downey's, her warm, sculptured thigh pressing against his own.

The man I've become is in demand, but not so sought after that I have to bother with offers that disrupt my tranquil mental state. I call my own shots and bask in my rarified celebrity. Twice a week I play poker with friends, all of them accomplished and most of them more famous than me—but accomplishment is subjective. We laugh because we're witty and experienced in the ways of the world. Sometimes I win at poker and sometimes I lose, but most of the time I break even. We play in my Victorian-red offices above the stage of the Diana Lew. I supply the sandwiches.

It's a fantasy that projects the early 1960s into infinity, the fantasy of a thirteen-year-old ill at ease with the concept of progress, part artistic reactionary, part believer in a perfectionist past he never experienced. I've never wanted to move forward as much as I've wanted to reenter the past. It's about being swept along while exerting minimum influence on my environment. No photographs, please. I want to be appreciated in the present and recollected in the past. I believe that everyone, no matter how famous and adored, will have to be explained to a future generation. George Brent was once a very famous man.

I have several bones to pick with the present: I don't accept that what is unmelodic is more complicated. Our present-day theater is distinguished by writers who hide behind the veneer of sophistication and categorically refuse to give us pleasure. Large themes and impulses are not old hat. Writing only about the inability to love or to connect is about as intellectually challenging as leafing through a coffee-table book.

Today's music and lyrics are no more complicated than those of Cole Porter, Richard Rodgers, Lorenzo Hart, Oscar Hammerstein, or George and Ira Gershwin. Most of the time they're about nothing at all. Plays that are about a single event don't represent an evolution in playwriting. The theme of the alcoholic pipe dream in *The Iceman Cometh* is universal, because we're all either medicated or searching for ways to be medicated in order to shut out the disappointment of being ourselves. *Awake and Sing* is about a dispirited country and the eternal hope of making it and our lives better. A play about standing in a line or buying a white on white painting is a clever conceit, but it doesn't humanize us in the same way as watching a family dissolve under the weight of the American capitalist dream.

In the two decades since AIDS has been exacting its devastating and disproportionate toll on the theatrical community, the most talented voices heard on the American stage have been those of Tony Kushner and the late August Wilson. Both men write about human imperfection, whether it manifests itself in nuclear accidents, colonialism masquerading another name, or social injustice. Both men aren't afraid to look directly at our ceaseless struggle to ward off the evil in ourselves.

The theater today is beset by a noisy, bitchy effeteness that can be ignored if you're not driven crazy by its provincialism. What other entertainment medium espouses such a threadbare standard for illusion? If a movie was utterly artificial you'd either hiss or leave the premises. Today's theater audience sits in a self-conscious, compliant stupor, either to justify the indecent expense involved or in the hope that they're exposing their children to culture. But the Broadway theater has become nothing more than a walking tour through Disneyland in which attractive young performers dance past you lip-syncing while you make your way to the nearest refreshment center.

"Calling all show queens! Or, if you prefer to be more formally addressed, may I have your attention please, devoted aficionados of musical theater. Have I got a show for you!" This is the beginning of a recent rave by *New York Times* drama critic Charles Isherwood. Or try this, from Ben Brantley's review of Julia Roberts in a Broadway revival of Richard Greenberg's *Three Days of Rain*. Brantley panned the show mercilessly but still dedicated his entire four-column review to Ms. Roberts's celebrity: "The only emotion this production generates arises not from the interaction on stage, but from the relationship between Ms. Roberts and her fans. And before we go any further, I feel a strong need to confess something. My name is Ben, and I am a Juliaholic.... Like a down-home Garbo, she is an Everywoman who looks like nobody else. And while I blush to admit it, she is one of the few celebrities who occasionally show up (to my great annoyance) in cameo roles in my dreams."

Not quite Brooks Atkinson's first impressions of *A Streetcar Named Desire*.

I don't mean to exacerbate the culture wars, but I don't believe in political correctness either. If a play or musical doesn't have a homoerotic subtext, Brantley, the *Times*'s first-string drama critic, isn't interested. It's time to broaden the canvas. And while we're at it, I don't believe a captive audience should be asked several times a year to contribute money to a charity that has been institutionalized, without anyone's permission, in my actor's union.

But there's still hope. Each year a few productions seem to slip in and re-animate the standard that was once nearly the norm. To quote Zelda Fichandler, "The theater is a neighborhood enterprise. It can be performed around a kitchen table." Yes, it can, but sitting in a velvet seat, surrounded by an architect's vision of culture, is so much more satisfying.

I remember as an adolescent walking the streets of New York with my father's actor friend John Marley. We had just seen *Fiorello!*, and after the performance we stopped into Reuben's for a snack. John had only recently become, after forty years, an overnight success, appearing in *Cat Ballou*, *Faces*, and later, *The Godfather* (as the movie mogul who wakes up next to a horse's severed head). He had a tough-guy persona, with a Hell's Kitchen gravelly voice, terrible skin, and a majestic mane of coarse silver hair. Marley embodied the difficulties of the independent actor's life. He was the family friend who, walking beside me that night, was unaware that his influence would endure throughout my life. There was something of the bum about him (my mother's definition), which was a major reason he seemed so compelling to me.

As you grow into late middle age, job opportunities increase as your contemporaries fall by the wayside. But what's lost is that late evening walk alongside the man you dream of being, an independent, fictious you, influential today but gone tomorrow. The thrill for me has always been to spend time in the company of clowns who know too much about a certain thing and are willing to pass it on. I've become one of the clowns, but what's gone now is the old heroic fool who teaches me how to survive in my tiny world. Those who've taught me are slowly passing out of this life or drifting into incoherence.

What's left to aspire to, besides giving back.

Afterword

In the summer of 2008, I performed the role of Tevye the dairyman in *Fiddler On The Roof,* at the Muny Theater in St. Louis, MO. At the age of sixty one, it was as if my life were passing before my eyes. I have always been amazed at the process of relearning a role previously performed. One only has to reread a play's text several times before it reactivates within your muscle memory. In the case of *Fiddler,* I had never learned the role of Tevye, but I had certainly heard it performed several hundred times forty years before. The memorization came so easily I doubted I had learned it, but I had. It's a great role because Tevye must deal separately with his five distinctly different daughters, as well as his wife of twenty five years. Similar to the role of *Semmelweiss*, I felt as if I lived a lifetime within every performance. Like Luther and Zero, I played him strong. (Brave and hopeful). The cadences of Zero's raging sense of social justice and comic timing burning in my ears. After the first week of performances the role become a merger between me and the men who have influenced my life. Zero, Luther, Sam Levene, David Burns, Nathan Lane. Those whose pain will forever make me howl with laughter.

Oh yes. There was a young actor who played the role of Mendel the Rabbi's son. Etai Benshlomo. A gifted young man, hopefully at the beginning of a long career. I helped him and with every performance he got better and better.

CHECK THESE TITLES! BearManorMedia.com
PO Box 71426 * Albany, GA 31708

Comic Strips and Comic Books of Radio's Golden Age
by Ron Lackmann

From Archie Andrews to Tom Mix, all radio characters and programs that ever stemmed from a comic book or comic strip in radio's golden age are collected here, for the first time, in an easy-to-read, A through Z book by Ron Lackmann!

$19.95 ISBN 1-59393-021-6

Perverse, Adverse and Rottenverse
by June Foray

June Foray, voice of Rocky the Flying Squirrel and Natasha on Rocky and Bullwinkle, has assembled a hilarious collection of humorous essays aimed at knocking the hats off conventions and conventional sayings. Her highly literate work is reminiscent of John Lennon, S.J. Pearlman, with a smattering of P.G. Wodehouse's love of language. This is the first book from the voice of Warner Brothers' Grandma (Tweety cartoons) and Stan Freberg's favorite gal!

$14.95 ISBN 1-59393-020-8

The Old-Time Radio Trivia Book
by Mel Simons

Test your OTR knowledge with the ultimate radio trivia book, compiled by long-time radio personality & interviewer, Mel Simons. The book is liberally illustrated with photos of radio stars from the author's personal collection.

$14.95 ISBN 1-59393-022-4

The Writings of Paul Frees

A full-length screenplay (The Demon from Dimension X!), TV treatments and songs written for Spike Jones—never before published rarities. First 500 copies come with a free CD of unreleased Frees goodies!

$19.95 ISBN 1-59393-011-9

How Underdog Was Born
by creators Buck Biggers & Chet Stover

The creators of Total Television, the brains behind Underdog, Tennessee Tuxedo and many classic cartoons, reveal the origin of one of cartoon's greatest champions—Underdog! From conception to worldwide megahit, the entire story of the birth of Total Television at last closes an important gap in animated television history.

$19.95 ISBN 1-59393-025-9

Daws Butler – Characters Actor
by Ben Ohmart and Joe Bevilacqua

The official biography of the voice of Yogi Bear, Huckleberry Hound and all things Hanna-Barbera. This first book on master voice actor Daws Butler has been assembled through personal scrapbooks, letters and intimate interviews with family and co-workers. Foreword by Daws' most famous student, Nancy Cartwright (the voice of Bart Simpson).

$24.95 ISBN 1-59393-015-1

For these books and more, visit www.bearmanormedia.com
Visa & Mastercard accepted. Add $5.00 postage per book.

www.ingramcontent.com/pod-product-compliance
Lightning Source LLC
Chambersburg PA
CBHW070230230426
43664CB00014B/2259